Plant-Based Diet for Better Health

By

Dr Nat Khublall
BSc (Lond), MSc (Rdg), DSc (Rdg), FRICS,
Barrister at law

Publisher: Dr Nat Khublall

Email: nat1938@ymail.com
Mobile phone: 07830647303 (UK)

© **Nat Khublall**
eBook and paperback 2023
ISBN: 9798869544292

Preface

Plant food in many countries is becoming popular and more and more people are changing their dietary lifestyle. This being the case, this book is to provide an idea of what is a whole food plant-based diet and what are the health benefits. Such a diet is likely to prevent or reduce the risk of many of the chronic diseases. For those who already have them they can eat wisely and doing moderate exercises with a view to remission in some cases. This is particularly relevant to those who are afflicted with diabetes type 2.

There are 19 chapters, many of which deal with matters not already covered in the author's two other books in the general area. For example, there is a chapter on obesity. This is a serious global weight gain issue. Another chapter deals with issues relating to eating excessive animal products. Sugar in one's diet is a very serious matter covered in Chapter 9. Sugar is from a few sources, one of which is that it is inherent in many foods, particularly carbohydrates. In this regard, there are 8 tables in Chapter 4; the sugar content for many foods is tabulated. Dietary fats and oils are dealt with in Chapter 10. A few authors claim that seed oil is toxic, but it appears that some oil manufacturers are claiming there is no scientific evidence for this. This is contrary to the views expressed by some objective scientists.

Many new topics covered in a few chapters are the effect of ultra-processed food, protein and fibre, food poisoning, food to avoid, and kidney and liver health. The remaining chapters are updates of matters already covered in the previous books. They deal with how diets can be used for relief in chronic diseases, support for plant-based foods, positive thinking for a healthy life, nutrition generally, and the final chapter is on vegetables and fruits. What are featured in almost all the chapters are plant foods. Your food is primarily your medicine, medication is secondary.

Many footnote references are given on the materials researched from books, articles and many You Tube videos available on the internet. Many of these videos are by US doctors and some in the UK.

The author wishes to acknowledge his gratitude to all the authors of published materials referred to in the course of writing this book. He is indebted for the reproduction of food images from the shelves of supermarkets and other sources, including The Daily Mail, and for many incisive quotes of learned and lay persons.

The author takes responsibility for all errors, though without legal liability. Professional advice should be sought before acting on the information in this book. Comments are invited and can be sent to nat1938@ymail.com

Dr Nat Khublall
20 November 2023

Contents

Preface iii
Chapter 1 Introduction 1

Chapter 2 Overweight and Obesity Epidemic 11

Chapter 3 Diets to Prevent Chronic Diseases 24

Chapter 4 Balanced Plant-Based Diet 59

Chapter 5 Nutrition for Health 70

Chapter 6 Effect of Excessive Meat Consumption 79

Chapter 7 Support for Plant-Based Diets 87

Chapter 8 WFPB Diet Can Reduce Brain Damage.. 96

Chapter 9 Effect of Sugar (Carbs & Glucose) 109

Chapter 10 Dietary Fats, Oil & Health Outcome 117

Chapter 11 Effect of Ultra-Processed Food 128

Chapter 12 Protein and Fibre 134

Chapter 13 Food Poisoning 142

Chapter 14 Food to Avoid 148

Chapter 15 Kidney Health and Liver Health 153

Chapter 16 Hydration: Water & Other Liquids 167

Chapter 17 Positive Thinking and Immune System 179

Chapter 18 Nutrition Generally 205

Chapter 19 Vegetables and Fruits 215

Other Books of Author 242

CHAPTER 1

INTRODUCTION

This is the author's third book in the general area of health and nutrition. Without delving into much academic aspects, this work concentrates mainly on plant foods as a primary factor for maintaining and/or improving your health. This theme is a common aspect throughout the book. It is with a view a view to improving your health, particularly with reference to reducing the risk of chronic diseases.

VARIETY OF TOPICS

This chapter includes many topics which are very briefly discussed as an introduction to what is to follow in this book. As the title of this book suggests, it is basically about whole food plant-based (WFPB) diets. This is discussed in relation to many health issues and chronic diseases. This is an area which was hardly taught in medical schools. When patients visit their physicians, very rarely this is discussed, however relevant and important it is and could be more beneficial to a patient than medication in many situations. Sometimes, mistakes are made in prescribing medications.

> "When diet is wrong, medicine is of no use. When diet is correct, medicine is of no need."
>
> Ayurvedic Proverb

Plant-based diet performs wonders, and some doctors themselves in the US and other countries were able to recover from their own ailments by resorting fully or partially to such a diet.[1] The correct diet in many cases can perform better than medicine but it must be right for the patient. Most medicines have side effects and some are even detrimental to patients. More than 237 million medication errors occur yearly in the NHS (in England), costing upwards of £98 million and more than 1,700 lives every year.[2]

Benefit of Whole Food Plant Based (WFPB) Diets. Research shows that plant-based diets are cost effective, low-risk, interventions and may lower body mass index (BMI), blood pressure, diabetes' risk (HbA1c), and cholesterol levels. If such a diet is followed, it may have the effect of

---

[1] To name a few, they are Dr Deen Ornish, Dr Brook Goldner, and Dr Mark Hyam.
[2] According to the Journal of the BMJ Quality & Safety. https://www.bmj.com

reducing the number of medications required to treat chronic diseases and lower ischemic disease mortality rates.[3]

Food Supporting Brain Health. Relevant here are Alzheimer's, Parkinson's and dementia. A suitable plant-based diet can reduce their risk. Foods such as leafy green vegetables, non-starchy vegetables, like broccoli, cauliflower, and Brussels sprouts should be part of your dementia-fighting diet. Other items are oily fish, beans, wine, nuts and olive oil. To reduce the risk of Parkinson's and other diseases, eat plenty of whole foods. They include fruits and vegetables, lean protein, beans, and legumes, and whole grains, and staying hydrated. They will help towards staying energised and healthy overall. The advice for Alzheimer's patients is for them to concentrate on regular exercise, social engagement, healthy diet, mental stimulation, quality sleep, stress management and vascular health.

TYPES OF DIET AND RELATED MATTERS

Those who do not eat meat or fish but still consume eggs and dairy are known as vegetarians. If eggs, dairy, honey and gelatine are eliminated as well, they will be regarded as vegans.[4]

A plant-based diet is any diet derived from plant sources. Such a diet can include vegetables, fruits, grains, pulses, legumes, nuts and any meat substitute, such as any made from soy products. People may interpret a plant-based diet differently. Some may include a small quantity of animal products (such as meat and fish) but at the same time they focus on mainly vegetarian foods. The term for this is semi-vegetarian or flexitarian diet. If meat is completely eliminated but there is a little fish in the diet, it is known as a pescatarian diet. As mentioned above, if a diet does not contain any trace of any animal product, it is referred to as vegan.

A vegetarian or vegan diet is likely to have good intakes of fibre and the vitamins and minerals present in vegetables and fruits, including foliate, vitamin C and potassium. These are all required for good health.

Not All Plant-Based Foods Are Healthy. This is usually the case if the foods are highly processed and packaged. While products such as refined sugar, white flour and certain vegetable fats fall within the category of "plant-based" (as they are from plants) they cannot be considered as healthy. Therefore, a healthy diet, if required, should only include a small portion of such products if the diet is to be considered a healthy diet. Carbohydrates contain a lot of sugar. Refer to the 8 tables in Chapter 4

---

[3] Nutritional Update for Physicians: Plant-Based Diets NCBI https://www.ncbi.nlm.nih.gov
[4] https://www.bbcgoodfood.com > w

showing the blood glucose (sugar) in food intake. For example, a portion of 150 grams of basmati or white rice contains 10.1 teaspoons of sugar.

Balanced and Nutritionally Adequate Diet. A well-balanced, plant-based diet should include: wholegrains, vegetables, fruit, legumes, nuts and seeds. Such a diet has many health benefits which include lower body mass index (BMI), lower cholesterol and a reduced incidence of chronic diseases, that include type 2 diabetes, and may protect from certain cancers (prostate, and breast cancers).

Quality and Nutritional Adequacy. Health benefits can only be assured in a diet if there is a replacement of refined typically "white" carbohydrates with wholegrains, avoiding sugary-laden drinks and confectionery and instead focusing on better quality plant-based protein and fats. Such fats can be obtained from nuts and seeds. Industrially produced seed oils (sold as vegetable oils) should be avoided as far as possible as they are toxic. Refer to Chapter 10 to understand the detrimental nature of most vegetable (or seed) oils. Manufacturers of such oils will naturally disagree with this view. They sometimes get scientists to publish articles in favour of seed oils.

THE FIVE FOOD GROUPS

Briefly set out below is a list of the major food groups of a plant-based diet, with examples:[5]

Fruits. There different types of fruits, including apples, bananas, grapes, strawberries, citrus fruits, etc. When a banana is fully ripe, the sugar content is 5.7 teaspoons. Therefore, it should only be eaten in moderation.

A variety of vegetables include peppers, corn, lettuce, spinach, kale, peas, collards, broccoli, and cauliflower, among others.

Tubers are starchy root vegetables such as ordinary potatoes, sweet potatoes, yams, and cassava (aka yuca).

Whole grains include grains, cereals, and other starches in whole form. These include quinoa, brown rice, whole wheat, oats, and popcorn, among others.

Legumes: they comprise beans of different types, lentils, and pulses, etc.

---

[5]For a breakdown of a WFPB diet, refer to The Forks Over Knives Diet Explained.

In addition to the above, there are many other foods you can eat, such as nuts, seeds, avocados, tofu, tempeh, whole-grain flours and breads, and plant-based drinks which are substitutes for dairy. Whatever foods are chosen, they should be eaten in moderation. The reason for the caution is because many of these foods are calorie-dense that can result in weight gain.

The 5 food groups.

EATING MORE PLANT-BASED FOODS

Resorting to a plant-based diet today is a general approach to eating. Many people the world over are switching wholly or partially to a plant-based diet. Once such a transformation is made, there is less emphasis in the need to count calories or about meeting certain macronutrient goals daily. Put simply, it is about consuming more plant-based foods and fewer or no animal-based ones.

Interpretation of a Diet. As there are many interpretations of a diet, perhaps they can be set out below:

(a) Vegetarian Diet. People who are vegetarian may eat eggs, cheese, and milk, but not meat in general (including beef, chicken, and pork). Instead of getting their protein from meat, it is obtained from a plant-based source, as explained later in this book. Refer to Chapters 18 and 19.

(b) Vegan Diet. People in this group forgo animal products altogether (including milk, cheese and honey); they exclusively confine themselves to plants in pursuing their vegan lifestyle.

(c) Raw Vegan Diet. Those who follow (a) and (b) above may choose to eat only raw plant-based foods. It is a matter of choice. However, most people may choose to cook their foods. This aids digestion.

(d) Flexitarian Diet. Some people are flexible in that they eat a little meat. Instead of confining themselves exclusively to plant-based foods, they try simply to cut down on their large meat intake; they primarily filled themselves with plants but with some animal products probably small amounts. People in the Blue Zones use very little meat as condiments for taste not as their main meal. There are 5 Blue Zones around the world: Okinawa in Japan, Sardinia in Italy, Icaria in Greece, Nicoya in Costa Rica, and Loma Linda in California, USA. Many people in these regions live beyond a century on account of their lifestyle.

Interchanging Terms

The term, *plant-based*, is sometimes used to mean a *vegetarian* or a *vegan* diet. These different terms are probably adopted for ethical or religious reasons. What is important to know is the specific diet and to ascertain the details of a person's diet without making any assumption of one's diet. The following is a summary of diets that restrict animal products. Note carefully the information below shows what a diet excludes, but the plant-based diet is defined by what it includes. Here are 8 diets:

(a) **Whole-foods, plant-based, low-fat diet:** This diet encourages plant foods in their whole form, especially vegetables, fruits, legumes, and seeds and nuts (in smaller amounts). To experience maximum health benefits, this diet excludes animal products. Total fat is generally restricted.

(b) **Mediterranean diet:** This is similar to (a) but allows small amounts of chicken, dairy products, eggs, and red meat once or twice per month. Fish and olive oil are encouraged. Fat is not restricted.

(c) **Vegan (or total vegetarian):** It excludes all animal products, especially meat, seafood, poultry, eggs, and dairy products. However, it does not require consumption of only whole foods or restrict fat or refined sugar.

> "A vegan diet is one of the best things you can do for your health and the well being of our planet."
>
> Robert Clarke

(d) **Raw food, vegan diet**: Same exclusions as for (c) as well as the exclusion of all foods cooked at temperatures greater than 118°F (47.78°C).

(e) **Lacto-vegetarian diet**: It excludes eggs, meat, seafood, and poultry but includes dairy products.

(f) **Ovo-vegetarian diet:** It excludes meat, seafood, poultry, and dairy products but includes eggs.

(g) **Lacto-ovo vegetarian diet**: It excludes meat, seafood, and poultry but includes eggs and dairy products.

(h) **Ketogenic Diet:** It includes 75% fats, 20% protein and 5% carbs.

From mainly animal foods

As can be seen in the above picture, the Keto diet contains a great deal of fat. It shares similarities with the Atkins and low carb diets.[6] The Keto diet is an eating pattern that includes high amounts of fat, low to moderate amounts of protein, and very little carbohydrates. This diet is typically rich in foods like butter, cheese, eggs, meat, nuts, oils, seafood and seeds.[7] Meat is included.

The Many Variations of a Plant-Based Diet

Some of the items can be recognised.

Vegetarian: This is also known as ovo-lactovegetarian. It includes all plant-based foods, as well as allowing eggs and dairy.

Vegan: This is a diet consisting of plant-based foods only and excludes meat, dairy, eggs, and often honey. Many who follow this lifestyle is for ethical or environmental reasons. Other lifestyle modifications are typically included in addition to the dietary changes.

Pescatarian: This is a largely vegetarian diet that also includes seafood.

Whole-foods, plant-based (WFPB): This is similar to a vegan diet; this diet eschews the ethical baggage and focuses on the health aspect. It is high in fruit, vegetables and whole grains while typically low in fat.

Flexetarian: This allows some flexibility by those who primarily follow a vegetarian or plant-based diet; it allows for some meat, dairy, and seafood on occasion.

6

The Ketogenic Diet: A Detailed Beginner's Guide to Keto
https://www.healthline.com › nutrition › ketogenic-diet-10
[7] 14 Feb 2023. https://foodinsight.org What to know Before Yoy Go Keto – Food Insighr

A 10-Year Long Study. Whereas meat consumption has been linked to an increased risk of developing diabetes, higher intake of fruits and vegetables has been shown to reduce the risk by as much as 50%. A prospective 10-year-long case-cohort study of over 300,000 individuals found an inverse relationship between the amount of fruits and vegetable servings eaten per day and risk of developing type 2 diabetes mellitus. This research, published in the BMJ in July 2020, found that increased produce intake was linked to higher levels of plasma vitamin C and carotenoids, markers of vegetable and fruit consumption, which was associated with a decreased development of diabetes. Participants who developed diabetes over the course of the study had markedly lower biomarkers of fruit and vegetable intake than those who did not develop diabetes. Following a whole food plant-based diet, or simply increasing daily fruit and vegetable consumption, is one step individuals can take to reduce their risk of type 2 diabetes.

WORLDWIDE INCREASE IN CHRONIC DISEASES

The burden of morbidity and mortality from diet-related chronic diseases is increasing across the world. This is attributable to poor diet and the consumption of too much calories and animal products.

In addition to the increase in chronic diseases, the global food production system is draining our planet's resources. This is bad for the environment and future food security. Population wellbeing and planetary health are closely intertwined. They will continue to be vulnerable unless appropriate actions are taken. Any move of global dietary patterns towards high-quality, plant-based diets could alleviate these health and environmental burdens. This requires a reduction in animal foods.

The typical Western diets with high amounts of animal products are seriously unhealthy. In comparison, plant-based diets are not only more sustainable, but have also been associated with lower risk of chronic diseases such as obesity, type 2 diabetes, cardiovascular disease, and some cancers. In disease management and prevention of unnecessary health risks, precision nutrition has the potential to offer some redress. What is required is the need to tailor individual characteristics, such as the genome, metabolome, and microbiome so that they become more effective. Studies in this area are still in the early stages. Regardless, public health nutrition strategies have the power to improve the health of many people. Therefore, a move worldwide towards healthy plant-based dietary patterns could ensure not only better health for individuals but also our planetary health.

PLANT-BASED DIETS THROUGH THE AGES

Over the centuries, different groups have been associated with plant-based diets. In ancient Greece, the philosopher Pythagoras advocated the health benefits of a vegetarian diet and disseminated the idea that slaughter of animals was immoral. Pythagoras studied in India in the BC era.[8] He returned to Greece as a vegetarian and in the belief of reincarnation. He disseminated his new–found knowledge to his followers. They ate a simple diet of bread, honey, and vegetables. Thus, until the 1800s, a plant-based diet was known widely as the Pythagorean Diet.[9] In those early days in India, many people believed in Ayurveda and were eating plant-based diets.

> "Ayurveda: The ancient Indian medical system, focusing on the prevention of disease through diet, lifestyle and herbalism."
> Gopi Warrier

Many religions feature a long tradition of adhering to a vegetarian diet, including three Indian religions: Hinduism, Buddhism and Jainism. As in the case of Pythagoras's followers, people in India in ancient times approached the plant-based diet in the belief that it was immoral to slaughter animals for consumption. Moving fast forward in the mid-1800s, the adherents of the newly formed Seventh-Day Adventist Church advocated and followed a vegetarian diet. In contrast, the aim was to promote human health and longevity instead of aligning with non-violence to animals and an ethical framework.

More Recently in the Early 21 Century. Plant-based consumption now has become popular. In the USA people who follow a vegan diet have increased some 600% from 2014 to 2018.Their interest in plant-based diets is driven by many factors:

(a) Some choose a plant-based diet partly in the pursuit of health, and partly out of concern to avoid violence to animals.
(b) Many people choose a plant-based diet as a way to reduce their environmental footprint.
(c) While some are driven partly by celebrity endorsement, attention in the media, and popular documentaries.

Whatever are the reasons, as above, more and more people in the US, and in many other countries as well, are seeking to include more plant-based foods into their diet.

---

[8] Ancient India had many universities. The first was established in the 7th century BC at Taxshisila. Many more followed, including the famous Nalanda. Almost all were destroyed around the 12th century AD by Islamic invaders.
[9] The famous Pythagoras theorem was learnt in India, though the West in the light of their Eurocentric attitude does not attribute the credit to India.

Corresponding to many households being driven by plant-based diets for one reason or another, many restaurants are incorporating meat substitutes into their menus. They are crafting and marketing dedicated plant-based foods in a variety of ways to suit the palates of their customers. In the supermarkets and other grocery stores, plant-based egg, cheese, and milk alternatives are on sale and in demand. Undoubtedly, there is an interest in plant-based alternatives. The market for plant-based foods has increased some 29% in the U.S. between 2017 and 2019 and is growing.

SUPPORT FOR A PLANT-BASED DIET

There is support from many national and international organisations that support a plant-based diet. However, the tabloid press and media are known to be against a vegan diet. From time to time mention is made that a vegan diet results in all kinds of nutritional deficiencies. This is incorrect.

The newspapers often give the vegan diet a bashing, mainly for the purpose selling newspapers. Veganism is used to fuel this fire. However, these so-called "experts" fail to mention what nutrients are missing in the Western diet. Many adults had intakes below the lower recommended level for both selenium and zinc. Iodine intakes have also been deficient. It is better for the press to pay better attention to the many deficiencies of the average UK diet. Instead, they are involved in making unfounded attacks on vegan diets.

Support for Plant-based diets from Certain Organisations

People would be better off in avoiding the typical Western diet and embracing a balanced plant-based one. This is supported by many health organisations:

1. Food and Agriculture Organisation & World Health Organisation.

2. British National Health Service (British NHS).

3. British Dietetic Association

4. British Nutrition Foundation

5. Academy of Nutrition and Dietetics

6. American Dietetic Association
7. Johns Hopkins Center for a Livable Future

8. Dieticians of Canada

9. The Dieticians Association of Australia

10. The National Health and Medical Research Council of Australia.

More information is given in Chapter 7 relating to support from the above 10 organisations. There is increasing support from some doctors that support WFPB diet and more recently its benefit to alleviate brain diseases.[10]

THE BENEFITS OF A WHOLE-FOOD, PLANT-BASED DIET

There are several major benefits to moving to plant-based nutrition, all supported by science. The benefits of a plant-based diet include:

Easy weight management: People who eat a plant-based diet tend to be of normal weight than those who do not, and the diet makes it easy to lose weight and keep it off, without counting calories.

Disease prevention: Whole-food, plant-based (WFPB) eating can prevent, halt, and in some cases reverse chronic diseases. This food is particularly overwhelming in relation to heart disease and diabetes. Research has also linked such diets to lower rates of arthritis, improved liver function, and healthier kidneys. Refer to Chapter 15 on kidney and liver health.

A lighter environmental footprint: A plant-based diet places much less stress on the environment.

A Guide to Plant-Based Diets

Starting a plant-based diet does not mean that you need to become a vegetarian and cut all sources of animal protein from your diet. You can choose to be a flexitarian. Questions that can be posed are these:

What is a plant-based diet, and is it good for your kidneys?
The beginner's guide to starting a plant-based diet.
Plant-based diet or vegetarian diet – what is the difference?
Myths and misconceptions about plant-based diets.

All the above are discussed in this book.

End

---

[10]Refer to Neuroscientists AKA "Brain Docs" Drs Ayesha and Dean Sherazi Pod Cast. Also, Dr Dale Bredeson and Dr Richard Johnson on this topic were recently interviewed by Tom Bilyeu in a You Tube video.

CHAPTER 2

OVERWEIGHT AND OBESITY EPIDEMIC

"More die in the United States of too much food than too little."
John Kenneth Galbraith

"If you keep on eating unhealthy food then no matter how many weight loss tips you follow, you are likely to retain weight and become obese. If only you start eating healthy food, you will be pleasantly surprised how easy it is to lose weight."
Subodh Gupta

MAJOR PUBLIC HEALTH CHALLENGE

At present, obesity is the biggest disease of mankind. It is bigger than even cancer. It has some effect on your self-confidence and it may make you mentally sick.

Obesity currently is a major public health challenge that affects possibly almost every country in the world. Globally, obesity rates have been advancing steadily for some decades now.[11] Obesity and overweight are defined as abnormal or excessive fat accumulation that may impair health.

The term "obese" describes a person who has excess body fat. In the UK it is estimated that around 1 in every 4 adults and 1 in every 5 children aged 10 to 11 are living with obesity. The most widely used method to check if you have a healthy weight is by body mass index (BMI). This is a measure of whether you have a healthy weight for your height. You can use the BMI healthy weight calculator (from the British NHS) to find out if you are underweight or overweight. For most adults, if your BMI is:

- Below 18.5 – you are in the underweight range.
- 18.5 to 24.9 – you are in the healthy range.
- 25 to 29.9 – you are in the overweight range.
- 30 to 39.9 – you are in the obese range.
- 40 or above– you are in the severely obese range.

If you have a South Asian, Chinese, other Asian, Middle Eastern, Black African or African-Caribbean family background you will need to use a lower BMI score to measure overweight and obesity. If you are:

- 23 to 27.4 – you are in the overweight range.

---

[11] https://world-heart-federation.org Obesity What We Do – World Heart Federation.

- 27.5 or above – you are in the obese range.

BMI score has some limitations because it measures whether a person is carrying too much weight but not too much fat. For example, those who are very muscular, like professional sports people, can have a high BMI without much fat. But for most people, BMI is a useful indication of whether they have a healthy weight.

Another measure of excess fat is the waist to height ratio. This can be used as an additional measure in adults who have a BMI under 35. This measurement is around your waist above your belly button, and you divide it by your height (using the same units, centimetres or inches. A waist to height ratio of 0.5 or higher means you have increased health risks. From the chart in Chapter 18 you can get an idea what your normal weight should be for your height. This is shown in the 2nd column of the chart.

Key Facts Worldwide about Overweight and Obesity. The main facts on obesity are these:

(a) In the whole world obesity has nearly tripled since 1975.

(b) By 2016, more than 1.9 billion adults, 18 years and older, were overweight. The proportion of these who were obese is over 650 million, and probably growing.

(c) Some 39% of adults aged 18 years and over were overweight in 2016, and 13% were obese. This was 7 years ago. These figures are very likely to be substantially more today.

(d) Most of the world's population live in countries where overweight and obesity are responsible for the death of more people that underweight.

(e) Some 39 million children below the age of 5 were overweight or obese in 2020 (3 years ago).

(f) Over 340 million children and adolescents aged 5-19 were overweight or obese in 2016.

(g) Most importantly, obesity is preventable (by making lifestyle changes, in particular with regard to diets and physical exercises).

Causes of Overweight and Obesity. The fundamental cause of overweight and obesity is an energy imbalance between calories consumed and calories expended. Any excess is stored as fat. This problem is experienced around the world:

(a) There is an increased consumption of energy-dense foods that are high in fat and sugars.

(b) To worsen the problem there has been a decrease in physical activity on account of increasingly sedentary lifestyle in many forms of work, changing modes of transportation and an increase in moving from rural areas to the towns (increasing urbanisation).

Changes in Dietary and Physical Activity. These changes are often attributable to the result of environmental and societal changes. Such changes are associated with development and a lack of concern for supportive policies in a number of sectors. Among such sectors are agriculture, transport, urban planning, environment, food processing distribution, marketing, education and health.

COMMON HEALTH CONSEQUENCES (Attributable to Overweight and Obesity)

The problem of overweight and obesity is a major risk factor with regard to non-communicable diseases. Among such diseases are:

(a) Cardiovascular diseases, mainly heart disease and stroke. In 2012, these were the main cause of death.

(b) Diabetes, mainly type 2, which can go into remission for most sufferers if dietary pattern is changed and being involved in some physical exercises.

(c) Musculoskeletal disorders. These relate especially to osteoarthritis, which is a highly disabling degenerative disease associated with the joints.

(d) Certain cancers. These include breast, endometrial, ovarian, prostate, liver, kidney, gallbladder, and colon.

Risk of Living with Obesity

Obesity is a serious health concern that increases the risk of many other health conditions as can be seen under (a) to (d) above.

Effect on Childhood. The risk of the above diseases increases with increases in BMI. Childhood obesity is associated with a higher chance of adult obesity, premature disability and early death in adulthood. In addition to these future risks, children with obesity may experience breathing difficulties, increased risk of fractures, high blood pressure, early markers of cardiovascular disease, insulin resistance and psychological effects.

Malnutrition and Obesity, Both in Some Countries

In some low- and middle-income countries, there may be the problem of facing a "double burden" of both malnutrition and obesity.

(a) Some of these countries may continue not only to deal with the problems of infectious diseases and malnutrition (or under nutrition), but also a rapid upsurge in other diseases attributable to overweight and obesity, particularly in urban areas.

(b) In the same country it is common to find under nutrition and obesity coexisting side by side. Sometimes, this is experienced in the same household.

The above apply to children who are more vulnerable in low- and middle-income countries. These children are exposed to high-fat, high-sugar, high-salt, energy-dense, and micronutrient-poor foods. Such foods tend not only to be lower in cost but also lower in nutrient quality. Together with lower levels in physical activity, the levels of fat, sugar and salt may cause a sharp increase in childhood obesity, while at the same time under nutrition still remains an issue.

PREVENTING OVERWEIGHT AND OBESITY

Overweight and obesity are largely preventable. What are required are supportive environments and communities. These are fundamental in shaping people's choices. They relate to healthier foods and regular physical exercises. People can:

- Limit energy intake from total fats and sugars.
- Increase consumption of fruit and vegetables, as well legumes, whole grains and nuts. Eat a balanced calorie-controlled diet as recommended by your GP or weight loss management health professional, such as a dietician.
- Engage in regular physical activity. This could be 60 minutes daily for children and 150 minutes or more spread throughout the week for adults. Engage in activities such as brisk walking, jogging, swimming or tennis. Going to a gym for intensive workout could cause injury.

The full effect can be experienced only where people have access to a healthy lifestyle. Therefore, if required, society should support this. If necessary, a tax can be imposed on sugar sweetened beverages. The food industry can play a significant role by promoting healthy diets:

(a) Reducing the fat, sugar and salt from processed foods.
(b) Ensuring that healthy and nutritious foods are available and affordable to consumers.
(c) Impose restrictions in marketing foods high in sugars, fats and salt, especially foods targeting children and teenagers.
(d) Ensuring the availability of healthy food choices and supporting regular physical activity for adults, especially in the workplace.

Treating Obesity with Medicine. If you are living with obesity, and lifestyle and behavioural changes alone do not help in losing weight, a medicine called orlistat may be recommended. It works by reducing the amount of fat you absorb during digestion. However, most medicines have side effects, and some can do more harm than good.

Living with Overweight and Obesity. This can also affect your quality of life and contribute to mental health problems, such as depression, and can also affect self-esteem.

CAUSES OF OBESITY (and Overweight)

Obesity is a complex issue attributable to many causes. Both obesity and overweight are caused when extra calories, particularly those from foods high in fat and sugar, are stored in the body as fat. Obesity is an increasingly common problem because the environment we live in makes it difficult for many people to eat healthy and do enough physical activity.

Genetics can also be a cause of obesity for some people. The genes can affect how the body uses food and stores fat.

There are also some underlying health conditions that can occasionally contribute to weight gain, such as an underactive thyroid gland (hypothyroidism). But these conditions do not usually cause weight problems if they are effectively controlled with medication.

Some medications can also make people more likely to put on weight, including steroids and some medicines for high blood pressure, diabetes or mental health condition.

Other Obesity Related Problems

Day to day problems that are related to obesity include:

- Breathlessness.
- Increased sweating.

- Snoring.
- Difficulty doing physical activity.
- Often feeling very tired.
- Joint and back pain.
- Low confidence and self esteem.
- Feeling isolated.

Serious Health Conditions

Obesity can also increase your risk in developing many potentially serious health conditions, including:

- Type 2 diabetes.
- High blood pressure.
- High cholesterol and atherosclerosis (where fatty deposits narrow your arteries). This can lead to coronary heart disease and stroke.
- Asthma.
- Metabolic syndrome, a combination of diabetes, high blood pressure and obesity.
- Several types of cancer, including bowel cancer, breast cancer and womb cancer.
- Gastro oesophageal reflux disease (GORD), where stomach acid leaks out of the stomach and into the gullet.
- Gallstones.
- Reduced fertility.
- Osteoarthritis, a condition involving pain and stiffness in your joints. Sleep apnoea, a condition that causes interrupted breathing during sleep, which can lead to daytime sleepiness with an increased risk of road traffic accidents, as well as greater risk of diabetes, high blood pressure and heart disease.
- Liver disease and kidney disease.
- Pregnancy complications, such as gestational diabetes or pre-eclampsia, when a woman experiences a potentially dangerous rise in blood pressure during pregnancy.

Obesity reduces life expectancy by an average of 3 to 10 years, depending on how severe it is. Through their research, Dr Kitahara and her colleagues made the stunning discovery that extreme obesity can reduce lifespan by as much as 14 years.[12] This is supported by an NIH study.

---

[12] 23 Jan 2020. https://irp.nih.gov Extreme Obesity Shaves Years Off Life Expectancy.

Outlook

There is no "quick fix" for obesity. Following weight loss programmes take time and commitment, and work best when fully completed. The healthcare professionals involved with your care should provide encouragement and advice about how to maintain the weight loss achieved.

Even losing what seems like a small amount of weight, such as 3% or more of body weight, and maintaining this for life, can significantly reduce your risk of developing obesity-related complications like diabetes and heart disease.[13]

Lifestyle Change

Most often, health care professionals treat overweight and obesity by helping to adopt lifestyle changes that may help people to lose excess weight safely and keep it off over the long term. In some cases, other treatments such as weight-loss medicines or weight-loss surgery can be helpful.[14] However, resort to medicine or surgery should be a last resort. It is far better to reduce your weight by making lifestyle changes as there is a risk in using medicine and a higher risk in surgery.

CONTROLLING GLOBAL OBESITY

Not many decades ago there was the problem of malnutrition in many countries. Now at the other end of the scale is a most blatantly visible (but yet most neglected) public health problems relating to obesity. Paradoxically coexisting with under nutrition, an escalating global epidemic of overweight and obesity – "globesity" – is taking over many parts of the world. The USA and UK rank 9 and 28 respectively in the global ranking with the fattest people. A failure to take immediate action, millions will suffer from an array of serious health disorders.

The table below shows that the very small country **Nauru** (94.5) in the south-west Pacific Ocean ranks as the No 1 country with the fattest people in the world. Because of its income from phosphate, it is a very rich country in the world, though only a few Nauruans are rich. **Israel** is shown as No 50 in the ranking. Out of a list of 194 countries (only 50 shown in the table), the ranking of **Guyana** is 97, **India** is 176 and **China** is 148. India and China have between them 2.6 billion in the total world population of about 8 billion. While the population in India is still growing, it is falling and aging in China.

---

[13] Source NHS 24. Last updated 10 March 2023.
[14] https://www.niddk.nih.gov Treatment for Overweight & Obesity – NIDDK.

Table with Countries of Fattest People

Rank	Country	Rank	Country
1	**Nauru** 94.5 Rank No 1	26	Bahrain
2	Micronesia, F/States 91.1	27	Andorra
3	Cook Islands. 90.9	28	**United Kingdom**
4	Tonga. 90.8	29	Saudi Arabia
5	Niue. 81.7	30	Monaco
6	Samoa. 80.4	31	Bolívar
7	Palau. 78.4	32	San Marino
8	Kuwait.70.2	33	Guatemala
9	**USA**	34	Magnolia
10	Kiribati	35	Canada
11	Dominica	36	Qatar
12	Barbados	37	Uruguay
13	Argentina	38	Jordan
14	Egypt	39	Bahamas
15	Malta	40	Iceland
16	Greece	41	Nicaragua
17	New Zealand	42	Cuba
18	United Arab Emirates	43	Germany
19	Mexico	44	Brunel Darussalam
20	Trinidad and Tobago	45	Slovenia
21	Australia	46	Peru
22	Belarus	47	Vanuatu
23	Chile	48	Finland
25	Seychelles	50	Israel

Effect and Problem of Obesity. Obesity is a complex condition. It has serious social and psychological dimensions that affect virtually all age and socioeconomic groups and threatens to overwhelm both developed and developing countries. In 1995, there were an estimated 200 million obese adults globally and another 18 million under-five children classified as overweight. By 2000, the number of obese adults has increased by over 100 million. Contrary to conventional wisdom, the obesity epidemic is not restricted to industrialised societies. In developing countries, over 115 million people suffer from obesity related problems.[15]

Although the rates of male overweight are higher than female, the rates of obesity are higher for female. Nevertheless, the obesity risk for both of the sexes is a major risk for serious diet-related non communicable

---

[15] World Health Organisation https://www.who.int Controlling the Global Obesity Epidemic

diseases, such as diabetes mellitus, cardiovascular disease, hypertension and stroke, and certain forms of cancer. The health consequences range from increased mortality to serious chronic conditions that reduce the overall quality of life.[16]

In collaboration with the University of Sydney in Australia, WHO is concerned about the global economic impact of overweight and obesity. WHO is also working with the University of Auckland in New Zealand in analysing the impact that globalisation and rapid socioeconomic transition have on nutrition and to identify the main political, socioeconomic, cultural and physical factors which promote obesogenic environments.

TREATMENT FOR OBESITY

The best way to treat obesity is to eat a healthy, reduced-calorie diet and exercise regularly. This entails eating a balanced, calorie-controlled diet as recommended by your GP or weight loss management health professional, such as a dietician. In addition, you may join a local weight loss group, if available.[17] Many doctors may not be knowledgeable about nutrition as it is hardly taught at medical schools (about 20 hours over a 4-year period, and many of these hours may be concentrating on inappropriate topics for nutrition).

Bariatric Surgery for Obesity. This term describes a variety of procedures to manage obesity and related conditions. Long-term weight loss through the standard of care procedures is largely achieved by altering gut hormone levels responsible for hunger and satiety, leading to a new hormone weight set point. This carries some long-term risks for patients, including dumping syndrome. This is a condition that can possibly lead to symptoms like nausea and dizziness, low blood sugar, malnutrition, vomiting, ulcers, bowel obstruction and hernias. All surgeries carry bleeding and infection risks, as well as risks associated with general anaesthesia.[18]

There is also what is known as gastric sleeve for weight loss. Gastric sleeve surgery restricts your food intake. Most of the left part of the stomach is removed. What is left is a narrow tube called a sleeve.[19] The most common complications of sleeve gastrectomy are bleeding, nutrient deficiencies and leakage.

---

[16] WHO Teams, Nutrition and Food Safety (WHO = World Health Organisation).
[17] 10 March 2023. https://www..nhsinform.scot Obesity causes & treatment – illnesses & conditions – NHS inform (NHS is for the National Health Service in the UK).
[18] https://www.dukehealth.org Weight Loss Surgery – Pros and Cons – Duke Health
[19] https://www.hopkinsmedicine.org Gastric Sleeve Surgery John Hopkins Medicine.

Drugs for Weight Loss

There are many side effects, such as nausea, constipation, and diarrhoea, which are common. It is better to concentrate on lifestyle changes rather than on medication or surgery. An Australian lady who used the pill, **Ozempic**, for weight loss died on account of *ileus,* blockage in the bowel.[20]

Treatment with Medication under the NHS. On 4 September 2023 Novo Nordisk announced that a limited supply of Wegovy will become available to people in specialist NHS weight management services who meet NICE eligibility criteria, or privately through a registered healthcare professional.[21] This drug in the US has a minimum monthly price of $1,303. It is expensive for the majority of US patients. Another medication is Ozempic and the most common side effects are nausea, vomiting, diarrhoea, stomach-area pain and constipation. Instead of using medication, your GP can advise about losing weight safely by eating a healthy, balanced diet and regular physical exercise. Limit your fullness to 80% as people in the Blue zones. They can also let you know about other useful services, such as:

- Local weight loss groups
- Exercise on prescription

Treatment for Obesity

Since the FDA in the US approved once-weekly semaglutide injection in 2021 for chronic weight management for adults with obesity or overweight with at least one weight-related condition, a multibillion-dollar market for anti-obesity medications has followed.[22] This is a usual scenario in the US. For example, the mainly public-funded Covid-19 medication has produced 9 billionaires.

Six Weight-loss Drugs Approved in the US. They are:

- Bupropion-naltrexone (Contrave).
- Liraglutide (Saxenda). This is available in the UK also.
- Orlistat (Xenical, Alli).

---

[20] Reported in The Daily Mail on 7 Nov. 2023. The Australian lady, Trish Webster, lost 35 lbs. Her cause of death was acute gastrointestinal illness.

[21] 4 Sept. 2023. https://www.diabetes.org.uk Wegovy made available in the UK for weight loss in people Diabetes UK

[22] 23 Aug 2023. https://www.healio.com Promising new drugs usher in 'transformational time' for obesity.

- Phentermine-topiramate (Qsymia).
- Semaglutide (Wegovy). This is available in the UK also.
- Setmelanotide (Imcivree).[23]

Simple Ways to Lose Weight

Common treatments for overweight and obesity include:

- losing weight through healthy eating;
- being more physically active; and
- making other changes to your usual habits.[24]

Multifaceted Approach

The obesity epidemic has no single or simple solution. It is a complex problem that requires a multifaceted approach. Policy makers, state and local organisations, businesses, school and community leaders, childcare and healthcare professionals and individuals must collaborate to create an environment that supports healthy lifestyles.

DIET (WFPB DIET)

As every individual is different, there is no single rule that applies to everyone. Most people can be advised to reduce their energy intake by 600 calories daily. For most men, they should consume no more than 1,900 calories daily. In the case of women, their intake should be no more than 1,400 calories a day. Ensure that your stomach is not more than 80 % full, as people in the Blue Zones, many of whom live to over 100 years.

To limit your calories intake as above, people of all ages should be discouraged from eating unhealthy and high energy foods, such as fast food, processed food and sugary drinks, including alcohol; they should go for healthier choices. A healthy diet should consist of:

(a) A lot of fruit and vegetables.
(b) Meals based on potatoes, bread, rice, pasta and other starchy foods, preferably high fibre and wholegrain varieties.
(c) Some milk and dairy foods or dairy alternatives (such as plant milks)
(d) Some meat, fish, eggs, beans and other non-dairy sources of protein.
(e) Just very small amounts of food and drinks high in fat and sugar.

---

[23] https://www.mayoclinic.org Prescription weight-loss drugs: Can they help you? – Mayo Clinic.
[24] https://www.cdc.gov Losing Weight Healthy Weight, nutrition, and Physical Activity.

You should try to avoid foods containing high levels of salt. Salt can raise your blood pressure. This is dangerous for people already experiencing obesity. You need to check calorie information for each type of food and drink to ensure you stay within the daily calorie limit. Eating out could create problems, but some eating places provide calorie information per portion. Be careful as some burgers, fried chicken, some curries or Chinese dishes can take you over your daily limit.

Diet Programmes and Fad Diets. Avoid fad diets that encourage unsafe practices, such as fasting (over long period of time) or cutting out entire food groups. Such diets do no work and can make you feel ill. They are not sustainable as they fail to impart long-term healthy eating habits.

Although some commercial diets are unsafe, many can be based on sound medical and scientific principles. They can work well for some people. A good diet programme should:

- Educate people about issues, as to portions, making behavioural changes and healthy eating.
- Not be too restrictive in terms of the types of foods you can eat.
- Be based on achieving gradual, sustainable weight loss instead of a short-term rapid weight loss, which may not last.

Very Low Calorie Diets

Very-low-calorie diets (VLCD) are defined as diets limiting energy intake to 1.88-3.35 MJ (450-800 kcal) daily while providing at least 50g of high-quality protein and amino acids, essential fatty acids and daily requirement of trace elements, vitamins and minerals.

These diets are dietary regimens that provide approximately 400-600kcal daily usually as a liquid formula. Vices have been shown to produce excellent initial weight losses (- 20kg at 12 weeks). This is partly attributable to the degree of caloric restriction and partly to decreased dietary variety and use of protein-controlled foods in these regimens. In the light of the large initial weight loss produced by Vices, it was hoped that by combining these diets with behavioural approaches would result in high long-term weight loss. Despite the Vices improve initial weight loss, they do not appear to have a better long-term weight loss than low calorie diets (Lads).

As Vices have been effective at decreasing intake, the effect of intermittent use of it, transiting to conventional foods, and then returning to a VLCD, on long term weight loss has also been investigated. The result is less than promising. The suggestion is that Vices may produce greater initial weight loss not only by restricting calories but also by increasing the structure of the diet.

Adverse Effect of Too Few Calories

This may put your health at risk in these ways:

- You will not meet your nutrient needs
- Your will slow your metabolism
- You will lose your mental edge
- You might get gallstones.[25]

CONCLUSION

Overweight and obesity is a global problem. In many countries by just taking a walk in a populated area you will appreciate the large number of people who are in the cusp of weight gain, if they are not already obese. This problem was initiated by the growth and marketing of the US fast-food industry, which has spread to almost every country in the world. What is now required as a matter of some urgency is for the authorities to educate the general public on the deleterious effects of overweight and obesity.

The best solution is to advise the general population to eat a balanced diet and to exercise regularly. Medication and surgery to remove body weight is not generally a solution to the problem. Indeed, they may have serious side effects, not to mention that they are expensive. A more desirable solution is to go for a mainly plant-based diet. This is likely to avoid many of the chronic diseases which emanate from being dependent on mainly animal products. In addition, by following such a diet, there will be enormous environmental changes beneficial to the planet.

Those who want to make lifestyle changes, particularly with regard to diet, should choose food that will not spike their blood glucose (sugar). Refer to Chapter 4 for 8 tables showing the sugar content in many foods. For example, a portion of basmati or white rice (150 grams) contains 10.1 teaspoons of sugar. This is not helpful for the reduction of weight.

> "The only successful way to reach and maintain a healthy weight is to find what works for you."
>
> Author Unknown

> "More than half of world's population will be classed as obese or overweight by 2035."
>
> BBC News 3 Mar. 2023

End

---

[25] 7 January 2021. https://www.eatright.org 4 Way Low-Calorie Diets Can Sabatoge Your Health.

CHAPTER 3

DIETS TO PREVENT CHRONIC DISEASES

"Healing takes courage, and we all have courage, even if we have to dig a little to find it."

Tory Amos

"Our food should be our medicine and our medicine should be our food."

Hippocrates

It is difficult to appreciate what it is like to endure a life with chronic illness unless you have been there. The pain of depression, the loneliness of dementia, the fight of those living with arthritis, MS and cancer, to be frank it is a lot, but there are things you can do to feel just a bit better.

Many of the chronic diseases that people suffer from are discussed particularly in relation to how a plant-based diet can help.

HEALTHY EATING AND ITS EFFECT ON CHRONIC DISEASES

This book throughout contains a great deal on the topic of healthy eating and how such eating can help to prevent or reduce the risk of chronic diseases. Healthy eating simply involves a prudent choice of what to eat.

Healthy Eating. This helps to prevent, delay and manage heart disease, type 2 diabetes and other chronic diseases. A balanced, healthy dietary pattern includes a variety of fruits, vegetables, whole grains, lean protein, and low-fat dairy products and limits added sugars, saturated fats, and sodium.[26] Many chronic diseases are caused by key risk behaviours. By making healthy choices, you can reduce your likelihood of getting a chronic disease and improve your quality of life.

Need for Physical Activity. In addition to eating healthy diets, regular physical activity can help you prevent, delay or manage chronic diseases. Avoid strenuous exercises; aim for moderate intensity of physical activity, such as brisk walking or gardening for at least 150 minutes weekly, with muscle-strengthening activities twice weekly.

Avoid Excessive Alcohol. Over time, excessive drinking can lead to high blood pressure, various cancers, heart disease, stroke, and liver disease. Refrain from excessive drinking with a view to reducing these health risks.

---

[26] https://www.cdc.gov > about > prev

Excessive drinking includes binge drinking and drinking by pregnant women and young persons below the legal age limit. Binge drinking includes women consuming 4 or more drinks during a single occasion, while for men it is 5 or more on a single occasion. Heavy drinking is defined as 8 or more drinks by women weekly, while for men it is 15. However, most people who drink excessively are not alcoholics or alcoholic dependent. Be that as it may, drinkers should be careful as the situation can change for the worse, by becoming addictive to alcohol.

> "Sobriety was the best gift I ever gave myself."
>
> Rob Lowe

Regular Visit to Healthcare Clinics. To prevent chronic diseases or catch them early, visit your GP and dentist regularly. This is not only for preventive services but most importantly for the detection of any early disease. You are more likely to be cured of a chronic disease if you are diagnosed early. While you may recover from a stage one cancer, it is very unlikely you can from stage 4.

Oral Diseases and Dental Visit. These range from cavities and gum disease to oral cancer. They cause pain and disability for millions of people around the world. To help prevent these problems, drink fluoridated water, brush your teeth with fluoride toothpaste at least twice daily and floss daily. Visit your dentist at least once a year, even if you have no natural teeth or have dentures. Some people try to avoid fluoride due to its toxic nature.[27]

Enough Sleep. Insufficient sleep has been associated with the development and poor management of diabetes, heart disease, obesity, and depression. Adults should try to sleep for 7 hours daily.

> "Early to bed and early to rise, makes a man healthy, wealthy, and wise."
>
> Benjamin Franklin

Family History and Health. If you have a family history of a chronic disease, e.g., osteoporosis, you may be more likely to develop that disease yourself. However, if you follow a healthy lifestyle, it does not necessarily follow that you will encounter the same fate. Taking precaution is important for longevity. Some health conditions that run in families are these:

- Asthma.

---

[27] S.Guth 2020, Toxity of fluoride: critical evaluation of evidence for human development, See also Harvard T H Chan School. https://www.hsph.harvard.edu

- Birth defects (such as spina bifida or a cleft lip).
- Cancer (including breast, ovarian, prostate, bowel/colon or melanoma skin cancer).
- Diabetes.
- Genetic conditions, such as cystic fibrosis or haemophilia.
- Heart disease or sudden heart attack.

Make healthy choices whether you are at home, school or at work. Choose healthy behaviours as part of your daily life. This can prevent conditions such as high blood pressure or obesity, which can raise your risk of developing the most common and serious chronic diseases.

Prevent the Spread of Infection

Most importantly, cultivate the habit of washing your hands frequently. Cover your mouth when you cough or sneeze as your germs can travel 3 feet or more almost instantaneously. Use a tissue and after its disposal safely wash your hands after.

You need to practice good environmental hygiene. Ensure that you clean kitchen and bathroom surfaces well, wash hands before and after handling food products; separate raw meat and poultry prep surfaces from uncooked vegetables (such as salad materials); pay attention to timely refrigeration, perishable product expiration dates, and appropriate cooking temperatures.

Take your flue vaccine and encourage friends and family to do so as well. Wear your mask and exercise social distancing if required to help stop the spread of Covid-19. As this disease has subsided largely, very few people wear a mask.

Avoid misuse and overuse of antibiotics, and question your healthcare you have questions about preventing germ transmission. Communicate infection control concerns and issues to your healthcare providers.

At the expense of repetition, wash your hands frequently. This is important. Be an infection prevention role model to your family and friends.

CHRONIC DISEASES

> "Chronic disease is a food borne illness. We ate our way into this mess, and we must eat our way out."
>
> Mark Hyam, MD.

A chronic disease is a condition that lasts one year or more and requires ongoing medical attention; it may limit one's activities of daily living. Chronic diseases such as heart disease, cancer (different types), and type 2 diabetes are the leading causes of death and disability in many countries including the US and the UK.

A plant-based diet can prevent or reduce the risk of developing a chronic disease which can take many forms. Some of the chronic diseases and conditions are these:

- Cancer (in the US about 1,700 persons die every day due to cancer).
- Arthritis.
- Type 2 diabetes.
- Stroke.
- Kidney disease.
- Alzheimer's disease and other dementias.
- Asthma.
- Chronic obstructive pulmonary disease (COPD).
- Crohn's disease, ulcerative colitis, other inflammatory bowel diseases, irritable bowel syndrome (IBS).
- Cystic fibrosis.
- Eating disorders.
- Heart disease.
- Obesity.
- Oral health.
- Osteoporosis.
- Reflex sympathetic dystrophy (RSD) syndrome.
- Sudden cardiac arrest (SCA) in youth.
- Tobacco use and related conditions.

Today, the top 7 most common chronic diseases in the West, in particular the US, are heart disease, cancer, chronic lung disease, stroke, Alzheimer's, diabetes and kidney disease. In Chapter 8, there is information on Alzheimer's, Parkinson's, strokes, other brain disorders, dementia and epilepsy. Kidney and liver diseases are discussed in Chapter 15.

Chronic diseases, such as heart disease, cancer, diabetes, stroke and arthritis, are the main causes of disability and death in New York State and throughout the US. More than 40% of adults in this State suffer from chronic diseases. Chronic diseases are responsible for 23% of all hospitalisations. Six of every 10 deaths are caused by chronic diseases. Cancer and heart diseases account for over half of all deaths. These statistics should not be occurring in a State within the most powerful and very rich country in the world. Something is definitely wrong.

Although common and costly, many chronic diseases are also preventable and those in being can go into remission in most cases. Many of such diseases are linked to lifestyle choices. They are within your control to change. By consuming nutritious foods, be involved in physical activity and avoiding tobacco and excessive alcohol, you can prevent developing many of these diseases and conditions. Even if you are already suffering from diabetes, heart disease, arthritis or another chronic condition, eating mainly plant-based diets and being involved in more physical exercises (whether a brisk walk, a bike ride, a jog or a swim) can enable you to better manage your illness, avoid complications and live longer.

In the State of New York, the Department of Health's division of chronic disease prevention implements innovative public health strategies. This is to reduce the incidence and burden of chronic diseases and related conditions.[28]

Chronic Disease and the NHS (in the UK). A long term physical health condition (also known as a chronic condition) is a health problem. It requires ongoing management over many years or decades. The condition is one that cannot currently be cured but can be controlled with the use of medication and/or other therapies.[29] The 7 most common chronic illnesses in the UK are these:

- Coronary heart disease (CHD). This is a long term damage, blockage or in worst cases both in the heart's major blood vessels.
- Cancer.
- Stroke.
- Chronic obstructive pulmonary disease (COPD).
- Dementia (including Alzheimer's disease).
- Liver disease (refer to Chapter 15 for a discussion on it).
- Diabetes.[30] Type 2 diabetes can go into remission by lifestyle changes. Doctors hardly provide advice on this as it is in their interest to prescribe metformin (medication).

Brief details below are given on some of the chronic diseases.

HEART DISEASE (Coronary Heart Disease)

Coronary heart disease (CHD) is not only common but is a serious condition. The blood vessels supplying the heart are narrowed and blocked. This disease does not always have obvious symptoms. For some people, it can cause chest pain (angina) or serious problems such as heart attacks. The main treatments for a coronary heart disease are healthy lifestyle changes and medicines. Some serious cases may need surgery.

---

[28] Refer to the Division of Chronic Disease Prevention Fact Sheet for more information.
[29] https://www.datadictioary.nhs.uk Long Term Physical HealthCondition – NHS Data dictionary
[30] 10 April 2023. https://bequest.com 7 Most common chronic illnesses in the UK - Bequest

The cause of this disease is a build-up of fatty substance in the blood vessels supplying the heart with blood. It is often linked to the consumption of unhealthy diets (e.g., eating a breakfast of ham, sausages and bacon). The risk of getting this disease can be reduced by making simple lifestyle changes. These are a healthy diet and being involved in regular exercises.

Major Cause of Death. Coronary heart disease (CHD) is a major cause of death worldwide, including the UK and the USA.

Symptoms of CHD. The main symptoms CHD are:

- Chest pain.
- Shortness of breath.
- Pain throughout the body.
- Feeling faint.
- Nausea, feeling sick.

Furring-up of Arteries. Over time the walls of your arteries can become furred up with fatty deposits. This process is known as atherosclerosis, and the deposits are known as atheroma. Atherosclerosis can be caused by lifestyle factors. Contributory factors can be smoking and consumption of excessive amounts of alcohol, in addition to unhealthy diets. You are at greater risk of developing atherosclerosis if you have conditions such as high cholesterol, high blood pressure (hypertension) or diabetes.

Diagnosing CHD. If a medical doctor is of the view that you are at risk of CHD, a risk assessment may be carried out. You will be asked about your medical and family history and your lifestyle. A blood test will be taken. Further tests may be required to confirm the CHD, including:

- A treadmill test.
- A radionuclide scan.
- A CT scan.
- An MRI scan.
- Coronary angiography.

Treating Coronary Heart Disease (CHD). This disease cannot be cured but treatment can help to manage the symptoms and reduce the chances of problems of possible heart attacks.[31] Treatment can include:

---

[31] A US doctor who was involved in treating patients for heart problems told a patient to follow a plant-based diet and to return in a few months' time as he could not schedule him for surgery immediately. When that patient returned a few months later, it was found that he no longer required surgery. The plaques in his arteries disappeared on account of the

(a) Lifestyle changes, such as regular exercise and quitting smoking.
(b) Taking medication.
(c) Angioplasty – balloons and stents are used to treat narrow heart arteries.
(d) As a last resort heart surgery.

An angioplasty or heart surgery may bring you back to a normal life if you had suffered a heart attack.

Prevention of CHD

The risk of CHD can be reduced by making lifestyle changes. These changes are:

- Eating a healthy, balanced diet (mainly plant-based).
- Being physically active (sedentary people should do some exercise).
- If you smoke, give up this deadly habit.
- Control your blood cholesterol and sugar levels.

Keeping a healthy heart will have other benefits as well. They may help to reduce your risk of stroke and dementia.

Improve Heart Health. A whole-food, plant-based diet is extremely effective at promoting cardiovascular health and preventing, halting, and in some cases even reversing heart disease. This is the leading cause of death in the United States and many other countries. A 2021 review of 99 studies found that diets rich in whole and minimally processed plant-based foods were associated with significantly lower risk of cardiovascular disease compared with diets high in meat and dairy products.

Effect of Animal-Based Food. Animal-based foods are high in saturated fat and cholesterol, which raise blood cholesterol levels, causing fatty, wax-like plaque to build up in the arteries. Highly processed foods often contain excessive salt, which raises blood pressure, damaging the lining of the arteries over time. By eliminating these harmful foods from your diet and replacing them with whole plant-based foods, you can bring down your cholesterol levels, blood pressure, and risk of heart disease.

A Plant-Based Diet May Keep Your Heart Healthy

Meat contains saturated fat. This can contribute to heart issues when eaten

---

new diet. Thereafter, the doctor converted his practice to that of a GP and he never carried out another stent operation. He felt he was better able to advise his patients.

in excess. So by cutting back on meat and eating more plant-based foods, you will improve your health. A published study found that eating a plant-based diet may reduce the risk of developing cardiovascular disease by 16% and of dying of this health condition by about 31%.[32]

Limiting Meat. Limiting meat consumption has enormous benefits and helps to prevent cardiovascular disease. Concentrate on foods that are anti-inflammatory. These foods happen to be mainly plant-based foods. They include green leafy vegetables, yellow vegetables, whole grains, walnuts, extra virgin olive oil, tomatoes, and fruits. You should also eat fatty fish. On the other hand, you should avoid pro-inflammatory foods. These are processed meats, processed foods, fried foods, and refined sugar.

Cardiac Health. In addition to helping improve insulin sensitivity and decrease BMI, a vegan diet may reduce risk of cardiovascular disease and improve cardiac function. This is of particular importance given that the CDC ranked heart disease as the leading cause of death in the US in 2020.[33] A plant-based diet affects cardiovascular outcomes in a positive way.

Based on lifestyle trials, diet could be the cause of atherosclerosis. In a study, patients with cardiac disease were switched from their omnivorous diets to either a plant-based diet or the American Heart Association Diet. The study found that 34% more patients on the plant-based diet had a reduction of atherosclerosis than those on the diet recommended by the American Heart Association. People who avoid meat have significantly lower rates of both ischemic heart disease and all-cause mortality.

There was a combined evaluation of five prospective analyses comparing omnivore vs. vegetarian rates of death from ischemic coronary disease. The vegetarians were found to have 24% lower rates of death from ischemic heart disease than those who ate meat after controlling for factors such as smoking status, age, and gender.[10]

CANCERS

"Our greatest weakness lies in giving up. The most certain way to succeed is always to just try one more time."

Thomas Edison

"Most of the important things in the world have been accomplished by people who have kept on trying when there seemed to be no hope at all."

Dale Carnegie

---

[32] Journal of the American Heart Association
[33] There have been many studies carried out on heart disease and can be easily found on the internet, if interested.

A cancer may be regarded as a chronic disease. It is a journey, but you are in the road alone. It is often the case with certain cancer types, such as ovarian cancer, chronic leukaemia, and some lymphomas that they are considered as chronic. Those that have spread or have returned in other parts of the body, like metastatic breast or prostate cancer, also become chronic cancers.[34] Chronic cancers often do spread.[35]

Late Stage Cancers Not Usually Curable. Cancers which are difficult to cure are these:

- Pancreatic cancer.[36]
- Mesothelioma.
- Gallbladder cancer.
- Oesophageal cancer.
- Liver and intrahepatic bile duct cancer.
- Lung and bronchial cancer.
- Pleural cancer.
- Acute monocytic leukaemia.[37]

Lung and bronchus cancer is responsible for the most deaths with 127,000 expected to die yearly from this disease (in the US). This is nearly 3 times the 52,550 deaths attributable to colorectal cancer. This is the second most common cause of cancer death. Pancreatic cancer is the third deadliest cancer responsible for 50,550 deaths.[38]

The highest five-year survival estimates were seen in patients with testicular cancer (97%) melanoma of skin (92%) and prostate cancer (88%). What is important is the stage at which the cancer is diagnosed. Even if a cancer cannot be considered 100% eradicated today, many can be effectively "cured" if detected early. A stage zero cancer such as ductal carcinoma in situ (DCIS) are in theory cancers that can be cured completely.[39]

---

[34] 14 Jan. 2019. https://www.cancer.org Managing Cancer as a Chronic Illness.

[35] https://www.lvhn.org Living with Cancer as a Chronic Illness – Lehigh Valley Health Network.

[36] But a few cases have been reported as being cured. One was a Brazilian doctor in Boston. He had stage 4 pancreatic cancer and went back to Brazil to seek a cure from herbs.
Another person with the same cancer is from New York (Ms Marisa Harris). She was cured by following plant foods, exercise and some chemo. Her doctor died but she survived.

[37] 21 Sept. 2022 https://www.livescience.com The 10 deadliest cancers, and why there's no cure – Live Science

[38] https://seer.cancer.gov Cancer Stat Facts: Common Cancer Sites

[39] 28 Feb. 2023. https://www.verywellhealth.com Will Cancer Ever Be Cured?

Herbal Remedies. There is no reliable evidence from human studies that herbal remedies can treat, prevent or cure any type of cancer. Some clinical trials seem to show that certain Chinese herbs may heal people to live longer, might reduce side effects, and help to prevent a return of the cancer.[40] An extract from wormwood plant kills breast cancer cells in a test tube.[41] Garlic is the most powerful anti-cancer spice. It is part of the cancer-fighting allium group (onions, shallots, scallions, leeks, chives). Garlic helps boost the immune system to help fight diseases, as well as colds and flu. It also decreases the growth of cancer cells.[42]

A Plant-Based Diet May Decrease Your Risk of Cancer. It is well-known that a plant-based diet has many health benefits. Can it help prevent cancer? Research suggests that the answer could be in the affirmative. The American Institute for Cancer Research says the best way to source cancer-protective nutrients, including fibre, vitamins, minerals, and phytochemicals, is to consume a diet rich in vegetables, fruit, grains, beans, nuts, seeds, and some animal foods. This also applies for cancer survivors. The protective benefits are there though moderate according to *Cancer Management and Research* Notes. The risk for certain cancers is lowered by about 10%. The lower risk is likely on account of the nutrients present in plant foods. Such foods are full of chemical compounds, called phytochemicals that protect the body from damage. Phytochemicals also interrupt processes in the body that encourage cancer production.[43]

Cancer Fighting Foods

At the top of the list are berries, broccoli, tomatoes, walnuts, grapes and other vegetables, fruits and nuts. The typical foods that reduce cancer risk are all plant foods that contain phytochemicals.[44]

Broccoli is a wonderful addition to your arsenal of cancer fighting foods. With broccoli specifically there is a high amount of phytochemical called sulforaphane. This is a cancer-fighting plant compound that has been linked to reducing the risks of prostate cancer, breast cancer, colon cancer and oral cancers.[45] Dark green leafy vegetables such as mustard, greens, lettuce, kale, chicory, spinach and chard have an abundance of fibre, foliate,

---

[40] https://www.cancerresearchuk.org Herbal medicine Complementary and alternative therapy.
[41] https://www.science.org Wormwood Extract Kills Cancer Cells Science AAAS
[42] 22 Sept 2016 https://www.mhs.net Six cancer-fighting herbs and spices - Memorial Healthcare System.
[43] 21 June 2022. https://www.mayoclinichealthsystem.org
[44] https://www.mdanderson.org 36 Foods That May Help Lower Your cancer Risk.
[45] 29 Sept. 2021. https://www.uclahealth.org Broccoli and other cruciferous veggies can significantly lower cancer risks.

and carotenoids. These nutrients may help protect against cancer of the mouth, larynx, pancreas, lung, skin and stomach.[46]

Carotenoids like beta-carotene (carrots), lycopene (tomatoes) and lutein (spinach) provide you with antioxidants. Antioxidants help protect your cells from damage that might turn them into cancer cells.

Bananas can be a great dietary addition for those recovering from cancer. Bananas are easy to tolerate for those with swallowing difficulties. Also, they are a good source of many important nutrients, such as vitamin B6, manganese, and vitamin C.[47] But a fully ripe banana has a lot of sugar.

The American Institute for Cancer Research recommends drinks in your diet that provide vitamins and phytonutrients that have demonstrated anti-cancer effects. Some of the recommended drinks are coffee, green tea, red wine, and 100% vegetable and fruit juices.[48] These are among the best choices.[49]

Using Diet to Reduce Cancer Risk. Filling your plate with food grown in the ground may be the best diet for cancer prevention. It was estimated that 1.9 million cases of cancer was discovered in the US in 2022.[50] Some people have a higher genetic risk to develop cancer, but according to research nearly 25% of cancer cases could be prevented with diet and nutrition alone. As many cancers can take 10 years or more to develop, it is prudent to choose your diet carefully for cancer prevention.

According to research, people who do not eat any animal products, including fish, dairy, or eggs appeared to have the lowest rates of cancer. The next lowest rate was for vegetarians, who avoid meat but may eat fish or foods originate from animals (eggs and milk). Plant-based diets also are high in fibre. Eating a plant-based diet has been shown to lower the risk of breast and colorectal cancer as well.

Plant Chemicals. In addition to protecting from damage, these chemicals interrupt processes in the body that encourages cancer production. Two of the most helpful phytochemicals are these:

(a) **Antioxidants**. This type protects the body from damage. Cancer develops when the DNA in cells is damaged, causing abnormal cells to

---

[46] 24 April 2022. https://www.webmd.com Cancer-fighting Foods: Resveratrol, Green Tea, and More - WebMD

[47] 28 Aug. 2019. https://www.healthline.com Fruits to Eat During and After Cancer Treatment _ Healthline

[48] By squeezing fruits for the juice will have the effect of getting rid of the fibre. It may be better to eat the whole fruit for both the juice and the fibre rather than just the juice.

[49] 9 Nov 2019. https://draxe.com Cancer-fifhting Drinks: Best 6 types and Dosage – Dr Axe.

[50] According to the American Cancer Society.

divide uncontrollably. This can infiltrate and destroy normal body tissue. Such cell damage can also be caused by radiation, viruses and exposure to other chemicals. In addition, the body's natural metabolism creates oxidants that can cause cell damage. Antioxidants neutralise such damage processes while protecting and restoring cells. Foods that include high levels of antioxidants include dark chocolate, apples with the skin, avocados, artichokes, red cabbage, tea, coffee, nuts and grains.

(b) **Carotenoids**. These are fat soluble compounds. They need to be accompanied by a fat source to be absorbed. They can be found naturally in many fruits, grains, oils and vegetables, such as sweet potatoes, carrots squash, spinach, apricots, green peppers and leafy greens. As they are highly pigmented, they look for natural foods which are red, orange, yellow and green in colour. Carotenoids include beta, carotene, lycopene and lutein. They are known to have reduced the risk of heart disease, cancer, macular degeneration and cataracts.

Some plant-based foods are high in provitamins known as alpha and gamma carotene. When eaten, these vitamins can be converted to vitamin A. This nutrient is important to vision, growth, cell division, reproduction and immunity, not to mention the antioxidant properties.

Phytochemicals and nutrients in plant-based foods appear to work both independently and together to decrease cancer and disease risk. Plant-based foods work best when eaten with other foods. A prostate cancer study showed that a combination of broccoli and tomato diet was more effective at slowing tumor growth than each eaten individually.

Plant-Based Fibre. The high fibre content of plant foods has been shown to reduce cancer risk and moderate insulin levels. Young women who ate the most fibre-rich diets were 25% less likely to get breast cancer later in life, according to a study. Another study finds that 10 grams of daily fibre could lower the risk of colorectal cancer by 10%.

Portions in Your Diet. You should try to obtain as far as possible those set out under (a) to (e) below:

(a) Fruits, 1.5 to 2.5 cups daily
(b) Vegetables, 2.5 to 4 cups daily
(c) Whole grains, 3 to 5 ounces daily
(d) Legumes, 1.5 cups weekly
(e) Protein, 5 to 7 ounces daily.

Legumes, dairy, tofu and eggs are excellent sources of protein. Or you can select lean cuts of meats, and avoid processed meats.

Fats should be limited to 3 to 5 servings daily. One serving is one teaspoon of oil, 4 walnut halves or one-sixth of an avocado.

Moving to a Plant-Based Diet

Consuming a plant-based diet does not have to be all or nothing. You can make a gradual change. This is more sustainable and realistic for most people. They can gradually increase their intake of a plant-based diet.

Seven Ways a Vegan Diet Fights Cancer. They are:

(a) Consume adequate fibre.
(b) Eat foods with many colours that reflect the rainbow.
(c) Eat and enjoy soy as it is associated with a reduced risk of cancer.
(d) Avoid the deli meat (this type of meat is deadly).
(e) Ditch the dairy. Studies have linked high-fat dairy products to an increased risk of breast and prostate cancers.
(f) Avoid hot dogs. When meat is grilled, it releases carcinogens known as heterocyclic armines (HCAs) including a compound called PHIP, which is linked to multiple cancers.
(g) Avoid alcohol. Consuming just one alcoholic beverage or more daily has been associated with an increased risk of colorectal cancer. Alcohol has been linked to an increased risk of breast cancer. Women should be careful.

Plant-Based Diet for Recovery from Cancer Treatment

Eating a plant-based diet has many proven health benefits. It may help cancer patients to better manage treatment-related side effects and help them stay strong during their recovery. A plant-based diet may provide a healthier alternative to the standard American diet, or Western diet, a high-calorie feast loaded with red meat, high-fat dairy products, heavily processed foods, fast foods, refined carbohydrates, added sugars and salt.

The American Institute for Cancer Research now promotes the New American Plate. It focuses on eating sensible servings, comprising a variety of whole foods, such as vegetables, fruits, and whole grains. Some studies have suggested that eating whole soy foods, such as tofu, endameme and soy milk, may reduce the risk of breast cancer. However, there were no rigorous clinical trials as yet.

With regard to cancers, there are studies that suggest up to 30 to 40% of all kinds can be prevented with healthy lifestyle and dietary measures. Particularly beneficial in reducing the risk of cancer are foods rich in certain vitamins, antioxidants and carotenoids. Those listed below are excellent sources:

(a) Garlic.
(b) Broccoli.
(c) Tomatoes.
(d) Berries.
(e) Carrots.
(f) Leafy greens.

So far for cancer, now how to avoid brain diseases?

BRAIN DISEASES

The chronic neurological diseases are:

(a) Alzheimer's disease, including dementia.
(b) Parkinson's disease.
(c) Dystonia.
(d) ALS (Lou Gehrig's disease).
(e) Huntington's disease.
(f) Neuromuscular disease.
(g) Multiple Sclerosis, and
(h) Epilepsy, among others.

The above diseases afflict millions of people around the world and account for tremendous morbidity and mortality.[51] The 5 common neurological disorders are headache, stroke, seizures, Parkinson's, and dementia.

Information from The Daily Mail. How to keep your brain sharp in your 50s and beyond: After alarming study rules pandemic had "lasting impact" on cognitive function, experts share their must-know tips in the picture below after this quote.

> "It was the alarming claim that made headlines this week [7 Nov. 2023] - Covid had a 'real lasting impact' on the brain health of people over 50. Scientists at the University of Exeter and King's College London found memory and cognitive function, such as decision making, declined quicker during the pandemic. It sparked the question of whether Britain could be facing a dementia time bomb. Experts claimed the effects were likely due to factors exacerbated by the pandemic and subsequent restrictions, such as not exercising enough and drinking too much alcohol, as well as loneliness and depression. Staying healthy in later life can prove tricky, especially if other health problems are in the mix. But,

---

[51] https://mbi.ufl.edu chronic Neurological diseases – McKnight Brain Institute.

generally speaking, is there anything people can do to help keep their cognitive function and memory sharp in their 50s and beyond? We asked some experts."[52]

There is evidence indicating that a vegan diet could be beneficial in preventing neurodegenerative disorders, including Alzheimer's disease.[53]

Brain Plant-Based Diets. These have been shown to have many benefits for brain health. Such diets provide the body with the essential nutrients necessary for maintaining brain function and protecting against many brain-health-related issues.[54]

There is evidence that vegetarians have a lower risk of dementia, and there is no evidence about the association of a vegan diet with dementia.[55]

Most people are choline deficient as they are not getting enough choline, while some people are genetically predisposed to a deficiency. Based on a study, the rising popularity of vegan and vegetarian diets is raising rates of deficiency. A male person requires about 550 mg daily (425 mg for women). The two richest sources of choline are beef liver and egg yolk, but most people would get theirs from eggs. Plant foods that are especially rich in choline include:

- Tofu.
- Soynuts.
- Soymilk.
- Cruciferous vegetables.
- Cooked dried beans.
- Quinoa.

[52] The Daily Mail on 7 Nov. 2023.
[53] 29 Nov. 2022. https://www.ncbi.nlm.nih.gov >pmc
[54] https://www.bluetribefoods.com > b Benefits of a Plant-Based Diet for Brain Health – Blue Tribe Foods
[55] 29 Nov. 2022 https://www.ncbi.nlm.nih.gov > pmc Effect of a Vegan Diet on Alzheimer's Disease – PMC - NCBI

- Peanuts peanut butter.

It is not clear how much choline is in more processed vegan foods as this has not been measured.[56]

Eating a Plant-Based Diet May Minimize Your Risk of Stroke

Your risk for stroke increases if you have high blood pressure, are overweight, have diabetes or heart disease, have high cholesterol, or smoke, drink, or use drugs. As noted above, most of those risk factors can be wiped out by following a plant-based diet and making healthy lifestyle choices. After all, half of strokes are preventable. One simple way to reduce your risk is by increasing your intake of fruits and vegetables. The highest consumers of fruits and veggies had a 21 percent lower risk of stroke than those who consumed the least, according to a study.

Ramping Up Your Plant Intake May Keep Your Brain Strong

The physiological benefits of following a plant-based diet are many, including possible mental ones, too. "There is some compelling research examining plant-based diets and their role in slowing the progression of Alzheimer's," Feller says.[57] A review of nine studies found that eating an extra 100 grams of fruits and vegetables daily (about one-half cup) led to a 13% reduction in the risk of cognitive impairment and dementia.

Polyphenols. What is the likely reason why fruits and vegetables are rich in polyphenols? According to an article published in *Nutrients,* fruits, vegetables, and whole grains (aka, the cornerstones of a plant-based diet) contain polyphenols. These may help slow the progression of Alzheimer's disease and may help to reverse cognitive decline, according to a study.[58]

ARTHRITIS

Arthritis is usually ongoing (chronic). This and other rheumatic diseases are more common in women than men. These conditions are often encountered by older people, but people of all ages may be afflicted.

Most forms of arthritis are thought to be caused by a fault in the immune system. That causes the body to attack its own tissues in the joints. It could be inherited genetically. Other forms of arthritis can be caused by problems with the immune system or by a metabolic condition, such as

---

[56] https://veganhealth.org Choline – Vegan Health.
[57] https://www.linkedin.com Michelle Feller – Alzheimer's Association.
[58] A review published published in *Current Pharmaceutical Biotechnology* (23).

gout.[59]Environmental factors that may contribute to the development of osteoarthritis include:

- Obesity which places added strain on joints.
- Activities that involve repetitive movements of a particular joint.
- Previous damage to a joint, such as from a sports injury.

People who smoke and are not involved in much physical activity are more likely to develop arthritis. If the arthritis is attributable to an infection it is called "reactive arthritis". This type is difficult to diagnose, and it can develop at an age, though it is more commonly seen in younger people. Reactive arthritis is temporary and can last from a few weeks to 6 months.

The most appropriate treatment depends on the type of arthritis you have, which joints are affected, and the symptoms you have. Treatment might include:

- Pain killers, anti-inflammatory medicines to slow down the disease.
- Pain management techniques, such as with medication.

In serious cases, surgery may be required to replace or repair damaged joints. If you are living with arthritis there are many things you can do to help in its management. Maintain a healthy lifestyle can help to control the symptoms.

Diet and Fats. Eating well is advocated for your overall health and wellbeing. A healthy diet can help towards maintaining a healthy weight. This reduces the pressure placed on the joints. Also, it might help to reduce joint pain. Eating healthy fats, such as monounsaturated and omega-3 fats, instead of the unhealthy polyunsaturated fats, can help reduce the symptoms of arthritis. These benefits are modest compared with benefits from modification, but they have no side effects, not to mention a reduction in the risk of heart disease. Those who suffer from arthritis should aim to eat:

- A healthy balanced diet.
- More Mediterranean-style diet, with a lot of fish, pulses, nuts, olive oil, fruit and vegetables.
- More saturated fats, such as in vegetable oils, avocados and many nuts and seeds.
- More omega-3 fatty acids, such as from oily fish.
- Less saturated fats, such as from red meat, poultry, and full-fat dairy.

---

[59] https://www.healthdirect.gov.au Arthritis – causes, symptoms and treatment – Healthdirect.

- Less energy dense foods, such as in fatty and sugary foods to avoid gaining weight.
- Adequate calcium dairy products do not cause arthritis but the calcium therein is important for strong bones, which is especially important for people with arthritis, who may be at increased risk of osteoporosis (weak and brittle bones). Consume plenty of calcium-rich foods including dairy products (milk, cheese and yoghurt), nuts, seeds and fish, such as sardines or whitebait (particularly if you eat the bones).

Some people believe that acidic fruits, such as lemons, oranges and grapefruit, and nightshade vegetables, such as potatoes, eggplants and capsicum, can make symptoms worse. But there is no proof of this, and the avoidance of these foods may do more harm than good.

Exercise Regularly. This is important for the effective treatment of arthritis. Exercise is beneficial in these ways:

- It helps with balance.
- It keeps muscles strong to support the joints.
- It helps to reduce joint stiffness.
- It reduces pain and tension in your joints.
- It helps in decreasing fatigue and depression.
- It keeps you mobile.
- It boosts your mood and energy.
- It improves sleep.

Three types of exercise combine to make up a good fitness programme. They are:

- Range of movement to help improve strength and flexibility and the promotion of good posture: try swimming, tai chi and golf.
- Strengthening your body to help build the muscles, which in turn provide better support for your joints: try weight training.
- Aerobic to raise your heartbeat, which helps to improve your fitness level by strengthening your heart: try brisk walking, cycling and tennis.

If you suffer from rheumatoid arthritis, try to get the correct balance between rest and activity. Swimming and cycling are good low impact choices. Pain can be caused by inflammation, damage to the joints and muscle tension. What to do to manage pain are:

- Take pain killers (be warned medication may have side effects).
- Exercise regularly to keep joints moving (avoid strenuous exercises).
- Use a hot heat pack or hot water bottle or cold ice pack treatments throughout the day.
- Look after your joints by avoiding activities that exacerbate the pain.
- Use therapies, such as massage, acupuncture, transcutaneous electrical nerve stimulation or mindfulness techniques.[60]

How to Avoid Arthritis

Keep your joints healthy as you age by observing these:

(a) Control your blood sugar.
(b) Exercise regularly.
(c) Do some daily stretching.
(d) Maintain a healthy weight as excess weight puts pressure on weight-bearing joints such as hips and knees.
(e) Be careful to avoid injury.
(f) Quit smoking if you are a smoker.
(g) Eat fish twice weekly (be advised the larger fish may have mercury).
(h) Arrange for routine preventive care.[61]

That is all for arthritis, now a look into diabetes.

DIABETES (Prevent or Reverse Type 2 Diabetes

> "I want to change the belief of millions of people who think there is nothing they can do to stop taking medications and reverse an existing case of Type 2 Diabetes."
>
> John M. Poothullil

Diabetes mellitus, or diabetes, is a disease that causes high blood sugar. It occurs when there is a problem with insulin. This is a hormone that takes sugar from foods and moves it to the body's cells. If the body does not make enough insulin or does not use insulin well, the sugar from food stays in the blood, resulting in high blood sugar.

Diabetes is a common life-long health condition, if steps are not taken towards a remission. There are over 3.5 million people diagnosed with

---

[60] Source: Arthritis Australia: *Understanding arthritis, Healthy eating and arthritis, 10 steps for living well with arthritis, etc, etc*
[61] Https://www.bluecrossmn.com How to prevent arthritis pain Bluecross MN.

diabetes in the UK and an estimated 549,000 people who have the condition, but are not aware of it.[62]

Two Main Types of Diabetes.

They are: type 1 and type 2. These 2 types are attributable to different causes. The difference between them is substantial as can be seen below.

Difference Between Type 1 and Type 2

(a) **Type-1 Diabetes**. In type 1, the pancreas does not make insulin as the body's immune system attacks the islet cells in the pancreas that make the insulin; the cells that produce insulin are destroyed.

(b) **Type-2 Diabetes.** This is present when the body does not produce enough insulin, or the body's cells do not react to insulin. The pancreas makes less insulin than it used to, and your body becomes resistant to insulin.[63] This means glucose stays in the blood and is not used as fuel for energy.

The type-2 is far more common than type-1. In the UK, around 90% of all adults with diabetes have type 2.

Type 2 Diabetes is often associated with obesity and tends to be diagnosed in older people. On account of increased obesity and overweight, type 2 is now being seen in young people of all ages. It is far more common than type 1. Type 2 is treated with changes in your diet and depending on the response of your blood glucose levels, sometimes with medication and insulin. In the early stage of type 2, a planned weight loss can even reverse the disease. Even some people with the disease for over 10 years have been able to go into remission.

Type 2 diabetes is a condition that causes too much sugar in your blood. It can cause serious health problems if it is not treated (managed or bring it into remission). The symptoms of this disease include the need to urinate a lot, feeling thirsty all the time and feeling tired. Treatment for type 2 diabetes includes medicines and changes to your diet and activity levels to control your blood sugar levels.

Help with Oxygen Therapy. Many people with diabetes make use of oxygen therapy. Breathing pure oxygen in gently pressurised oxygen could alter the response of the immune system to the development of diabetes. In this manner more oxygen gets into the bloodstream than usual. This helps to accelerate the body's natural healing process. It is particularly helpful in the

---

[62] Diabetes UK https://www.diabetes.org.uk
[63] https://uvahealth.com Type 1 vs Type 2 Diabetes – UVA Health

43

treatment of Diabetic Foot Ulcers, even in the stubborn case where there is a risk of amputation. Oxygen Therapy can help to:

(a) accelerate healing;
(b) reduce pain;
(c) increase energy;
(d) reduce inflammation; and
(e) combat infection.

Diabetes Worldwide

In the US, the rate of new cases rose sharply in the past (from the 1990s), but it fell between 2008 and 2015 and it continues to fall.[64] Meanwhile, the number of adults with diabetes continues to rise. The most common diabetes is type-2, and some 90 to 95% of people have this type compared to just about 5% with type-1.

Causes. The risk of developing diabetes increases with age. Type-2 is thought to result from a combination of lifestyle and genetic factors. While scientists are not aware of the exact cause, the risk factors appear to include:

(a) excess body fat;
(b) high blood pressure or cholesterol;
(c) having a close family member with the condition;
(d) a history of gestational diabetes; and
(e) higher age (elderly people are more prone to the disease).

In view of the increasing prevalence of obesity in the past few decades, there has been a corresponding increase in type-2 diabetes as well. While in 2013 more than 1 in 3 people in the US were considered to be obese, over 2 in 3 were either overweight or had obesity. There is a link between obesity and diabetes. This link is well known, but the reasons for the link remain unclear.[65] However, obesity does not always lead to diabetes.

Diabetes and Ethnicity

Diabetes varies among ethnic groups in the US. There may be a combination of factors, such as genetics, health conditions, lifestyle, finances, environment and access to healthcare. It is found that, among people aged 20 years and over, diabetes affects:[66]

---

[64] According to the Centers of Diabetec Control and Prevention, Diabetes Report 2017.
[65] Journal of Clinical Endocrinology and Metabolism.
[66] CDC's National Diabetes Statistics Report, 2017

(a) Non-Hispanic whites - 7.4%;
(b) Asian Americans - 8.0%;
(c) Hispanics - 12.1%;
(d) Non-Hispanic blacks - 12.7%; and
(e) American Indians and Alaska Natives - 15.1%.

Seriousness of Diabetes. This is because it can have serious health consequences. More Americans die from diabetes yearly than from AIDS and breast cancer combined. Adults with diabetes are significantly more likely to die from a heart attack or stroke. Over a quarter of all Americans with diabetes have diabetic retinopathy. This can cause vision loss and blindness. Every year, nearly 50,000 Americans begin treatment for kidney failure on account of diabetes. This dreaded disease also accounts for 44% of all new cases of kidney failure. Moreover, each year, diabetes causes about 73,000 lower limb amputations. This accounts for 60% of all lower limb amputations (not including amputations due to trauma).

Costs. Because of its high prevalence and link to numerous health problems, healthcare costs attributable to diabetes are very significant in the US. It contributes to productivity loss for reduced performance at work. In 2012, the loss amounted to 113 million days, or $20.8 billion. Diabetes cost the US $327 billion in 2017, including $237 billion in medical costs and $90 billion in reduced productivity. These are not the only costs; there are others as well too numerous to consider here.

Management of Diabetes. Despite its complications, people can manage their diabetes with a comprehensive plan. This includes both lifestyle changes and proper medical care. Once they manage their blood sugar levels well, many people with diabetes can lead full, active lives.

Reversing Type-2 Diabetes

The word "reversing" might connote a permanent disappearance of the disease. This is not the case as the condition could return since there is no guarantee that your diabetes has gone forever. But it is possible to take steps to cause your diabetes to go into remission. This is when your blood sugar levels are below the range that indicates that you can live without diabetes medication.

Determination for Type 2 Diabetes. The A1C test measures your average blood sugar level over the past 2 or 3 months. An A1C below 5.7% (99 mg/dl) is normal, between 5.7 and 6.4% (100 – 125 mg/dl) indicates you are in the prediabetes stage, and 6.5 (126 mg/dl) or higher indicates you have diabetes. Within the 5.7 and 6.4 prediabetes range, the higher your A1C, the greater your risk in developing type 2 diabetes.[67] If you have diabetes, an ideal HbA1c level is 6.5% (48 mmol/mol).[68] The figures are shown in the table below

Table showing figures for NHS, UK and US

Stage	NHS Hba1c	UK AIC	US mg/dl
Normal	Below 43	5.7 %	99
Prediabetes	42 – 47	Between 5.7 & 6.4 %	100 - 125
Diabetes	48 & above	6.5 %	126

NHS Figures Regarding Type 2. A normal Hba1c is below 42 mmol. In prediabetes, the Hba1c is between 42 and 47 mmol. Diabetes is diagnosed when the Hba1c is 48 mmol and above.[69]

Reversing Diabetes. The strongest evidence available at present suggests that type-2 diabetes can be put into remission by weight loss. If you take steps immediately after you are diagnosed with type-2 diabetes to reduce your weight, it is possible that your diabetes can go into remission. However, it is known that people with a diabetes history of over 25 years after diagnosis have been able to get rid of their diabetes. Reversing type-2 diabetes is possible, but it requires meal planning, healthy eating and regular exercise. Once you can take these steps and you are able to lose enough weight, you may be able to go into remission and to get rid of its complications.[70]Thus, through diet changes and weight loss, you may be able to reach and hold normal blood sugar levels without medication.[71]

Going into remission does not mean that you are completely cured as this type-2 diabetes is an ongoing disease. Going into remission simply means that your blood sugar levels are in a healthy range without taking medication. The chances are that the symptoms will return. However, it is possible for some people to stay in remission for years without the trouble of controlling their glucose and the health concerns associated with diabetes.

Refer to the 8 tables in Chapter 4 showing various foods in relation to blood glucose (sugar). To reduce overweight eat those which are low in sugar. This will help towards type 2 remission.

Low-Calorie Diet. Studies in England looked into the question of low-calorie diet on diabetes. People were requested to follow a mostly liquid diet

---

[67] https://www.cdc.gov All About Your A1C - CDC
[68] https://https//www.diabetes.org.uk What is HbA1c Blood Test Target Levels – Diabetes UK
[69] https://www.foresthehealthcentre.nhs.uk The Diabetes Forest Health Care.
[70] Permanent Cure for Diabetes Type 2 https://www.info.co.uk
[71] Can You Reverse type 2 diabetes? https://www.webmd.com

of 625-850 calories daily for 2 to 5 months. This was followed by a less restricted diet to help in keeping off the weight that had been shed. The studies found that about half of the people took part reversed their diabetes and maintained their blood glucose near the normal range for at least 6 to 12 months.

The people who took part in the studies got rid of about 30 pounds at least. It is important to start taking steps to lose weight once you are diagnosed with type-2 diabetes. Not everyone who loses this amount of weight, or even more, will be able to put their diabetes into remission. However, losing 30 pounds or 15 kg comes with a lot of health benefits, even if it does not lead to remission. These benefits include:

(a) fewer medications;
(b) better blood sugar levels; and
(c) a lower risk of complications.

Methods of Losing Weight. Mention is made above in following a low-calorie diet. Physical exercises are important on a regular basis. The best would be brisk walking for at least 30 minutes per day. You can harm yourself by being involved in more strenuous and weight-lifting exercises. Though not recommended on account of some risk, some people go for weight loss surgery (called bariatric surgery). There is no such thing as a special diet for people with diabetes with the aim of its remission. In trials that looked at diabetes remission, 57% of people on low carb plans had gone into remission.[72] There is also what is known as the Mediterranean diet or a low carb diet. Perhaps, a dietician or other health professional can assist in preparing a diet programme to follow. There are also YouTube videos on remission.

Serious Health Problems. Diabetes can cause serious long-term health problems. It is the most common cause of vision loss and blindness in working people. Everyone with diabetes aged 12 or over should have their eyes screened yearly for diabetic retinopathy. Also, diabetes is responsible for most cases of kidney failure and lower limb amputation. In the event you are at risk of type 2 diabetes, you may be able to prevent it developing by adopting lifestyle changes. These include:

(a) losing weight if you are overweight, and maintain a healthy weight;
(b) eat a healthy, balanced diet;
(c) drinking alcohol in moderation (do not start if you have not consumed it before);
(d) if you are a smoker, get rid of this detestable habit (vaping is bad as well); and

---

[72]Go Low-Carb for type 2 Diabetes Remission? https://www.webmd.com

(e) engage in regular exercise.

If you already have the disease, it may be possible to control your symptom by making the above changes. They will minimise your risk of developing complications. Many sufferers can go into remission.[73]

Evidence suggests that a plant-based diet can help patients with type 2 diabetes achieve weight loss and improve glycemic control. The American Diabetes Association (ADA) Standards of Medical Care in Diabetes recognises a plant-based diet as a viable option for patients with type 2 diabetes. Multiple studies have shown an inverse relationship between a vegan diet and diabetes type 2. In a study,[74] 21 patients with type 2 diabetes simultaneously changed to a diet free of animal products and began an exercise regimen. They experienced notable improvements: these included a decrease in triglycerides, total cholesterol, fasting blood glucose, and insulin resistance. Within a period of 2 weeks, their fasting blood glucose dropped an average of 35%, and 5 participants improved so much that they no longer required glucose-lowering medications. During long-term follow-up for 4 years, 17 out of the 21 patients had remained on the vegan diet and continued with an exercise programme. These patients continued to have improved glycemic control.

Healthy plant-centred diets are associated with significantly lower rates of type 2 diabetes and improved outcomes in those who already have this dangerous chronic condition.

In 2018 it was found[75] that for people with diabetes type 2, plant-based diets were more beneficial than the diets recommended by several diabetes associations, offering greater improvements in physical and emotional well-being.

Plant-based diets are low in saturated fat (a culprit behind insulin resistance) and high in fibre, which helps the body to regulate blood sugar and properly absorb nutrients. Plant-based diets also reduce the risk of being overweight or obese, a primary risk factor for diabetes type 2.

A study found that eating a plant-based diet filled with high-quality plant foods reduced the risk of developing diabetes type 2 by 34%. This is likely as plants are lower in saturated fats than animal foods, which raises cholesterol levels and your risk of developing diabetes type 2, as noted by the American Diabetes Association. Another study, published in *Diabetes Care*, found the prevalence of diabetes type 2 was 7.6% among non-vegetarians and only 2.9% for vegans.

---

[73] A Dr David Unwin of Liverpool, England, in a You Tube video says that over 200 of his patients went into remission by making lifestyle changes.
[74] Research published in the Journal of Nutritional Medicine in 1994
[75] In a report in *BMJ Open Diabetes Research & Care*.

48

HYPERTENSION (High Blood Pressure)

High blood pressure (HBP) is when the pressure in your blood vessels is unusually high. It can be serious if it is not treated. HBP does not usually have any symptoms. You can get it checked to find out the level. Lifestyle changes, such as eating a healthy diet and being involved in regular exercises, can help lower your HBP. Some people may be prescribed medication. What may increase your chances of HBP are overweight, consuming unhealthy diet, smoking and lack of adequate exercise. People with HBP (usually 180/120 or higher readings) can experience symptoms, such as:

- Severe headaches.
- Chest pain.
- Dizziness.
- Difficulty breeding.
- Nausea.
- Vomiting.
- Blurred vision or other vision changes.
- Anxiety.[76]

Main Cause of Hypertension (or HBP)

HBP can be caused by unhealthy lifestyle choices such as by not getting enough regular exercises. Certain health conditions, such as diabetes and being afflicted with obesity can also increase the risk for developing HBP.[77]

What Can Be Done. While there is no cure for HBP, it is important for patients to take steps that matter. These steps can include making effective lifestyle changes and taking BP-lowering medications prescribed by your doctors.[78] You can try a few tips immediately without medication:

- Take a deep breath and try to relax.
- Consume some water.
- Try some physical activity.
- Eat some dark chocolate.
- Take a cold shower.
- Limit your alcohol intake and quit smoking.

---

[76] 16 March 2023 https://www.who.int Hypertension – World Health Organisation (WHO)
[77] https://www.cdc.gov High Blood Pressure symptoms and Causes cdc.gov
[78] 6 March 2023 https://www.ama.assn.org Patients can take these steps to lower their high blood pressure. Medication usually have side effects which can damage your health.

A banana a day keeps HBP at bay. This fruit is packed full of potassium. This is an important blood pressure-lowering mineral. Potassium helps balance sodium in the body. [79]

A range of blood pressure (in mm Hg) for various age groups is shown in the table below.

Table showing blood pressure for women and men

Age Range in Years	Women	Men
18 – 39	110/68	119/70
40 – 59	122/74	124/77
40 – 59	122/74	124/77
60+ years	139/68	133/69

As a general guide:

- HBP is considered to be 140/90 mmHG or more if your reading was taken at a GP surgery or clinic (or an average of 135/85 mmHg if taken at home)
- If you are over 80 years, HBP is considered to be from 150/90 or more if taken by a medical professional (or an average of 145/85 mmHg if taken at home)
- An ideal blood pressure is usually considered to be between 90/60 mmHg and 120/80 mmHg, while the target for people over the age of 80 is below 150/90 mmHg (or 145/85 mmHg if taken at home).

Readings from 121/81 mmHg to 139/89 mmHg could mean you are at risk of developing HBP if you do not take steps to keep your blood pressure under control. The pressure varies from person to person; what may be normal for one person may be high for another person. If it is too high, it puts extra strain on your blood vessels, heart, and other organs, such as the brain, kidneys and eyes. Persistent HBP can increase your risk of a number of serious and potentially life-threatening health conditions. These are:

- Heart disease.
- Heart attacks.
- Strokes.
- Heart failure.
- Peripheral arterial disease.
- Aortic aneurysms.

---

[79] https://bethelmedicalassociates.com Beyond Salt: Eight foods That Help Lower Blood Pressure.

- Kidney disease.
- Vascular dementia.

Even a small reduction can help to lower your risk of these health conditions.

In recent decades health professionals' tendency is to lower the figures in the table above by medication; more patients are put on medication to lower their blood pressure. This increases the revenue of pharma companies significantly each time there is a downward shift.

Eat Fruits to Lower HBP. The top fruits for lowering blood pressure include bananas, apples, pears, apricots, grapes, raisins, kiwis, mangoes, watermelon, pomegranate, plums, prunes, avocado, cantaloupe, honeydew melon, tomatoes, citrus fruit, berries and more.[80]

Risk of Getting HBP

It is not always clear what is the cause of HBP. You might be more at risk if you are:

- Overweight.
- You consume too much salt but not enough fruit and vegetables.
- You do not exercise enough.
- You drink too much alcohol or coffee (or other caffeine-based drinks).
- You smoke.
- You experience too much stress.
- You are over 65 years old.
- You have a relative with HBP.
- You are of black African or black Caribbean descent.
- You live in a deprived area.

By making lifestyle changes you can sometimes help to reduce your chance of getting HBP and help to lower your blood pressure if it is already high. You can bring your blood pressure to a safe level by making lifestyle changes and/or with medication. Lifestyle changes can include:

- Reduce amount of salt you eat and have generally a healthy diet.
- Cut back on alcohol.
- Reduce your weight if you are overweight.

---

[80] https://www.emedicinehealth.com 25 Best Fruits to Lower Blood Pressure & Maintain Healthy Diet.

- Exercise regularly.
- Cut down on caffeine.
- Stop smoking if you are a smoker.

Some people who are diagnosed with HBP may be prescribed one or more medication to keep it under control. But medication has side effects.

Studies and Analysis. A meta-analysis and systematic review of 24 studies published between the years 1984 and 2019 was conducted to analyse the effect that dietary changes had on blood pressure in patients with diabetes type 2. The vegan diet was reviewed alongside other popular diets including the Dietary Approaches to Stop Hypertension (DASH) diet and the Mediterranean diet. All dietary changes were analysed against a control, defined as patients making no dietary changes. The vegan diet, along with several others, was found to significantly lower both systolic and diastolic blood pressure.

Review of Vegan Diet. A similar systematic review, as that above, published in 2020 found that a vegan diet is associated with a significant decrease in blood pressure in those with hypertension (WMD[81] = −3.118, 95% CI = −4.540, −1.696). Those that followed either a vegetarian diet or a vegan diet reported decreases in blood pressure, although the decrease was more significant in those that followed a fully vegan diet.

High blood pressure contributes to many other health complications and can compound the risks that those with diabetes already have. Hypertension is an independent risk factor for both heart disease and stroke; however, those with both diabetes and hypertension have the highest risk of a fatal stroke. With more emphasis on dietary change, patients could see a substantial decrease in blood pressure while decreasing polypharmacy and the side effects that anti-hypertensive medications can provoke.

A Plant-Based Diet May Lower Your Blood Pressure

High blood pressure, or hypertension, can increase the risk for health issues, including heart disease, stroke, and diabetes type 2. Fortunately, the foods you eat can make a difference. Several studies have shown that sticking with a plant-based diet can reduce blood pressure, thereby reducing your risk for those conditions. A meta-analysis explored data from 39 studies and concluded that people who followed a vegetarian diet had lower blood pressure on average than those who followed omnivorous diets, meaning those including plants and meat. And another study found that vegetarians

---

[81] This abbreviation is for weighted mean difference.

had a 34% lower risk of developing hypertension than non-vegetarians. A consumption of vegetarian diets is associated with lower blood pressure.[82]

DYSLIPIDEMIA

Dyslipidemia is the imbalance of lipids such as cholesterol, low-density lipoprotein cholesterol, triglycerides, and high density lipoprotein (HDL). This condition can result from diet, tobacco exposure, or genetic and can lead to cardiovascular disease with sever complications.[83]

Dyslipidemia can be classified primary and secondary types. Primary causes are single or multiple gene mutations that result in either overproduction or defective clearance of triglycerides (TG) and low-density lipoprotein (LDL), in underproduction or excessive clearance of high-density lipoprotein (HDL).[84]

Secondary dyslipidemia is caused by unhealthy lifestyle factors and acquired medical conditions, including underlying diseases and applied drugs. It accounts for about 30-40% of all dyslipidemia.[85]

CHOLESTEROL

Cholesterol is the principal sterol of all higher animals. It is distributed in the body tissues, especially the brain and spinal cord, and in animal fats and oils. Cholesterol is biosynthesised by all animal cells and is an essential structural component of animal cell membranes. Your body needs some cholesterol to make hormones, vitamin D, and substances that help you digest foods. Your body makes all the cholesterol it needs.[86]

Eating too much saturated fat or transfats can result in unhealthy cholesterol levels. Saturated fats are found in fatty cuts of meat and full-fat dairy products. Trans fats are often found in packaged snacks or desserts.[87]

Recommended Level of Cholesterol. It is recommended that healthy adults should have a total cholesterol level below 5 mmol/L. The total level includes LDL (bad cholesterol) and HDL (good cholesterol). The risk of coronary heart disease is particularly high if you have a high level of LDL and a low level of HDL. The levels vary for different persons.

---

[82] See Jama Network Vegetarian diets and Blood Pressure: a Meta analysis https://jamanetwork.com

[83] 10 July 2023. https://www.ncbi.nlm.nih.gov Dyslipidemia – StatPearls – NCBI Bookshelf

[84] https://www.ncbi.nlm.nih.gov Secondary dyslipidermia: its treatment and association with atherosclerosis.

[85] *Ibid.*

[86] 10 Dec. 2020. https://medlineplus.gov Cholesterol Medline Plus.

[87] 11 Jan. 2023. https://www.mayoclinic.org High cholesterol – Symptoms and Causes – Mayo Clinic.

Table Showing Cholesterol Levels (US in mg/dl)

Total Cholesterol	Below 5 (below 193 mg/dL)
Non-HDL or bad cholesterol	Below 4 (below 155 mg/dL)
LDL Cholesterol	Below 3 (below 116 mg/dL)
HDL or good cholesterol	Above 1 for men and 1.2 for women*
Total Cholesterol HDL ratio	The lower the better – above 6** is considered a high risk

*Above 39 mg/dL for men, & above 46 mg/dL for women
**Less than 5.6 mmol/L (100 mg/dL) is normal. The figures within brackets are for the US.
Your HDL is the one number you want to be high ideally above 3.3 mmol/L (60 mg/dL) Your LDL should be below 5.6 mmol/L (100 mg/dl). Your total should be below 11.1 mmol/L (200 mg/dL).

What Contributes to Atherosclerosis. Consumption of dietary cholesterol found in meat and dairy products contributes to atherosclerosis and heart disease. Since humans are capable of synthesising all needed cholesterol, further dietary intake is not required for optimal function.

A study published in May 2020 analysed the correlation between meat consumption and low-density lipoprotein (LDL) levels in patients diagnosed with coronary artery disease. The mean LDL level in the omnivorous[88] group was found to be 34.75 points higher than the mean of the vegetarian group. Similarly, a large review of vegetarian diets and health outcomes, published in 2020, found there to be a clinically significant decrease in both total and LDL cholesterol levels in those who do not consume meat or fish products.

High levels of LDL are known to increase both the risk and severity of coronary artery disease including heart disease, angina, and myocardial infarction. Therefore, reducing dietary cholesterol by eliminating meat and dairy from one's diet may represent one option to reduce risk of coronary disease.

High-Density Lipoprotein. This is one of the 5 major groups of lipoproteins. These are complex particles composed of multiple proteins which transport all fat molecules around the body within the water outside cells. Typically, they are composed of 80 -100 proteins per particle.

A Plant-Based Diet May Improve Your Cholesterol

High cholesterol can lead to fatty deposits in the blood. This can restrict blood flow and potentially lead to heart attack, stroke, or heart disease. But

---

[88] An omnivore is an organism that eats plants and animals.

a healthy diet can help keep cholesterol levels in check. Therefore, it is advisable to ditch mainly animal products for primarily a plant-based diet. This course of action can lower LDL ("bad") cholesterol by between 10 and 15%, while those following strictly a vegan diet can lower their LDL cholesterol by as much as 25%.[89]

FIGHTING CHRONIC DISEASES WITH PLANT-BASED FOODS

In early 2021 some 6 in 10 US adults had a chronic disease. Some may have many such diseases at the same time. These diseases are the leading cause of disability and death in the US. One in every 3 deaths is caused by cardiovascular diseases (CVD). About 90% ($3.43 trillion) of the US health care costs are attributable to chronic and mental health conditions.[90] In the light of such high costs, it is imperative to prioritise chronic disease prevention. Despite the use of medications and cessation of smoking by many with a view of reduction of chronic diseases, the problem is getting worse. Perhaps, as a preventative measure, the adoption of a plant-based diet can perform wonders in curtailing the growth of chronic diseases. It can also reverse them.

Healthy Plant-based Diet

A healthy plant-based diet has the ability to decrease the risk of type 2 diabetes, CVD, and obesity. This is linked in part to its antioxidant properties. It is mentioned elsewhere that healthy plant-based foods are rich in polyphenols (PPs). They have antioxidant effects and may also contribute to a reduction of risk in cardiovascular diseases.

Polyphenols found in food are in four classes: flavonoids, ligands, phenolic acids, and stilbenes. The flavonoid class of PPs, in particular, have been found to reduce the risk of developing cardiovascular diseases. Foods and drinks rich in flavonoids are green tea, blueberry, dark chocolate, and capers. They increase the availability of nitric oxide (NO) and endothelium-derived hyperpolarizing factor (EDHF) to maintain vascular homeostasis and prevent endothelial dysfunction.

Studies on CVD also demonstrated improved endothelial functions after consuming flavonoid-rich foods. In a review of 12 cohort studies, an increased intake of flavonoids resulted in a decrease in age-adjusted coronary heart disease (CHD) mortality. Overall, PPs were found to decrease the inflammatory activity of reactive oxygen species (ROS) and reduce the production of potent LDL oxidant peroxynitrite which is

---

[89] This is according to a review of 27 studies published in *The American Journal of Cardiology.*

[90] Ashely Dao, PharmD Candidate c/o 2024. Combating Chronic Diseases with a Plant-Based Diet. 1 December 2021.

responsible for triggering endothelial injury and inflammation. Additionally, a healthy plant-based diet is correlated with high unsaturated fatty acids and low saturated fats, which have also been shown to have anti-inflammatory effects.[91]

Increased Risk Attributable to Animal Products

Many people around the globe are ditching reliance primarily on animal foods. This is because animal foods have been proved to be associated with an increased risk of CVD. This is due to the abundance of heme iron. Also, processed meats consist of sodium nitrates. Such nitrates may increase blood pressure, impair insulin response and lead to endothelial dysfunction.

Proteins Necessary in Diet. Protein is a staple in our diet. While animal proteins contain essential amino acids, a high intake of such proteins is correlated with an increase in inflammation and CVD by triggering what is known as reactive oxygen species (ROS) production.

Plant protein consists of non-essential amino acids. When people ditch animal proteins for plant proteins there is a decrease in leucine intake. This was associated with positive changes in BMI and energy intake. In addition, plant protein intake decreased histidine intake which was associated with decreased insulin resistance. Utilising this information, pharmacists and other health care providers can better assist patients by encouraging them to implement a plant-based diet to prevent the development of chronic diseases or at the very least minimise their progression.

Customise A Healthy Plant-based Diet. This diet can be customised to suit each patient on the basis of accessibility, affordability, and personal preference. This can lead to increased adherence to the diet with a consequent decrease in associated health care costs.

All Hospitals to Provide a Healthy Diet. Some hospitals are already implementing a healthy plant-based diet into their treatment plans, such as Montefiore's Cardiac Wellness Program and UC Davis's Integrative Medicine (in the USA). In the light of various studies, other hospitals should follow this course of action.

Advice from Pharmacists. Every patient deserves the opportunity to utilise a healthy plant-based diet. Such a diet is likely to prevent or even reverse existing chronic diseases. In the course of patients collecting their medication, Pharmacists who may have face to face contact with patients have the ability to ensure that this happens.

---

[91] Ashely Dao, PharmD Candidate c/o 2024. Combating Chronic Diseases with a Plant-Based Diet.1 December 2021.

 Picture showing plant foods.

CONCLUSION

This is a longest chapter in the book; it deals with many of the chronic diseases and how a plant-based diet can help in preventing or reducing the risk of getting such diseases. In both sides of the Atlantic, the chronic diseases are about the same. There are many types as listed in the chapter.

Particular attention is given to a few of the most common types. These are coronary heart disease (CHD), cancers, strokes, brain diseases, arthritis, diabetes type 2, Alzheimer's and other dementias, and liver disease. As appropriate, the causes, symptoms and for some of them the treatment are mentioned. In particular, as discussed, diabetes type 2 can go into remission by making appropriate lifestyle changes.

A common approach to prevent or reduce the risk of almost all of these chronic diseases is to go on a plant-based diet. A healthy plant-based diet has the ability to decrease the risk of diabetes type 2, CVD, and obesity.

Polyphenols found in food have the effect to reduce the risk of developing cardiovascular diseases. Foods and drinks rich in flavonoids are green tea, blueberry, dark chocolate, and capers. They increase the availability of nitric oxide (NO) and endothelium-derived hyperpolarizing factor (EDHF) to maintain vascular homeostasis and prevent endothelial dysfunction.

Studies on CVD demonstrated improved endothelial functions after consuming flavonoid-rich foods. An increased intake of flavonoids can result in a decrease in age-adjusted coronary heart disease (CHD) mortality. Overall, polyphenols (PPs) were found to decrease the inflammatory activity of reactive oxygen species (ROS) and reduce the production of potent LDL oxidant peroxynitrite which is responsible for triggering endothelial injury and inflammation.

Animal proteins can be replaced with plant proteins as the latter is associated with positive changes in BMI and energy intake. In addition, plant protein decreases histidine intake which is associated with a decrease in insulin resistance. This information can be used to encourage patients to adopt a plant-based diet to prevent the development of chronic diseases or at the very least minimise their progression.

This diet can be customised to suit each patient on the basis of accessibility, affordability, and personal preference. Everyone deserves the opportunity to utilise a healthy plant-based diet. It is likely to prevent or even reverse existing chronic diseases.

> "Sometimes you will be in control of your illness and other times you'll sink into despair, and that's OK! Freak out, forgive yourself, and try again tomorrow."
>
> Kelly Hemingway

> "Never let the things you cannot do prevent you from doing the things you can."
>
> John Wooden

End

CHAPTER 4

BALANCED PLANT-BASED DIET

"Nothing will benefit human health and increase the chances for survival of life on earth as much as the evolution to a vegetarian diet."

Albert Einstein

"People eat meat and think they will become strong as an ox, forgetting that the ox eats grass."

Pino Caruso

A healthy, balanced plant-based diet would include proper portions of whole grains, vegetables, fruits, nuts, legumes and healthy oils.[92] It should be noted that many oils produced from seeds industrially and marketed as vegetable oils are toxic. Less healthy plant-based diets may comprise more sugar-sweetened beverages, refined grains (eg, white flour), fried potato chips or crisps and deserts (sweets).

Plant-based diets including vegan and vegetarian diets can be healthy, as long as they are balanced and nutritionally adequate. When followed consistently, a well-balanced, plant-based diet that focuses on whole grains, fruit, vegetables, legumes, nuts and seeds may provide health benefits.[93] The exact composition of healthy, balanced plant-based diets can differ, but commonly include: high consumption of vegetables, fruit and wholegrains.

WHAT SHOULD A BALANCED DIET LOOK LIKE

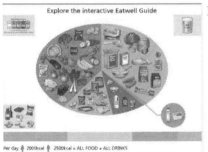

Picture showing what can be in this diet.

Meals should be based on potatoes, bread, rice, pasta or other starchy carbohydrates, ideally wholegrain, according to the NHS and many researchers:

---

[92] 30 March 2021 https://www.health.harvard.edu
[93] https://www.bbcgoodfood.com What is a plant-based diet? BBC Good Food

(a) Eat at least 5 portions of a variety of fruits and vegetables daily. They can be all fresh, frozen, dried and canned fruit and vegetables. They all count.

(b) Base meals on potatoes, bread, rice, pasta or other starchy carbohydrates, ideally wholegrain.

(c) Fibre should amount to 30 grams daily. This is the same as eating all of the following 5 portions of fruits and vegetables, 2 whole-wheat cereal biscuits, 2 thick slices of wholemeal bread and a large baked potato with the skin.

(d) Have some dairy or its alternative, such as soya drinks. Go for lower fat and lower sugar options (preferably unsweetened).

(e) Consume some beans, pulses, fish, eggs, lean meat and other proteins. Include in your diet 2 portions of fish weekly, one of which should be oily.

(f) Choose unsaturated oils and spreads and consume in small amounts:

(g) Drink water and/or other liquids for hydration:
    6– 8 cups/glasses of water daily

(h) An adult should have less than 6g of salt and 30g of standard fat (for male) and 20g for female. Note that some oils are toxic (refer to Chapter 10).

The Many Variations of a Plant-Based Diet

Picture showing a variety of foods.

How to Maintain a Balanced diet as a Vegetarian or Vegan? A vegetarian or vegan diet can have many health benefits. However, these diets also have risks if they are not properly balanced. Dr Kimberly Gudzune[94] explains how to get the key vitamins and nutrients required if you decide to go meatless or plant-based.

---

[94] Kimberly Gudzune, MD, MPH, a specialist in internal medicine in the John Hopkins Healthful Eating, Activity and Weight Program.

Risks of an Unbalanced Vegetarian or Vegan Diet. Either of these diets is very different from what most Americans and Westerners are accustomed to. Converting to either diet is a really big, sudden change. People that normally consume processed, fatty foods and suddenly eliminate them may not know what to eat. A change to either diet requires some planning. Foods are required to be selected that are nutritionally balanced for the body.

As vegetarians do not eat meat, they are at risk of missing out on protein and vitamin B12. In the case of vegans who do not eat any animal products, they follow a more restrictive diet. In the absence of not eating eggs and dairy, they need to keep an eye on their calcium, vitamin D intake, vitamin B12 and protein intake. As these diets exclude certain foods, other foods are chosen, such as fruits, vegetables and whole grains. If you eliminate meat and other animal products, you need to rely on quick carbohydrates and processed foods such bagels, macaroni and cheese or other items. These are not a healthy vegetarian or vegan diet.

NUTRIENTS AND VITAMINS FOR VEGANS AND VEGETARIANS

A meatless diet can be healthy, but vegetarians and especially vegans need to make sure they are getting enough vitamin B12, calcium, iron, and zinc. The Academy of Nutrition and Dietetics in particular warns of the risk of vitamin B12 deficiencies in the diets of vegans and vegetarians.[95]

Choosing Foods as Replacement. Products such as "faux meats" (a meat alternative or meat substitute) can be very processed with a lot of salt included. It is necessary to read food labels carefully to check for sodium, saturated fat and sugar content. Those who limit their sodium intake to no more than 2,300 milligrams daily can help to avoid the risk of high blood pressure. It is recommended that men limit their added sugar to no more than 9 teaspoons (36g) and women to no more than 6 teaspoons (25g) daily, while only 5% of their daily calories should come from saturated fat.[96]

Choose High Protein Foods

For vegetarians, the sources include eggs and dairy products, such as yogurt and cottage cheese. But for vegans the great sources are legumes (beans, lentils and peas), seeds and nuts. You can learn about protein-packed meatless meals. If you suffer from certain health conditions, eg, such as history of breast cancer or kidney disease, discuss it with your physician (GP) as to suitable sources for you. Some GPs may not have a good

---

[95] https://www.webmd.com Vegetarian & Vegan Diets Explained – WebMD.
[96] The American Heart Association (AHA) recommendations.

grounding of nutrition as their learning is limited to about 20 hours in a 4-year period at medical schools. Of these hours, most of the time may be spent on peripheral matters.

Avoid too Much Carbohydrates. Limit your carbohydrates when you cut out meat. However, too many refined carbs can lead to weight gain, blood sugar elevation and other health issues. You should opt for whole grains such as oatmeal, brown rice or quinoa. Refer to the 8 tables later in the chapter showing the sugar content of various foods.

Seek Enough Vitamin B12. Any sizable deficiency can cause anaemia, especially those who follow a vegan diet. Taking a vitamin that contains B12 may solve the problem. Some plant milks are fortified with B12.

Adhere to Calcium Requirements. Calcium needs depend on your age, gender and family history of conditions such as osteoporosis. Dairy products are rich in calcium. For vegans, it can be found in vegetables such as cooked kale or collard greens. You have the choice of consuming a calcium supplement that contains vitamin D. This helps with calcium absorption.

Vitamin D Fortified Foods. In addition to getting this vitamin (small amount) from safe sunshine, vegans can choose foods such as orange, cereal or plant-based milks fortified with vitamin D.

Consult a Dietician for an Experienced Physician

If you are thinking of becoming a vegetarian or vegan you should first make a nutrition plan. In this regard, you may seek assistance from a health professional, especially if you have pre-existing health conditions, such as diabetes, heart disease, obesity or a gastrointestinal disorder. You may need to:[97]

(a) start slowly;
(b) stay practical using a meal plan that is consistent with your budget and schedule; and
(c) find support among other vegans or vegetarians.

Balanced Diet. This is a diet that contains differing kinds of foods in certain quantities and proportions so that the requirements for calories, proteins, minerals, vitamins and alternative nutrients are adequate and a

---

[97] https://www.narayanahealth.org How to maintain a balanced diet – Narayana Health.

small provision is reserved for additional nutrients to endure the short length of leanness.

The 5 Importance of a Balanced Diet. A healthy diet helps to boost immunity, reduces the risk of developing type 2 diabetes, cardiovascular diseases, and some cancers, maintains a healthy weight, and helps recover quickly from diseases and trauma.[98]

In summary, a plant-based diet for a vegan should consist of minimally processed fruits, vegetables, whole grains, legumes, nuts and seeds, herbs, and spices and excludes all animal products, including red meat, poultry, fish, eggs, and dairy products. While the diet for a vegetarian includes all the items a vegan consumes, some that are excluded for a vegan are included, such as fish, dairy and some meat

BLOOD GLUCOSE (SUGAR) FROM FOOD INTAKE

This is a topic that should be considered in a balanced diet. It deals with blood glucose spike by some foods. This is particularly relevant to people dealing with type 2 diabetes. The information is set out in 8 tables. Dr David Unwin of Liverpool, UK, has a YouTube video on this topic. He was able to get hundreds of patients to go into remission regarding their type 2 diabetes.

Eight Tables Showing Sugar Content in Various Foods

Table 1 showing blood glucose in chocolate intake (tsf of sugar)

Types of Chocolate	Grams of Sugar per 100g	Weight of 4 grams for each tsf of sugar
Milk	56	14 tsf
70% dark	29	7.25 tsf
85% dark	11	2.75 tsf
90% dark	9	1.75 tsf

tsf= teaspoon full of sugar (4 grams). However, a rounded teaspoon has 5g.

What is very significant in the above table is the 14 tsf of table sugar. Some chocolate milk shakes have a shocking 39 teaspoons of sugar, over 6 times the recommended daily amount of sugar for a 7-10-year old.[99]

---

[98] https://www.maxhealthcare.in Balanced Diet – Definition, Importance, Benefits & Diet Chart.
[99] https://www.actiononsugar.org Milkshakes – Actioon on Sugar.

Table 2 showing blood glucose of different types of bread

Types of Bread	GI **	Serve Size g	Glycaemic	Tsf of Table Sugar****
White	71	30	10	3.7
Brown	74	30	9	3.3
Rye	78	30	11	4.0
Wholegrain barley	85	30	15	5.5
Wholemeal strong ground flour	59	30	7	2.6
Pita wholemeal	56	30	8	2.9
Oatmeal batch	62	30	9	3.3

**Glycaemic index from scientific literature.
****How does one small 30g slice of bread affect blood glucose. Each tsf has 4 grams of table sugar.
What is significant in the above table is the 5.5 tsf of table sugar for wholegrain barley, whereas the figure for white bread is 3.7 tsf.

Table3 showing blood glucose for cereal

Types of Cereal	Serving in gram/ml	Glycaemic Index	tsf of Table Sugar
Coco pops	30	77	7.3
Cornflakes	30	93	8.4
Mini wheats	30	59	4.4
Shredded wheat	30	67	4.8
Special K	30	54	4.0
Bran flakes	30	74	3.7
Oat porridge	150 ml	63	4.4

In this table, for 30 g of cornflakes the GI is 93 and table sugar is 8.4 tsf. Based on calculations, it is the glycaemic response, not the carbohydrates content of food, that matters in diabetes and obesity.

Table 4 showing blood glucose of some fruits (table sugar)

Food Item	GI **	Serving Size g	Glycaema Load g	tsf of Table Sugar***
Banana	62	120	16	5.9
Grapes, black	59	120	11	4.0
Apple, golden delicious	39	120	6	2.2
Watermelon	80	120	5	1.8
Nectarines	43	120	4	1.5
Apricots	34	120	3	1.1
Strawberries	40	120	3.8	1.4

** Glycaemic index from scientific literature
***Shows the extent in which 120 g of each food affect blood glucose.
What is significant in this table is that a fully ripe banana of 120 g has 5.9
tsf of sugar while many of the other fruits are far less.

Table 5 showing blood glucose spike (tsf of table sugar)

Food Item*	Glycaemic Index	Serving size g	Tsf of Table Sugar
Basmati rice	69	150	10.1
Potato, white, boiled	96	150	9.1
French fries, baked	64	150	7.5
Spaghetti, white, boiled	39	180	6.6
Sweet corn, boiled	60	80	4.0
Frozen peas, boiled	51	80	4.0
Banana	62	120	5.7
Apple	39	120	2.3
Wholemeal, small slice	74	30	3.0
Broccoli	15	80	0.2
Eggs	0	60	0

*Other foods in the very low glycaemic range would be chicken, oily fish,
almonds, mushroom, cheese, and meat. 150 grams = 5.291 ounces.

Table 6 showing blood glucose (tsf of table sugar)

Food Item*	Serving Size	tsf of Table Sugar
White rice	150 g	10.1
Baked beans	150 g	4.8
Black-eyed peas	150 g	4.0
Pea, frozen, boiled	150 g	2.8
Red kidney beans	150 g	1.8
Wheat flour, white	100 g	13.3
Gram chickpeas flour	100 g	2.1
Chick pea Hummus dip	150 g	2.0
Lentils, green, dried, boiled	150 g	1.8
Broad beans, frozen, boiled	150 g	2.0

*Other foods in very low glycaemic range would be ghee, broccoli, walnuts,
almonds, butter, olive oil, mushrooms, cheese, cauliflower, and celery.
The above table shows how each food may affect blood glucose compared
with 4 grams of tsf table sugar. What is significant in the above table is the
13.3 teaspoons of sugar for 100 g of white flour (g = gram). 150g = 5.291
ozs.

Table 7 showing blood glucose spike (tsf of table sugar)

Food Item	Serving Size g/ml	Tsf of Table Sugar
Bran flakes	30 g	3.7
Milk	125 ml	1.0
Brown toast 1 slice	30 g	3.0
Pure apple juice	200 ml	8.6

Many people consume the above for breakfast. It is better to eat the whole apple with the skin so that you will have the benefit of the fibre therein.

Table 8 showing some vegetables & fruit blood glucose

Food Item	GI**	Serving Size g	tsf of Table Sugar
Potato, boiled	96	150	9.1
Sweet corn	60	80	4.0
Frozen peas	51	80	1.3
Cabbage	10	80	0.1
Raisins	64	60	10.3
Banana	62	120	5.7
Apple	39	120	2.3
Strawberry	40	120	1.4

**Glycaemic index from scientific literature. The tsf for raisins is very high but only a small amount should be consumed.

A total of 8 tables showing how you can check on the amount of blood glucose (table sugar) for various types of food. This sugar spikes the blood glucose level and is particularly relevant for diabetes and obesity control. If you wish your type 2 diabetes to go into remission or to prevent its development, you should note how much sugar is being consumed in respect of each food item. The same applies if you wish to prevent weight gain or to get rid of your overweight or obesity. This sugar is not what is added when you prepare your meal but what is inherent in the food you acquired from the grocery store.

With regard to planning for a balanced diet, you can do better by noting the sugar spike inherent in each food item that you intend to include in you meal. You can choose food items which do not have much sugar.

TOO LOW BLOOD SUGAR

There are foods which can help you to increase your blood sugar levels. You should eat about 15g of carbohydrates if the level falls below 3.9 mmol/L or 70 mg/dl.[100] Wait for 15 minutes to check your blood sugar. Repeat this process until the level reaches a safe level. When the level falls

---

[100] Conversion factor: 1 mg/dL = 0.0555 mmol/L (70 mg/dL = 3.885 mmol/L).

too low you can eat to safely raise the level. Foods that can help in this regard are:

(a) **Fresh Fruits**. These are full of naturally occurring sugars and carbohydrates and can help to raise your blood sugar. Eat roughly half of a banana, 15 grapes or a small apple or orange

(b) **Fruit Juice**. Most of such juices have enough carbohydrates to help to raise your blood sugar level. You can have a glass of roughly 120 ml of juice, such as apple, orange, or pineapple. It will increase your blood sugar level. Avoid drinking too much as it can cause a significant spike in the blood sugar level.

(c) **Fat-Free Milk.** Milk has a lot of vitamin D and carbohydrates. It can help to increase your blood sugar when the levels start to fall.

(d) **Honey.** This is made up mainly of fructose and glucose. It has a high glycaemic index score. This means it will raise the levels relatively quickly. You can consume a tablespoon of honey as a snack if your blood sugar levels start a downward trend

As people are more troubled these days by too high blood sugar levels, how to deal with it is discussed below.

TOO HIGH BLOOD SUGAR

If your blood sugar level is too high, choose foods that lower blood sugar levels and help to keep it under control. You can also make other lifestyle changes by drinking more water that can also help to lower your blood sugar. Below are ways to bring your blood sugar levels down.

Increase Your Fibre Intake

(a) **Note Your Intake of Carbohydrates**. Your body breaks down carbs into glucose. This raises blood sugar. This is the reason why cutting down on refined or processed carbs like white bread or sugar-laden cakes and biscuits can help to control blood sugar. This has been proved by several studies.

(b) **Choose Low-GI Foods**. GI is for glycaemic index. It shows how quickly the food consumed raises blood glucose levels. The higher the GI level of a food the more quickly it releases glucose than foods with lower GI that release glucose slowly and steadily. Some low GI foods are:

- Some fruit and vegetables (as in some of the tables set out earlier).
- Pulses.
- Whole grains.

(c) **Boost Your Fibre Intake**. Foods with high fibre help blood sugar level to rise gradually. Sources of soluble fibre like porridge, apples, nuts, celery and flaxseeds, and wholegrains especially, have been shown to lower blood sugar level. Also, they may protect older women from developing diabetes type2. Fruit, beans, whole grains, and vegetables slow down how quickly the body absorbs sugar and digest carbohydrates.

(d) **Drink Water**. According to studies, drinks which contain sugar raise blood glucose levels, raise the risk of diabetes and lead to weight gain. But water has been linked with lowering blood sugar and may reduce possibility of developing diabetes. Try to drink 6-8 glasses of water daily.

(e) **Increase Your Chromium Levels**. Chromium is a mineral that helps the body to break down fats and carbohydrates. Also, it is thought to help control blood sugar levels for those who have diabetes type 2. Chromium-rich food includes:

- Wholegrains.
- Egg yolks.
- Bran cereals.
- Nuts.
- Meat.
- Vegetables, such as broccoli.

(f) **Consume Few Spoons of Apple Cider Vinegar.** This is thought to help lower glucose levels. It will help you to feel fuller after eating carbohydrates. Mix 2 teaspoons into a glass of water or use it as a salad dressing. You may need to check with your GP if you are already using medication to lower you blood sugar.

Your blood sugar levels may be affected by many factors. Therefore, you may need to seek advice from an expert who may be able to make you understand the nature of the problem

CONCLUSION

A balanced diet includes foods from various groups to help sustain a healthy mind, body and spirit. These groups are carbohydrates, vitamins, fats, minerals and proteins (5 in total). They must be incorporated in every diet. A lack of carbs could lead to exhaustion and fatigue

Eat at least 5 portions of a variety of fruit and vegetables daily. Choose various colours. Your meal can include potatoes, bread, rice, pasta, or other starchy carbohydrates. In particular, choose wholegrain as far as possible. You should have some fortified dairy alternatives, such as soya drinks and yogurts. You should choose lower-fat and lower-fat options. The importance of a balanced diet:

(a) It meets the nutritional demands of your body and will prevent malnutrition.
(b) This diet will keep up your energy levels and maintain your normal body functions.
(c)It will boost your immune system and optimise cell repair.
(d) Sticking to this diet will prevent lifestyle disease, including type 2 diabetes, cardiovascular diseases and possibly some cancers.

A balanced diet fulfils nutritional needs. Everyone needs a certain amount of calories and nutrient to stay healthy. Such a diet provides all the nutrients a person requires. Once followed, there is no need to go into the recommended daily calorie intake.

"Weight loss doesn't begin in the gym with a dumbbell: it starts in your head with a decision."

Toni Sorenson

"The only successful way to reach and maintain a healthy weight is to find what works for you."

Author Unknown

End

CHAPTER 5

NUTRITION FOR HEALTH

"Exercise is king; nutrition is queen. Put them together and you've a kingdom."

Jack La Lanne

"If you keep on eating unhealthy food then no matter how many weight loss tips you follow, you are likely to retain weight and become obese. If only you start eating healthy food, you will be pleasantly surprised how easy it is to lose weight."

Subodh Gupta

WHAT IS NUTRITION?

Nutrition is the study of nutrients in food, how the body uses them, and the relationship with diet, health, and disease. Nutritionists use ideas from molecular biology, biochemistry, and genetics to understand how nutrients affect the human body.[101]
Nutrition is a method in which food is consumed by the organisms and utilising the nutrients from the food. It is the process of taking in food and converting it into energy and other vital nutrients necessary for life. In this process, organisms utilise nutrients.[102]

Critical Part of Health. Nutrition is a critical part of health and development. Better nutrition relates to improved infant, child and maternal health, stronger immune system, safer pregnancy and childbirth, lower risk of non-communicable diseases, such as cardiovascular disease (CVD), diabetes, and longevity. Also, healthy children learn better.[103]

Provision of Energy. Nutrients provide energy to your body and enable bodily functions. These functions fall into 2 major groups: macronutrients in the form of protein, and carbohydrate, or fat, primarily provide energy to your body. The different macronutrients serve different energy pathways and functions in the body.[104] Vitamins and minerals are micronutrients.

Different Kinds of Nutrients. There are over 40 different kinds of nutrients in food. They can generally be classified into these major 7 groups:

---

[101] 9 Jan. 2020. https://www.medicalnewstoday.com Nutrition: Nutrients and the role of the dietitian.
[102] https://byjus.com Define Nutrition – BYJU'S
[103] https://www.who.int Nutrition – World Health Organisation (WHO)
[104] https://www.niehs.nih.gov Nutrition, Health, and Your Environment

- Carbohydrates.
- Proteins.
- Fats.
- Vitamins.
- Minerals.
- Dietary fibre.
- Water.[105]

The first 3 items above are macronutrients. There are many processes which are taken care of in the body without any conscious control. These are breathing, temperature regulation, movement, digestion and cell repair, all of which require energy.[106] Water and fibre are macronutrients, too.

As mentioned above, vitamins and minerals are micronutrients. These are required in smaller amounts than macronutrients, but are essential for the body to function properly.[107]

Supplements. Some supplements may be necessary for vitamin B12 which is essential. In the USA, the recommended dietary allowance (RDA) is 4-7mcg, but some experts believe that adults can benefit from 4-7mcg of vitamin D for optimal B12 status and a supplement of 500-1000mcg daily for the over 65. In the UK, guidelines state that adults only need about 1.5mcg of B12 daily. In the case of vitamin D, if you are not exposed to the sun, you can get it from brown mushrooms and fortified foods, such as plant milks and cereals. Other supplements you can get from algae oil (fish get it from algae), and flax seeds. Iodine can be obtained from seaweed and fortified foods, selenium notably from Brazil nuts, and zinc from a balanced diet of pulses such as baked beans and oats.

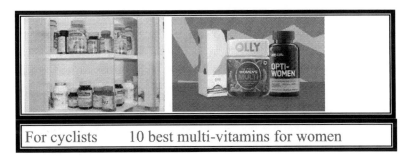

For cyclists   10 best multi-vitamins for women

---

[105] 4 Dec. 2017. https://www.chp.govhk Nutrient Classifications – Centre for Health Protection.
[106] Rhiannon Lambert, *The Science of Nutrition*, Penguin Random House, London, 2021
[107] 27 Sept 2017. https://www.canr.msu.edu Food Micronutrients explained – The necessary essentials – MSU Extension.

Favourite Spices. American doctor and physician Dr Mark Hyam has some of his most favourite spices and the main properties of those spices in his Instagram page. You can take a look at Dr Hyam's list of his favourite spices (Image Credit source: Pix abay). All the ingredients are present in our kitchen. He says this is a treasure trove of anti-bacterial properties to anti-inflammatory, anti-oxidant, and anti-cancer properties.[108]

Hyam says that there is no need to go to the pharmacy for anti-bacterial and anti-inflammatory medicine as such "medicines" are in your kitchen. They are spices you use for cooking.

Organism Uses Food for Support. Nutrition is the biochemical and physiological process by which an organism uses food to support its life. It provides organisms with nutrients, which can be metabolised to create energy and chemical structures. Any failure to obtain enough nutrients causes malnutrition.

Nutrition for Growth. Nutrition is the process of providing or obtaining the food necessary for growth. Nourishment is the branch of science that deals with nutrients and nutrition, particularly for humans.

PLANT-BASED DIET THROUGH THE AGES

Throughout human history, different groups have adhered to plant-based diets. As mentioned in Chapter 1, the philosopher Pythagoras of Greece advocated the health benefits of a vegetarian diet and was of the view that animal slaughter was immoral.[109] He and his disciples ate a simple diet of bread, honey, and vegetables. Thus, until the 1800s, a plant-based diet was known widely as the Pythagorean Diet. This diet was even adopted by people practising Indian religions before the time of Pythagoras. Like Pythagoras, this diet was viewed through the lens of nonviolence. In contrast, in the mid-1800s, the newly formed Seventh-Day Adventist Church advocated a vegetarian diet for its adherents, although its aim was to promote personal health and longevity rather than adhere to an ethical framework.

Plant-Based Eating Continues to be Popular. The number of Americans who follow a vegan diet increased 600% from 2014 to 2018. Interest in plant-based diets is driven by a number of factors. Many people choose a plant-based diet in the pursuit of health, out of concern for animal welfare,

---

[108] https://www.newsncr.com/.../no-need-to-go-to-the.../

[109] Pythagoras was a student in India during the BC era as India had many ancient universities (first in the world). He acquired his knowledge of the famous Pythagoras theorem in India and he returned to Greece as a Hindu, believing in reincarnation and non-violence.

or as a way to reduce their environmental footprint. Some have also been driven in part by celebrity endorsement, media attention, and popular documentaries. Regardless of the reasons for their change, more Americans are seeking to incorporate more plant-based foods into their diet.

As interest in plant-based diets has grown, so too has the market for it. Many restaurants are incorporating meat alternatives into their options, with some crafting and marketing dedicated plant-based menus. Items like the Beyond Burger are popular among vegans and meat-eaters alike. In grocery stores, plant-based egg, cheese, and milk alternatives have driven sales. The interest in plant-based alternatives is evident. The plant-based foods' market has increased 29% in the US between 2017 and 2019.

Public Health Nutrition Strategies

To improve human health certain public health nutrition strategies have been adopted. These strategies often include education, other policies, or interventions in various ways; all of which could be utilised to promote healthy plant-based diets. Policies, when based on consistent scientific evidence, can be especially effective. This is because they have the power to shape food environments and encourage people generally to make healthy choices. In this regard, some countries have introduced laws to limit trans fats in food products. This is based on extensive evidence linking them to CVD.

Denmark was the first country in the world to introduce a law to regulate successfully trans fats. Between 2007 and 2011, New York State restricted trans fat in 11 counties in all public eating places, vending machines and concessions. After 3 years since its implementation, the restriction caused a decline of 6.2% in hospital admissions compared with the non-restricted counties. In 2006, the FDA mandated the labelling of trans fat on all food products. This caused many companies to reformulate their products to reduce trans fat content. In June 2018, partially hydrogenated oils, which are the primary source of artificial dietary trans fats, were banned from the US food supply. This was an important step in creating a healthy food environment. In the same vein, many other countries introduced certain policies, including taxes, with a view to a healthier food environment.

Salt (Sodium and Potassium)

Sodium and potassium exist in a variety of foods. Their imbalance can cause adverse effects on major end organs such as the brain, eyes, heart and kidneys. Sodium and potassium assist with fluid and blood volume maintenance. Therefore, they cause an impact on blood pressure in contrasting ways. An excess of sodium and a low potassium intake can increase blood pressure.

High Risk Regarding Kidney. For those with abnormal kidney function, a high potassium intake may pose a health risk. Those who are affected should consult with their nephrologist before modifying their diets.

For healthy individuals with normal kidney function, a diet abundant in potassium is optimal. On account of its role in reducing blood pressure, potassium is an essential electrolyte for promoting cardiovascular health and preventing end organ damage. Also, diets high in potassium are linked to a reduction in risk for stroke.

Sodium Risk and Blood Pressure. Proper management of blood pressure is crucial to decrease end organ damage and mortality. As of 2021, the most recent public health guidelines indicate that hypertension can be diagnosed when blood pressure is 130/80 or greater. Only about 25% of adults in the United States have their blood pressure under control. This problem applies more or less in many other countries, as in the case of the obesity pandemic.

Refocus on What to Eat and Drink. To combat the epidemic of health misinformation, it is helpful to refocus on the basics of what to eat and drink.

Simple and manageable adjustments to diet and beverage choice can lead to dramatic improvements in health. Also, these improvements can serve as preventive measures against silent killers such as obesity, hypertension (elevated blood pressure) and diabetes. The beneficial result is protection of the health of the main organs, such as the brain, eyes, heart and kidneys, and increasing life span.

HOW A PLANT-BASED DIET CAN BOOST HEALTH

Moving to a plant-based diet is a powerful step you can take to improve your health, boost energy levels, and prevent chronic diseases. Those who have seen *Forks Over Knives*[110] may appreciate that according to the science shown by changing nutrition people can live longer. They will reduce the risk of falling sick due to chronic and other illnesses. In addition, a general improvement in health, via a WFPB diet, can help the environment.

The scientific evidence shows that many chronic diseases can be prevented, controlled, or even reversed with a whole-food, plant-based

---

[110] This is a 2011 American advocacy film and documentary. It advocates a low-fat, whole-food, plant-based diet that excludes all animal products and processed foods as a way to avoid or reverse several chronic diseases. https://en.m.wikipedia.org

(WFPB) diet. There is landmark book *The China Study* which shows that a plant-based diet can reduce the risk of type 2 diabetes, heart disease, certain types of cancer, and other major illnesses. Some people also report benefits in fitness, greater energy, reduced inflammation, and better health after adopting the plant-based diet.

Colourful foods

Throughout Human History. As already mentioned above, different groups have adopted the plant-based diets. For example, a plant-based diet was extensively used in India and Greece. This was known in Greece as the Pythagoras diet.[111] Until the 1800s, a plant-based diet was known widely as the Pythagorean Diet. Many Indian religions feature a long tradition of adhering to a vegetarian diet.

Today, plant-based eating continues to be popular. The number of Americans who follow a vegan diet increased 600% from 2014 to 2018. Many choose a plant-based diet in the pursuit of health, out of concern for animal welfare, or as a way to reduce their environmental footprint. Regardless of the reasons for their change, more and more Americans are seeking to incorporate more plant-based foods into their diet.

In view of the increasing interest in a plant-based diet, many eating places are incorporating meat alternatives into their options, with some crafting and marketing dedicated plant-based menus. The interest in plant-based alternatives is evident; as the plant-based foods market has increased 29% in the U.S. between 2017 and 2019.

THE BENEFITS OF A WHOLE-FOOD, PLANT-BASED DIET

Several major benefits can be obtained from plant-based nutrition, all supported by science. These benefits include:

(a) Easy Weight Management: People who eat a plant-based diet tend to be leaner than those who don't, and the diet makes it easy to lose weight and keep it off—without counting calories.

---

[111] Around the 7th century BCE, Pythagoras studied at an ancient Indian university and returned to Greece as a vegetarian Hindu. India was the first country in the entire world to have established institutions for higher learning that attracted students from many countries. Some Chinese scholars who attended these institutions wrote about it.

(b) Disease Prevention: Whole-food, plant-based eating can prevent, halt, and in some cases reverse chronic diseases. The scientific evidence is especially overwhelming when it comes to heart disease and diabetes, but research has also linked plant-based diets to lower rates of arthritis, improved liver function, and healthier kidneys.

(c) A Lighter Environmental Footprint: A plant-based diet places much less stress on the environment.

Eating a Plant-Based Diet Could Help You Lose Weight

Your risk of obesity decreases when you move to plant-based diet. Weight loss may be a by-product of replacing and reducing certain foods. Eating more plants can help you drop pounds, too. A small study found that 65 overweight adults who followed a whole-food, plant-based diet for a year lost 9.25 pounds on average.

One reason for the weight loss is that whole grains and vegetables are relatively low on the glycemic index. This means they are digested more slowly. Fruit contains **antioxidants** and **fibre**, which helps prolong fullness. People have to be careful in choosing what to eat they can also eat a very unhealthy plant-based diet.

A high sugar, high fat, processed food-laden diet has contributed significantly to the burden of obesity and chronic disease in America. Not only do Americans consume fewer than the recommended daily servings of fruit and vegetables, but the average American eats approximately 200 pounds of red meat and poultry each year. This volume is higher than needed to meet the average daily calorie and protein requirements of a healthy diet. America is No 9 in the global ranking of fattest people.

Many Americans will go to extreme lengths to lose weight, as is evident from the proliferation of fad diets like the South Beach diet and the cabbage soup diet. Many physicians recommend plans such as the Mediterranean diet to help patients manage and pursue their health goals. Though perhaps less often recommended by physicians, a whole food, plant-based diet is another evidence-based option which can promote weight loss and ameliorate many so-called lifestyle diseases. Physicians need to understand the benefits and possible risks of alternative diets in order to effectively counsel patients on their adoption.

SAVE MONEY ON GROCERIES

Whole and minimally processed plant-based foods are not only the healthiest and most sustainable foods around; they are also some of the most affordable. In fact, going plant-based can cut grocery bills by $750 a year per person, according to research published in the *Journal of Hunger &*

Environmental Nutrition. Perhaps, the savings will be greater in the UK, as the prices for fruits and vegetables are much cheaper than in the US.

When you stock your kitchen with WFPB staples such as brown rice, potatoes, and dried beans, you can assemble nutritious, satisfying meals for just a few dollars.

 Vegetables & fruit

Dietary Patterns and Planetary Health

In addition to their associated health benefits, plant-based diets also tend to have less environmental impact than animal-based diets. Globally, food production is the largest contributor to biodiversity loss and is responsible for 80% of deforestation, more than 70% of fresh water use, and 30% of human-generated greenhouse gas (GHG) emissions. Meat has been identified as the food that has the greatest impact on GHG emissions and land use. Producing 1000 kcal (kilocalories) of lamb or beef generates 14 and 10 kg of GHG emissions, respectively, compared with just 1 and 3 kg for 1000 kcal of lentils or tofu. Producing 1 serving of beef or pork requires 1211 and 469 L of water, respectively, compared with 220, 57, and 30 L required to produce 1 serving of dry beans, tofu, or tomatoes

The GHG is comparatively high for the production of meat, and the same applies for the use of water in their production, when compared with the production of plant based foods.

Table showing generation of greenhouse gas

Items	Quantity Produced*	GHG** Emission
Lamb	1000 kcal	14 kg
Beef	1000 kcal	10 kg
Lentils	1000 kcal	1 kg
Tofu	1000 kcal	3 kg

*kcal is for kilocalories. **Greenhouse gas.

CONCLUSION

Nutrition is the study of food and how it affects the health and growth of the body. Nutrients are substances found in foods suitable for our bodies

Consuming a healthy diet that includes lots of fruit, vegetables, whole grains and moderate amount of unsaturated fats, meat and dairy can help us to maintain a steady weight. Making use of a good variety of these foods daily leaves no room for unhealthy foods that are high in fat and sugar, a leading cause of becoming overweight or obese.

Nutrition involves consuming, absorbing and using nutrients needed by the body for growth, development and staying healthy. In order to get enough appropriate nutrition, you need to consume a healthy diet, consisting of a variety of nutrients to nourish the body. As such, they will ensure we grow, reproduce and survive.

Nutrition and health are important as healthy eating patterns enable people to live longer and are at lower risk of contracting serious health problems such as heart disease, type 2 diabetes and obesity, among others. Those who have chronic diseases can eat healthy foods that help to manage these conditions and prevent complications. In many cases a whole food plant-based diet can help in this regard.

"Came from a plant, eat it; was made in a plant, don't."
Michael Pollan

"It is health that is real wealth and not pieces of gold and silver."
Mahatma Gandhi

End

CHAPTER 6

EFFECT OF EXCESSIVE MEAT CONSUMPTION

"The longest-lived people eat a plant-based diet. They eat meat but only as a condiment or a celebration. Nothing they eat has a plastic wrapper."

Dan Buettner

This chapter is intended to show how a diet of animal products could cause many health problems. On the other hand, a plant-based diet is regarded as a healthier diet. This is supported by the above quote. Dan Buettner has carried out research on people living in the Blue Zones[112] and how they live healthy lives to an advanced age on account of their lifestyle.

Pertinent Clip from The Daily Mail

Slapping cigarette-style warnings on MEAT would help people eat less and save the planet, according to researchers. Also, it will help with health issues.

Scientists at Durham University, who tested the alerts on 1,000 people, found they forced up to a tenth of participants to choose a fish or veggie option instead. Warnings that eating meat 'contributes to climate change' or 'poor health' (pictured) were perceived as most effective, while warnings meat-eating can trigger pandemics was viewed as least credible, results showed. The researchers said eating lots of meat is 'bad' for health and contributes to deaths from pollution and climate change. Warning labels could 'reduce these risks' and help the UK 'reach net zero' if introduced

DETRIMENT OF EATING RED MEAT

Consuming too much of red meat could be bad for your health. Eating red meat and processed meat can raise the risk of type 2 diabetes, coronary heart disease, stroke and certain cancers, such as colorectal cancer.[113]

---

[112] There are 5 regions: Okinawa in Japan, Sardinia in Italy, Icaria in Greece, Nicoya in Costica Rica, and Loma Linda in California (USA). These people have 9 common habits.
[113] 2 Dec. 2020. https://www.scripps.org Is Eating Red Meat Bad for You?

Eating meat increases your LDL cholesterol levels, blood pressure, risk of heart disease and stroke. This is because meat contains harmful saturated fats, animal protein and haem iron. Avoiding meat altogether can lower your cholesterol levels and blood pressure and it may even reverse heart disease.[114]

Meat-eating is particularly linked to colon cancer, prostate cancer, breast cancer, lymphoma, and stomach cancer. The reason is two-fold: animal-derived foods contain many substances that can directly increase the risk of cancer, such as haem, nitrates, heterocyclic amines, and polycyclic amines.[115]

The carnivore diet consists entirely of meat and animal products, excluding all other foods. The claim is that it aids weight loss, mood issues, and blood sugar regulation, among other health issues. But as the diet is extremely restrictive, it is likely to be unhealthy in the long term.[116] This diet could damage the colon and degrade gut health. In fact, changes to the microbiome eating nothing but meat could colonise the gut with bacteria that increase the risk for heart disease. Animal protein is high in L-Carnitine, a type of amino acid.[117]

The long-term side effects of an all meat diet include hypoproteinemia, kidney stones and vitamin deficiencies.[118]

Almost 24,000 participants died during a study, including about 5,900 from cardiovascular disease and about 9,500 from cancer. Those who consumed the most of both unprocessed and processed red meat had the highest risk of all-cause of mortality, cancer mortality and cardiovascular disease mortality.[119]

Of all the animal-based foods, red meat appears to be especially detrimental to health. It has been linked to premature mortality and type 2 diabetes, among other diseases. Among men in the Health Professionals Follow-Up Study over 22 years and women in the Nurses' Health Study (for 28 years), an increase in 1 serving of processed and unprocessed red meat per day was linked to a 13% and 20% increased risk of mortality, respectively. Replacing 1 serving of red meat per day with other foods fish, poultry, legumes, nuts, low-fat dairy, or whole grains, resulted in a 7–19% lower risk of premature death.

---

[114] https://viva.org.uk Why Animal Products Harm – Meat Viva! The Vegan Charity.
[115] https://www.peta.ork.uk Meat and Your Health Animals Are Not Ours to Eat – PETA UK.
[116] https://www.healthline.com Carnivore Diet Review: Benefits, Downsides, and Sample Menu.
[117] 7 Feb 2023. https://www.mygenefood.com 7Reasons the Carnivore Diet is Healthy and What to Try Instead.
[118] https://bluebirdprovisions.co Carnivore Diet Pros and Cons: Is it Really a Safe Option for Weight Loss?
[119] 26 March 2012. https://www.nih.gov Risk in Red Meat? National Institutes of Health (NIH)

The cooking methods used for red meat also appear to influence health. Higher frequency of open-flame and higher-temperature cooking methods was significantly associated with type 2 diabetes risk. Those who broiled or barbecued red meat 2 times weekly had an increased type 2 diabetes risk.

Red meat broiling and barbecuing were also associated with a significantly greater risk of obesity and weight gain. Another analysis found a similar association between type 2 diabetes risk and high-temperature and open-flame cooking of chicken, further indicating that meat cooking methods may play a role in the development of type 2 diabetes

Environmental Consequences

Apart from health implications of eating red meat, worldwide dietary changes also have environmental consequences. The production of animal food is more environmentally damaging and resource intensive than plant food production. The cost of producing animal protein is eleven times on average more than for grain-based protein. The land use for livestock is enormous. It takes around 100 times more land to produce a kilocalorie of beef or lamb than plant-based alternatives.[120]

The increasing demand for animal products, especially meat, is becoming unsustainable, using modern food-production systems. The systems of production cannot continue to support future population growth without drastic changes. What compounds the situation is the threat of climate change that will further threaten the environment and food supply. It follows that major interventions are necessary to change the food environment. This is to enable the general population to make diet and lifestyle choices that are both healthy and sustainable. Most importantly, the general populations should be encouraged to move towards healthy plant-based diets. This could be an important target for interventions in preventing and managing diet-related chronic diseases and ensure future food *security.*

Recent Studies on Metabolomics[121]

Many recent studies have also focused on discovering metabolomic signatures of specific foods and dietary patterns to provide more accurate assessment of dietary intake of the populations. For example, plasma and urinary anserine has been associated with chicken consumption, and urinary

---

[120] 4 March 2021. https://ourworldindata.org If the world adopted a plant-based diet we would reduce global agricultuiral.

[121] This word means the scientific study of the set of metabolites present within an organism, cell or tissue, "the potential of metabolomics in the early detection of cancer is also being explored".

trimethylamine-N-oxide and carnitines have been associated with red meat and fish intake. However, metabolomics is not yet able to accurately distinguish between most dietary patterns and specific foods. Perhaps, it can be used in conjunction with existing dietary assessment methods to measure dietary intake and assess compliance to dietary interventions, but should not replace the established dietary assessment methods.

Raising Animal for Food Inefficient.

This is alluded to already. Raising animals for food is an incredibly inefficient use of resources. Crops are grown to feed animals. This "introduces a major extra step of waste relative to the efficiency of us just eating the plant foods directly." A 2018 analysis found that livestock provides just 18% of calories consumed globally but takes up 83% of farmland. What a waste of resources! Refer to the table in Chapter 5 showing the excessive greenhouse gas being produced in the production of animals for food. This is not good for the planet.

Outcome of Not Eating Meat

Limiting foods with saturated fat, including meat, can lower "bad" or LDL cholesterol in your body. Research indicates that both processed and red meats are high in saturated fat and can lead to ongoing inflammation. The consequence is that it could raise the possibility of developing cancer and other diseases. Process meat includes bacon, deli meat, and hot dogs, while red meat includes, beef, pork and lamb.

However, if meat is eliminated and not substituted you are likely to be at risk of iron or B12 deficiency, anaemia, and muscle wasting.[122]

Sources of Vitamin B12. Bananas are rich in vitamin B12. Mushrooms, oranges and spinach are also sources of this vitamin. Other plant foods are almonds, pistachios, cashews dates, raisins, pumpkin seeds, sunflower seeds and figs. Some notable animal products are eggs, milk and salmon, among many others. Nutritional yeast is also a source.

Meat Not Essential for Survival. Although meats provide certain nutrients that plants do not, eating meat is not necessary for your health or survival. By appropriate planning and consuming supplements, plant-based diets can supply the nutrients your body needs.[123]

---

[122] Wollins explains on 23 Feb. 2023. https://www.realsimple.com > health
[123] 23 Aug. 2021 https://www.healthline.com > are-hu...

There are 9 essential amino acids, and the sources of complete protein include: dairy products, poultry, beef, pork, eggs, quinoa, whole sources of soy such as tofu, edamame, and tempeh.

Most plant sources of protein are incomplete. Regardless, you can get all the essential amino acids you need from plant foods, but you need to eat a variety of them. The sources are nuts, seeds, whole grains, vegetables, legumes such as beans, peas, and lentils.

Some Benefits from Animal Protein

Animal protein also has some health benefits. Low fat sources of animal protein from poultry and fish, rather than red meat, are god for health in view of these benefits:

(a) lower risk of diabetes type;
(b) lower risk of heart disease;
(c) lower risk of colorectal, stomach, pancreatic, and prostate cancer; and
(d) better weight control.

Risk of Animal Protein

A study of 100,000 people has shown that eating unprocessed and processed red meat has been linked to a shorter lifespan. Eating one additional serving of unprocessed red meat each day increases the risk of death by 13%. Consuming an additional serving of processed red meat increases the risk of death by 20%.[124]

Plant Protein
Protein from plant may be more important than the amount. This type of protein provides plenty of nutrients, fibre, and antioxidants that can increase your overall health. The benefits of plant protein may include:

(a) Protection against heart disease.
(b) Protection against cancer.
(c) Protection against stroke.
(d) Protection against diabetes type 2.

Some Plant-Based Diets Unhealthy. When considering overall plant-based dietary patterns, it is crucial to examine the types of foods included in your diet because not all plant-based diets are healthy. For example, white rice and white bread are plant-based but they are not healthy. As they are highly

---

[124] Medically reviewed by Dan Brennan, MD, on 15 Nov. 2021, written by WebMD Editorial Contributors.

processed, they have been depleted of many heart-healthy nutrients and in consequence they have a high glycaemic index. This means they can make blood sugar levels spike, leading to increase hunger and overeating.

Among more than 200,000 female and male health professionals, an overall plant-based diet index (created by positively scoring plant foods and negatively scoring animal foods) was associated with lower risk of coronary heart disease.

FOOD CONTRIBUTING TO OBESITY AND CHRONIC DISEASES

A high sugar, high fat, processed food-laden diet has contributed significantly to the burden of obesity and chronic disease in America and elsewhere. Not only do Americans consume fewer than the recommended daily servings of fruit and vegetables, the average American eats approximately 200 pounds of red meat and poultry each year. This excessive meat consumption is responsible for most of their chronic diseases, one of which is cancer. According to Dr John McDougall, some 1,700 Americans die daily from cancer. His programme on health does not allow the eating of meat, poultry, fish, cow's milk, butter, cheese, cottage cheese, yogurt, sour cream, ice cream, eggs, mayonnaise, vegetable oils, refined and sugar-coated cereals, chocolate (carob powder), and coconut.[125]

Outcome of Not Eating Meat

Those who are not involved in eating meat, known generally as vegetarians, eat fewer calories and less fat. The consequence is that they weigh less. In addition, they tend to have a lower risk of heart disease than non-vegetarians do. A study shows those who eat red meat are at a higher risk of death from heart disease, stroke and diabetes.[126]

The consequences of not eating meat may cause you to feel tired and weak if you cut out meat from your diet suddenly. This is due to missing an important source of protein and iron, both of which provide energy. The body absorbs more iron from meat than from other foods, but it is not your only choice.[127] You can cut down on meat gradually/

Meat Substitutes. They are:

---

[125] Dr McDougall is a renowned expert on plant-based recipes. He has a free 12-day programme on plant-based recipes.

[126] https://www.mayoclinic.org Meatless Meals: The benefits of eating less Meat – Mayo Clinic.

[127] 2 Dec. 2022. https://www.webmd.com What Happens When You Stop Eating Meat - WebMD

(a) Tofu. 1/10. This is a plant-based choice that packs a protein punch – half cup has over 11 g.

(b) Tempeh. 2/10. It is made from fermented soybeans. Tempeh has even more protein than tofu.

(c) Seitan. 3/10.

(d) Jackfruit. 4/10.

(e) Mushrooms. 5/10

(f) Beans. 6/10.

(g) Textured vegetable protein. 7/10.

(h) Chickpeas. 8.10.[128]

Whether you are thinking of giving up meat entirely or eating less, the benefits are clear: less risk of disease and improved health and well-being. More importantly, less meat decreases the risk of heart disease or stroke. Some of the substitutes for animal products are pulses, soya beans, quinoa, nuts, seeds, cereals and grains.

CONCLUSION

On account of the health risk attributable to eating meat, it is advisable to choose an alternative diet. The evidence against eating meat is stark. The Americans on average consume 200 pounds of meat yearly, and this has a tragic toll on their health, causing some 1,700 to die daily from just cancer. For this and among other reasons there is a need to move to mainly a plant-based diet.

The requirement to eat enough protein does not mean you only have to eat meat. There is growing evidence that replacing animal proteins with more plant-based proteins can benefit your health. Vegetarian and vegan foods are not only high in protein but also heart-healthy. Nut provides a good dose of protein. Like nuts, seeds contain healthy unsaturated fats and protein. Whole grain breads, rice and pasta have more protein, fibre and iron than white versions. Like soya, quorn is a complete protein. It is made from an edible fungus, has a meat-like texture, low in saturated fat and contains a lot of fibre, more than bake beans, wholemeal bread or brown rice.

Good meat substitutes are tofu, tempeh, seitan, jackfruit, mushrooms, beans, textured vegetable protein, and chickpeas.

> "We cannot have peace among men whose hearts find delight in killing any living creature."
>
> Rachel Carson

---

[128] 5 Nov. 2021. https://www.webmd.com

"For as long as men massacre animals, they will kill each other. Indeed, he who sows the seed of murder and pain cannot reap joy and love."

Pythagoras

"We manage to swallow flesh, only because we do not think of the cruel and sinful thing we do."

Rabindranath Tagore

"Animals are my friends and I don't eat my friends."

George Bernard Shaw

End

CHAPTER 7

SUPPORT FOR PLANT–BASED DIETS

"Nothing will benefit human health and increase the chances for survival of life on Earth as much as the evolution to a vegetarian diet."

Albert Einstein

"I always say that eating a plant based diet is the secret weapon of enhanced athletic performance."

Rich Roll

DIFFERENT TYPES OF DIETS

Many studies have explored the relationship between plant-based dietary patterns with an emphasis on plant foods. These include vegetarian, vegan or Mediterranean-style diets. Refer to Chapter 1 for these diets. They have shown to be linked with reduced risk of heart disease, strokes and type 2 diabetes. This is compared to less healthy dietary patterns.[129]

Strategies used by some practitioners to support patients in plant-based eating are:

(a) To advise them not to buy costly and highly processed animal products but to buy mainly foods suitable for vegetarians and vegans.
(b) To suggest inexpensive frozen vegetables.
(c) To buying items in bulk, such as legumes, brown rice, potatoes and oatmeal.
(d) To discuss nutritional value and nutrient-to-cost ratio of legumes as compared to meat.[130]

Eating more plants does not have to be all or nothing, as this mentality can quickly backfire and make a person resistant to plant–based diets. Instead, people can be encouraged to add more of such foods into their current diet without cutting out completely animal products.[131] Reducing animal products can be done gradually.

---

[129] https://www.nutrition.org.uk Plant-based diets – British Nutrition Foundation.
[130] https://www.ncbi.nlm.nih.gov Strategies for practitioners to support patients in plant-based eating – PMC.
[131] 7 June 2022. https://nutrium.com How to encourage clients to eat more plants – Nutrium Blog.

Support for Vegetarian Diet

The results of an evidence-based review showed that a vegetarian diet is associated with a lower risk of death. Vegetarians also appear to have lower low-density lipoprotein cholesterol levels, low blood pressure, and lower rates of hypertension and type 2 diabetes than non vegetarians.[132]

Practitioners Can Promote a Healthy Eating Environment.

Although physicians lack training in nutrition (only about 20 hours in 4 years at medical schools), there is no reason why they should not improve their knowledge over time in the course of their practice. Those who have acquired relevant knowledge can help towards a healthy eating environment in these respects:

(a) encouraging mealtimes to be relaxed and comfortable;
(b) getting the whole family to sit and eat together;
(c) being positive regarding healthy foods the children are eating;
(d) those who are fussy should be encouraged to eat new foods; and
(e) regard themselves as a role model in the foods they eat.[133]

Encouraging People to Eat Healthy Diets. The encouragement can take these forms:

(a) Trust and rapport can be built with each client.
(b) Tolerate mistakes which can be corrected.
(c) Structure first, freedom second.
(d) Clients' habits should relate to their wants and needs.
(e) Clients should be surrounded in environments that reinforce their habits
(f) Connect with your client and model your habits.
(g) Provide education regarding nutritional needs.
(h) Skill competency.

National Initiatives in Support of Healthy Eating. Extensive initiatives locally and nationally should promote healthy eating. This can be beneficial to families, including children and adults. Some notable examples are Change4Life[134] Campaign, the Nursery Milk Scheme, the Schools Fruit & Vegetable Scheme, and the 5-a-day Campaign.[135]

---

[132] 3 March 2022. https://viva.org.uk 10 Top Health Organisations that Endorse a Plant-based Diet – Viva!
[133] https://heas.health.vic.gov Promoting healthy eating in early childhood education and care
[134] This is the UK government's behaviour change programme which aims to inspire a societal movement through which government, the NHS, local authorities, businesses,

UK Government Promote Healthy Eating. The Eatwell Guide is a visual representation regarding the types and proportions of foods required for a healthy balanced diet to promote long-term health of the public. It includes key messages such as eat at least 5 portions of a variety of fruit and vegetables daily.[136]

A Healthy Eating Plan. This can include fish, poultry, beans, and nuts: limit red meat and cheese: avoid bacon, cold cuts, and other processed meats. Eat a variety of whole grains, such as whole-wheat bread, whole-grain pasta, and brown rice. Limit refined grains such as white rice and white bread.[137]

Reasons for Eating More Veggies and Fruits. There are 3 main reasons:

(a) Healthy eating feels good. Plant-based diets are in demand because of an increased focus on living a healthy lifestyle.
(b) The environment is a big deal.
(c) Social consciousness cares about animals[138] (non violence).

Unheathiest Diet in the World. It is a carnivore diet. It is not a sustainable diet. There are healthier ways to lose weight if this is the objective. Not only is the carnivore diet extremely high in saturated fat, which can increase cholesterol levels, it can also leave out a lot of foods that are good for health.[139]

The carnivore diet is a fad diet in which only animal products, such as meat, eggs, and dairy are eaten. This diet is associated with pseudo scientific health claims. But such a diet can result in deficiencies of vitamins and dietary fibre, and increase the risk of chronic diseases.[140]

A fad diet is based on a plan to produce results such as fast weight loss. But there is no scientific evidence in support. Popular ones include plans involving eating a very restrictive diet with few foods or an unusually

---

charities, schools, families and community leaders can all play a part in improving people's diets and activity levels.
[135] Https://eyanswers.co.uk Evaluate national and local initiatives which promote healthy eating.
[136] 10 January 2023 https://www..gov.uk Healthy eating: applying All Our Health – Gov.UK.
[137] https://www.hsph.harvard.edu Healthy Eating Plate The Nutrition Source
[138] 26 Feb. 2021. https://www.hatcocorp.com Three Reasons Why the Plant-Based Movement Is Strong.
[139] https://www.everydayhealth.com the Best and Worst Diets for Sustained Weight Loss.
[140] According to Wikipedia.

combination of foods. There is restriction to eating certain foods at certain times.[141]

SUPPORT FROM 10 ORGANISATIONS

The truth is most of us would be better off waving goodbye to the typical Western diet and embracing a well-planned plant-based one. And you do not have to take our word for it: check out what these 10 world-leading health organisations have to say about a vegan diet. This is already alluded to in Chapter 1.

1. Food and Agriculture Organisation & World Health Organisation

"Households should select predominantly plant-based diets rich in a variety of vegetables and fruits, pulses or legumes, and minimally processed starchy staple foods. The evidence that such diets will prevent or delay a significant proportion of non-communicable chronic diseases is consistent."

2. British National Health Service

"With good planning and an understanding of what makes up a healthy, balanced vegan diet, you can get all the nutrients your body needs."

3. British Dietetic Association

"Diets centred on a wide variety of plant foods offer affordable, tasty and nutritious options. Plant-based diets rich in beans, nuts, seeds, fruit and vegetables, wholegrains (such as oats, barley and quinoa) and minimally processed foods can provide all the nutrients needed for good health."

4. British Nutrition Foundation

"A well-planned vegetarian or vegan diet can provide the nutrients we need [...] vegetarian dietary patterns may have a health benefit when compared to more traditional dietary patterns. Vegetarian or more plant-based diets are typically higher in fruit and vegetables, whole grains and dietary fibre while being lower in saturated fat, sweets and non-water beverages (such as sugar-sweetened beverages and alcohol)."

5. Academy of Nutrition and Dietetics

"It is the position of the Academy of Nutrition and Dietetics that appropriately planned vegetarian, including vegan, diets are healthful, nutritionally adequate, and may provide health benefits for the prevention and treatment of certain diseases. These diets are appropriate for all stages of the life cycle, including pregnancy, lactation, infancy, childhood, adolescence, older adulthood, and for athletes [...] Vegetarians and vegans

---

[141] https://www.bda.uk.com Fad diets – British Diebetic Association.

are at reduced risk of certain health conditions, including ischemic heart disease, type 2 diabetes, hypertension, certain types of cancer, and obesity. Low intake of saturated fat and high intakes of vegetables, fruits, whole grains, legumes, soy products, nuts, and seeds (all rich in fibber and phytochemicals) are characteristics of vegetarian and vegan diets that produce lower total and low-density lipoprotein cholesterol levels and better serum glucose control. These factors contribute to reduction of chronic disease."

6. American Dietetic Association

"It is the position of the American Dietetic Association that appropriately planned vegetarian diets, including total vegetarian or vegan diets, are healthful, nutritionally adequate, and may provide health benefits in the prevention and treatment of certain diseases [...] The results of an evidence-based review showed that a vegetarian diet is associated with a lower risk of death from ischemic heart disease. Vegetarians also appear to have lower low-density lipoprotein cholesterol levels, lower blood pressure, and lower rates of hypertension and diabetes type 2 than non vegetarians. Furthermore, vegetarians tend to have a lower body mass index and lower overall cancer rates."

7. Johns Hopkins Center for a Livable Future

"A strong body of scientific evidence links excess meat consumption, particularly of red and processed meat, with heart disease, stroke, type 2 diabetes, obesity, certain cancers, and earlier death. Diets high in vegetables, fruits, whole grains and beans can help prevent these diseases and promote health in a variety of ways."

8. Dieticians of Canada

"Anyone can follow a vegan diet – from children to teens to older adults. It's even healthy for pregnant or nursing mothers. A well-planned vegan diet is high in fibre, vitamins and antioxidants. Plus, it's low in saturated fat and cholesterol. This healthy combination helps protect against chronic diseases.

Vegans have lower rates of heart disease, diabetes and certain types of cancer than non-vegans. Vegans also have lower blood pressure levels than both meat-eaters and vegetarians and are less likely to be overweight."

9. The Dieticians Association of Australia

"With planning, those following a vegan diet can cover all their nutrient bases, but there are some extra things to consider."

10. **The National Health and Medical Research Council of Australia**

"Appropriately planned vegetarian diets, including total vegetarian or vegan diets, are healthy and nutritionally adequate. Well-planned vegetarian diets are appropriate for individuals during all stages of the lifecycle. Those following a strict vegetarian or vegan diet can meet nutrient requirements as long as energy needs are met and an appropriate variety of plant foods are eaten throughout the day. Those following a vegan diet should choose foods to ensure adequate intake of iron and zinc and to optimise the absorption and bioavailability of iron, zinc and calcium."

Some doctors are bcoming more involved in helping their patients to adopt healthier lifestyles. Healthier eating may be best achieved with a plant-based diet. This diet encourages whole, plant-based foods (WPBF) and discourages meats, dairy products, and eggs as well as all refined and procfessed foods. Various studies have shown that these diets are cost-effective, low-risk interventions that may lower body mass index (BMI), blood pressure, HbA1c, and cholesterol levels, and may also reduce the number of medications needed to treat chronic diseases.

SUPPORT FROM SOME DOCTORS

Students at medical schools around the world are not given enough grounding on plant-based diets. Unless practising doctors acquire the knowledge later, they hardly discuss the benefits of a plant-based diet with their patients. They concentrate mainly on prescribing medications.

Doctors Supporting Plant-Based Diets.[142] The doctors below, among others, support plant-based diets. They have devoted their lives to medical research, nutrition and optimal living:

(a) Neal Barnard. A plant-based powerhouse.

(b) Colin Campbell (The China Study) 86 years young.

(c) Caldwell Esselstyn.

(d) Dean and Dr Ayesha Sherzai.

(e) Garth Davis.

(f) Michael Klaper.

(g) Deen Ornish (you can look at his YouTube videos).

---

[142]7 Plant-Based Doctors You Should Be Following - Oops Vegan 22 April 2021. https://oopsvegan.com › blog › vegan-plant-based-doctors.

The pictures of many doctors are set out below. These doctors embrace a plant-based diet which they acquired mainly on their own, rather than being wholly thought at medical school. In addition, many other doctors are following this diet themselves and some of them advocate it to their patients for a healthy lifestyle.

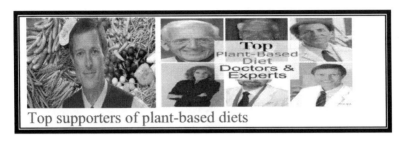
Top supporters of plant-based diets

Plant-based top doctors

Top vegan doctors

In addition to the doctors in the pictures, there are many more that support a plant-based diet. But many who pass through med schools have no proper clue as to this diet, and they may not be showing an interest.

Plant–based diets in comparison to diets from animal products are more sustainable. The main reason for this is because they use fewer resources and they are having a lesser impact on the environment.[143].

Nutritional Support Services

The Nutrition Support Service (NSS) is a multidisciplinary team comprising physicians, a pharmacist, a nurse and dietitians with certification in nutrition support. This body provides inpatient consultation for all aspects of nutrition support: Assessing nutritional status.[144]

The provision of enteral or parenteral nutrients to treat or prevent malnutrition. Nutrition Support Therapy is part of Nutrition Therapy which is a component of medical treatment that can include oral,enteral, and parenteral nutrition or restore optimal nutrition status and health.[145]

CONCLUSION

There are many studies show that plant-based diets are cost-effective, low-risk interventions that may lower body mass index, blood pressure, HbA1c and cholesterol levels. Most importantly, they may reduce the number of medications required to treat chronic diseases and lower ischemic heart disease mortality rates. Such diets in comparison with animal products are more sustainable as they require fewer natural resources and are less taxing on the environment.

In the light of the benefits set out above, there is a great deal of support for such diets. As set out in the chapter, there are support by 10 important national and international organisations and a long list of American doctors.

A plant-based diet is important for health. It provides all the protein, calcium and other essential nutrients your body needs as shown in a few other chapters. A plant-based diet makes sense for many reasons, including:

(a) an increase in vitamins and nutrients.
(b) it boosts fibre intake.
(c) it prevents chronic conditions and diseases.
(d) it manages your weight.

The top science papers of 2022 support plant-based nutrition. Many medical professionals now support plant-based nutrition, not just those listed in the chapter but many more listed in a table in Chapter 19. This is a

---

[143] https://www.sciencedirect.com sustainability of plant-based diets: back to the future – Science-Direct.com.
[144] https://nutritionalscience.wustl.edu Nutritional Support Services.
[145] https://www.nutritioncare.org Aspen What is Nutrition Support Therapy

major turning point in the narrative within the medical profession, having regard to the fact that their studies at med schools regarding nutrition was generally less than 20 hours in 4 years.

> "The Gods created certain kinds of beings to replenish our bodies: they are the trees and the plants and the seeds."
>
> Plato

End

CHAPTER 8

WFPB DIET CAN REDUCE BRAIN DAMAGE

"Boost your brain health nature's way, with the best vegan foods to nurture your body and brain from within."

Stephanie Masterman

The acronym WFPB is for whole food plant-based diet or food. This diet is becoming popular in many countries, and there is a good reason for it. It helps the brain to prevent or to get rid of brain diseases. There are numerous brain diseases. The main types of Brain Disorders are:

- Alzheimer's disease.
- Dementias.
- Brain cancer.
- Epilepsy and other seizure.
- Mental disorders.
- Parkinson's and other movement disorders.
- Stroke and transient ischemic attack (TIA).

A few of the well-known brain diseases are briefly set out below, starting with Alzheimer's disease.

ALZHEIMER'S DISEASE

This is a progressive, degenerative disease of the brain, in which build-up of abnormal proteins cause nerve cells to die. This disrupts the transmitters that carry messages, and causes the brain to shrink. It begins with mild memory loss and can lead to loss of ability to carry on a conversation and respond to the environment.

Alzheimer's disease is the most common type of dementia. This disease involves parts of the brain that control thought, memory and language.[146] It is a brain disorder that slowly destroys memory and thinking skills and, eventually, it interferes with the ability to carry out the simplest tasks. In most people with this disorder, those with the late-onset type symptoms first appear in their mid-60s.[147]

The disease is characterised by an accumulation of abnormal plaques and neurofibrillary tangles. Plaques are spherical microscopic lesions that

---

[146] https://www.cdc.com What is Alzheimer's Disease? – CDC.
[147] 8 July 2021. https://www.nia.nih.gov What is Alzheimer's Disease? National Institute of Aging.

have a core of extracellular amyloid beta-peptide surrounded by enlarged axonal endings.[148]

Alzheimer's Disease in the US and the UK. More than 5 million people suffer from the disease in the US, where it is the 6th leading cause of death, and more than 1 million Britons had it. But currently about 850,000 to 900,000 people are said to have this disease in the UK.[149] Based on total population, the rate of getting the disease in the US is higher than in the UK.

Causes of Alzheimer's. The exact causes are not fully understood. But at a basic level, brain proteins fail to function as usual. This causes a disruption of the work of the brain cells, also called neurons, and triggers a series of events. The neurons become damaged and lose connections to each other.[150]

This most common type of dementia affects an estimated 850,000 people in the UK. Dementia is a progressive neurological disease. It affects multiple brain functions, including memory.[151]

Things that Trigger Alzheimer's Disease. They are:

- Education level.
- Cognitive activity.
- Hypertension in mid-life.
- Orthostatic hypotension.[152]
- Diabetes.
- BMI (body mass index).
- Head trauma.
- Hyperhomocysteinemia.[153]

Foods that increase the risk of Alzheimer's disease are:
- Red meat.
- Refined carbohydrates.
- High-age foods (red meat, certain cheeses, fried eggs, oils, etc).
- Food with high cholesterol.
- Gluten[154](certain grains, often refers to only wheat proteins).

---

[148] https://www.ncbi.nlm.nih.gov Alzheimer's Disease – StatPearls – NCBI Bookshelf.
[149] https://www.alzheimers.org.uk Local dementia statistics Alzheimer's Society.
[150] 30 Aug. 2023. https://www.mayoclinic.org Alzheimer's disease – Symptoms and Causes – Mayo Clinic.
[151] 13 Feb. 2023. https://www.nhsinform.scot
[152] A condition in which your blood pressure suddenly drops when you stand up from a seated or lying position. Hypotension means low blood pression.
[153] Refers to the condition where there is greater than 15 micromol/L of homocysteine in the blood. It is present in many diseases and in many cases it is an independent risk factor.

What Happens?

As brain cells die, the functions they provide are lost. That includes memory, orientation and the ability to think and reason. The progress of the disease is slow and gradual. On average, patients live five to seven years after diagnosis, but some may live for 10 to 15 years.

Early Symptoms. They are:

- Loss of short-term memory.
- Disorientation.
- Behavioural changes.
- Mood swings.
- Difficulties dealing with money or making a phone call.

Later Symptoms. They are:

- Severe memory loss, forgetting close family members, familiar objects or places.
- Becoming anxious and frustrated over inability to make sense of the world, leading to aggressive behaviour.
- Eventually they may lose ability to walk.
- May have problems eating.
- The majority will eventually need 24-hour care.[155]

Dementia is linked with an abnormal build-up of proteins in the brain, called amyloid and tau. When these toxic proteins build-up in the brain, the organ launches an inflammatory response to keep the damage at bay.

Diets and Other Help

According to a Ms Tracy Parker,[156] berries, such as strawberries, blueberries and blackberries, also have many brain protective benefits. Emerging research suggests that compounds in blueberries known as flavonoids may improve memory, learning and general cognitive function, including skills in reasoning, decision making, verbal comprehension and numerical ability.[157]

Red meat, fried food and sweets should be avoided. Choose at least two servings of poultry and one of fish, instead. According to experts, these foods

---

[154] Information from the internet.

[155] Source: Alzheimer's Association.

[156] Tracy Parker, the heart health dietician at the British Heart Foundation. 2 Oct. 2023.

[157] 1 Jan. 2011 https://www.scientificamerican.com Your Brain on Blueberries: Enhance Memory with Right Foods.

contain high levels of antioxidants, which help protect against some of the damage to brain cells which is associated with dementia.

They can also increase the levels of proteins in the brain that protect brain cells from this damage, according to the **Alzheimer's Society**. The diet is low in cholesterol, which recent research has suggested may be associated with memory and thinking problems.

But diets such as MIND, which are packed with vegetables and fruit, high in antioxidants, can reduce inflammation, according to Harvard School of Public Health. The diet, recommended by Ms Parker, contains vitamins such as C and E, and beta-carotene, which all act as antioxidants. These antioxidants help prevent disruption and damage caused by free-radicals, which contribute to brain ageing, according to the Alzheimer's Society.

The charity says the brains of people with Alzheimer's have higher levels of natural antioxidants which are thought to be responsible for "clearing up" excess free radicals, suggesting the brain is trying to combat damage. Therefore, eating more antioxidants can help battle free radicals and prevent damage, according to experts.

Studies of the diet in people living in retirement communities suggest that those who most closely follow it have brains that are equivalent to seven-and-a-half years younger compared to those who do not.

Although it could have brain boosting powers there is not enough research yet for the MIND diet to be part of national dietary guidelines, says Ms Parker. She said: "We need further studies to refine the specific foods and quantities included."[158]

MIND Diet. This diet focuses on plant-based foods linked to dementia prevention. It encourages eating from 10 healthy food groups: leafy green vegetables at least 6 servings per week, and other vegetables at least a daily serving.[159]

Avoiding Alzheimer's Disease. Is Remission Possible?

You can have a cognoscopy to test whether you are likely to get this disease. Two US doctors[160] were interviewed in a You Tube video on this disease. They were of the view that a suitable diet can help and that sugar should be avoided? To date, there has been no clinically validated remission

---

[158] Tracy Parker, the heart health dietician at the British Heart Foundation. 2 Oct. 2023.
[159] 27 Nov. 2019. httpa://www.nia.nih.gov What Do We Know About Diet and Prevention of Alzheimer's Disease?
[160] They are Dr Dale Bredeson and Dr Richard Johnson who appeared in Tom Bilyeu Podcast. According to the discussinon people with this disease can go into remission contrary to consensus of general opinion that it is life long. Refer also to Neuroscientists AKA "Brain Docs" Drs Ayesha & Dean Sherazi, MD, You Tube.

of Alzheimer's disease.[161] Currently, this disease has no cure, but can be avoided or prevented.

PARKINSON'S DISEASE

This is a condition that also affects the brain. It causes problems like shaking and stiffness that get worse over time. The main symptoms are shaking (tremors), slow movements and stiffness. Treatment for this disease included therapies to help with movement problems, medicines and sometimes brain surgery.

Cause of Parkinson's. It is due to loss of nerve cells in part of the brain. There is no clear explanation why this happens. The life expectancy of a person with this disease can be normal or near normal. Patients usually live between 10 and 20 years after diagnosis, according to Michael J. Fox Foundation.[162]

Diets of Plant-Based Food

Adhering to a healthy plant-based dietary pattern was associated with a reduced risk of developing Parkinson's disease, especially among older people, according to a large-scale UK study. A higher intake of vegetables, nuts, and tea in the regular diet is linked to the lowest Parkinson's risk, data show.[163]

Snack on small quantities of walnuts, cashews and other nuts to promote brain health. Also, try to incorporate berries, which contain beneficial antioxidants, and foods that may have anti-inflammatory effects in the brain, like salmon, tuna and dark, leafy green vegetables.[164]

Berries, green leafy vegetables, eggs, fish and oil have neuroprotective properties which can reduce cognitive decline and improve memory function. Yogurt, kefir and raw sauerkraut, and natural probiotics can also increase natural dopamine production. This is good for Parkinson's disease.[165] Vitamin B12 may have the effect of preventing or reducing tremors on the hand and leg.[166] Check food labels for vitamin B12 (such as soy milk).

---

[161] 30 Aug. 2023. http://alzheimer.ca Bredeson Protocol offers false hope of reversing it.
[162] 6 Dec. 2022. https://www.grisworldhomecare.com Parkinson's disease Life Expectancy – Grisworld Home Care.
[163] 25 Aug. 2023. https://parkinsonsnewstoday.com Healthy plant-based diet lowers Parkinson's risk, UK study asserts.
[164] https://www.parkinson.org Diet & Nutrition Parkinson's Foundation.
[165] https://www.theracycle.com Dopamine foods for Parkinson's disease – Theracycle.
[166] https://parkinsonsnewstoday.com B12Injections for Stopping Tremors- Parkinson's News Today.

There is usually no cure for Parkinson's disease. However, Howard Shifke fully recovered from it.[167]

STROKES

A stroke is sometimes called a brain attack. It occurs when something blocks blood supply to part of the brain or when a blood vessel in the brain bursts. In either case, parts of the brain become damaged or die. A stroke can cause lasting brain damage, long-term disability or even death.[168]

Brain During a Stroke

The brain controls movements, stores memories, and is the source of our thoughts, emotions, and language. It also controls many functions of the body, like breathing and digestion.

To work properly, your brain needs oxygen. Your arteries deliver oxygen-rich blood to all parts of your brain. If something happens to block the flow of blood, brain cells start to die within minutes, because they cannot get oxygen. This causes a stroke. To save the life of a person requires emergency care. Act fast by calling 112 (UK) or 911 (US) right away, if there is a sign of a stroke. Time lost is brain lost, and every minute counts.

Types of Stroke

They are Ischemic stroke and Hemorrhagic stroke. A transient ischemic attack (TIA) is sometimes called a "mini-stroke." It is different from the major types of stroke. This is because blood flow to the brain is blocked for only a short time, usually no more than 5 minutes.

Ischemis Stroke. Most strokes are ischemic strokes. This type occurs when blood clots or other particles block the blood vessels to the brain. Fatty deposits called plaque can also cause blockages by building up in the blood vessels.

Hemorrhagic Stroke. This stroke happens when an artery in the brain leaks blood or ruptures (breaks open). The leaked blood puts too much pressure on brain cells. That blood damages the brain cells. High Blood Pressure and aneurysms – balloon-like bulges in an artery that can stretch and burst – are examples of conditions that can cause a hemorrhagic stroke

---

[167] https://www.amazon.com Fighting Parkinson's and Winning: A memoir of my recovery.
[168] https://www.cdc.gov About Stroke cdc.gov

Transient Ischemic Attack (TIA or "mini-stroke). TIAs are sometimes known as "warning strokes." It is important to know the following:

(a) A TIA is a warning sign of a future stroke.
(b) A TIA is a medical emergency, just like a major stroke.
(c) Strokes and TIAs require emergency care (call 112 (UK) or 911 (US) right away if there is a sign of a stroke or you notice a sign of someone in your presence).
(d) There is no way to know in the beginning whether symptoms are from a TIA or from a major type of stroke.
(e) Like ischemic strokes, blood clots often cause TIAs.
(f) Over a third of people who have a TIA and do not get treatment have a major stroke within 1 year. As many as 10 to 15% of people will have a major stroke within 3 months of a TIA.

TIAs can lower the risk of a major stroke. If you have a TIA, your health professionals can find the cause and take steps to prevent a major stroke.

Steps to Prevent a Stroke

These are the most important steps to take to lower your risk of a stroke:

- Keep your blood pressure in the normal range.
- If you are a smoker, quit.
- Keep your blood sugar (glucose) in the normal range.
- Seek treatment for any heart disease.
- Keep your cholesterol levels in the normal range.
- Maintain a healthy weight.
- Be active daily (if necessary do some exercises, such as brisk walking).[169]

Brain Cancer (Tumor)

A brain tumor is a growth in your brain. It can be non-cancerous (benign) or cancerous (malignant). Symptoms of a brain tumor include headache, seizures (fits), memory problems and changes in your personality. Treatments for brain tumours include medicines, surgery, radiotherapy and chemotherapy.

The cause of most brain tumours is unknown. Things that increase the risk of a tumor include getting older or being exposed to radiation.

---

[169] 1 Dec. 2021. https://health.gov Reduce Your risk of Stroke – MyHealthfinder
health.gov

Diets to Reduce Risk of Stroke

Studies found that a healthy plant-based diet – in addition to being linked with 10% lower overall stroke risk – was associated with a modest reduction in risk of ischemic stroke, the most common type of stroke, which occurs when blood flow to the brain is blocked.[170] Foods that help to prevent strokes are these:

- Fruits at least 5 servings daily.
- Healthy fats, such as fatty fish or seafood, nuts, seeds, avocado, and extra virgin oil.
- Bean and other legumes.
- Vegetables, at least 3 servings daily.
- Whole grains, such as quinoa.[171]

Diet Chart for Brain Cancer. Included in the chart are:

- Broccoli: This is a vegetable that suitable for the diet of brain tumor patients.
- Garlic. It is a commonly eaten food that has been found to have anti-cancerous properties. Garlic has allicin.
- Turmeric. It contains curcumin (should be eaten with a little blackpeper which helps to absorb the curcumin).
- Ginger.
- Hearty chicken broths.
- Nuts.
- Eggs.
- Leafy vegetables.[172]

The anti-oxidants present in curcumin reduce free radicals from the body, thereby improving health and immunity. It has gained popularity as a cure for brain tumours as well.[173]

---

[170] 10 Mar. 2021. https:P//www.hsph.harvard.edu Healthy plant-based diet associated with lower stroke risk.
[171] 10 April 2023. https://www.massgeneralbargain.org Foods That Help Prevent Stroke – Mass General Bargain.
[172] 6 June 2022; https://www.drhimanshugupta.com Diet Chart for Brain Tumor Patients in 2022 – Dr Himanshu Gupta.
[173] 6 Nov. 2019. https://www.pavtan.com Ayurvedic Remedies for the Treatment of Brain Tumor – Pavtan.

OTHER BRAIN DISORDERS

Some of the disorders of the brain, including a few of those discussed above, are these:

- Dementias.
- Brain cancer.
- Epilepsy and other seizure disorders.
- Alzheimer's disease.
- Mental disorders.
- Parkinson's and other movement disorders.
- Stroke and transient ischemic attack (TIA).

DEMENTIA

Plant-based foods are beneficial to the brain and may help prevent Alzheimer's disease and other forms of dementia. A decline in brain health is not an inevitable part of aging. How we eat and live can help us protect our memory and stay sharp into old age.[174]

Except for the first item, the foods linked adversely to dementia are these:

- Red Meats. These are great source of iron, which is necessary for preventing anaemia.
- Refined carbohydrates. A diet rich in starch and sugar also puts older adult at risk.
- High-Age foods.
- Foods with high cholesterol.
- Gluten.[175]

Many medical organisations have recommended a plant-based diet to optimise cognitive health and potentially prevent dementia. To maintain cognitive health and prevent cognitive aging, consuming a plant-based diet can be a low-risk and beneficial lifestyle change.[176] Eat green leafy vegetables, such as spinach, cabbage, spring greens, kale and salad leaves

---

[174] https://www.pcrm.org Alzheimer's Disease – Physcians Committee for Responsible Medicine. Many doctors in You Tube videos are of the view that this disease can go into remission. They are Drs Ayesha & Dean Sherazi, Dr Dale Bredeson, Dr Richard Johnson.
[175] 4 May 2023. https://www.homecareassistanceoshkos 5 Foods that Raise the Risk of Alzheimer's Disease - Home
[176] 29 Nov. 2022. https://www.ncbi.nlm.nih.gov Effect of a Vegan Diet on Alzheimer's Disease – PMC – NCBI.

(one or more servings daily). One or more daily servings of other vegetables, nuts on most days and beans and lentils 3 or more servings weekly should be eaten.

Nuts and berries are ideal snacks for dementia; both have been linked to better brain health. Blueberries and strawberries, in particular, keep your brain working at its best and may slow symptoms linked to Alzheimer's.[177] Eating plenty of apples, bananas, and oranges can also be the best foods for dementia patients to eat.[178] But very ripe bananas have a lot of sugar.

There is evidence suggesting that drinking green tea might reduce the risk of dementia, Alzheimer's disease and cognitive impairment. According to a study published in Translational Psychology, tea drinkers are 16% less likely to develop dementia compared with non-drinkers.[179]

EPILEPSY

Epilepsy is a common condition where sudden bursts of electrical activity in the brain causes seizures or fits. There are many possible symptoms of epilepsy seizures, including uncontrollable shaking or losing awareness of things around you.

The main treatment for epilepsy is medicine to stop the seizures. It is often not clear what causes epilepsy. It may run in the family or is caused by damage to the brain, such as from injury.

Remedies for epilepsy and seizures, and how effective they are proven to be, are these:

- Medicines called anti-epileptic drugs, these are the main treatment.
- Surgery to remove a small part of the brain that is causing the seizures.
- A procedure to place a small electrical device inside the body that can help control seizures.
- A special ketogenic diet that can help control seizures.

How effective the above are is beyond the scope of this book, and information should be sought from an experienced doctor or the internet.

Foods to Help Treat Epilepsy. Foods with a low glycemic index are recommended. A diet of such foods does not spike the blood glucose level. Foods with a low glycaemic index affect blood glucose levels slowly, if at

---

[177] 28 Aug. 2023 https://www.webmd.com Brain Foods That May Help Prevent Dementia – WebMD.

[178] 15 June 2022. https://lonestarneurology.net Brain Foods and diets that May Help Prevent Dementia.

[179] 3 June 2022. https://www.athomecaregivers.com 5 Best Drinks for Dementia, Says Dietitian – At Home Caregivers.

all. Refer to various tables in Chapter 2. It is not understood why low blood glucose levels control seizures in some people. Foods on this diet include meat, cheese, and most high-fibre vegetables.[180]

If you suffer from epilepsy, fruits and vegetables are suitable to increase your antioxidant intake. Incorporate a variety of colourful fruits and vegetables, such as berries, cherries, citrus fruits, tomatoes, spinach, kale, broccoli, and Brussels sprouts into your diet regularly.[181] Specialised diets, such as kitogenic diet, have been shown to help improve seizure control in people with epilepsy. However, the keto diet is not risk-free. Side effects occurring with long-term diet use include: low bone density and bone fractures, and constipation.[182]

who eat four or less.

ULTRA–PROCESSED FOOD

Ultra-processed food is bad for the body, and it is well publicised. First there are the large quantities of calories, salt, fat and sugar that are increasing the risk of weight-gain along with heart disease. Then there are the plethora of additives, such as emulsifiers, artificial sweeteners and other flavourings, which are said to destroy the healthy bacteria in our gut – which can protect against disease – and interfere with natural hunger signals, making us eat when we're full.

Until recently, the supposed harms to the brain were relatively unknown. A number of studies were carried out in France and Italy in which a group of people were give ultra processed food. The studies have shown that eating a lot of such food is likely to cause people to develop depression and anxiety disorders. At the end, and once back to the normal diet three weeks later, completed cognitive assessments are required to test the area of the brain called the hippocampus. This is involved with memory, learning, emotional processing and mood. Their results were compared with another group who ate a typical, nutritious diet. Scientists found that the waffles and takeaway group performed far worse on the tests at the end of the week.

The authors argued that the results suggested that just a small amount of ultra-processed food can impair the hippocampus. Previous studies have found that those who eat diets high in ultra-processed food were more likely than others to have an unusually small hippocampus. Some experts believe the explanation lies in the nutrients missing from most junk food products.

---

[180] https://nyulangoned.org Dietary Therapies for Epilepsy & Seizure Disorders.
[181] https://.www.lybrate.com Diet Chart for epilepsy - Lybrate
[182] 6 Oct. 2020. https://myclevelandclinic.org Ketogenic diet For Epilepsy Seizures Cleveland Clinic.

 Example of junk food

Studies from Brazil and Mexico involving more than 30,000 people have

noted that the more junk food a person eats, the more likely they are to be deficient in vitamins and minerals that are vital for brain health.

Over the past decade, scientists have identified foods that fuel our microbiome, as well as those that kill them off. Experts say some foods interact with gut bugs to generate inflammatory chemicals – substances that send the immune system into "attack" mode.

Foods that are known to benefit healthy gut bacteria are high in fibre and naturally fermented. They are fruits, vegetables, oats, pulses, including chickpeas, lentils, and yogurt. Eat more to improve both your physical and mental health. The consumption of an extra 7 grams of fibre daily (equivalent to 2 large bananas) has been shown to improve mental health. Only about one in 10 UK adults get their daily recommended intake of 30g of fibre. The same may apply in many other countries.

BRAIN FOODS

Brain foods for potential memory-boosting powers are these:

- Nuts and seeds. Nuts such as walnuts, almonds, and peanuts, as well as sunflower and pumpkin seeds, are brain foods high in protein and omega fatty acids.
- Salmon.
- Beans.
- Blueberries, dark and leafy greens.
- Lean red meat.
- Avocados.
- Tomatoes

Certain fruits such as oranges, bell peppers, guava, kiwi, tomatoes, and strawberries contain high amounts of vitamin C. This vitamin helps prevent brain cells from becoming damaged and supports overall brain health. It can potentially prevent Alzheimer's.[183] Drink coffee as the caffeine therein has

---

[183] Httpr://premierneurologycenter.com 10 Foods That Improve Brain Health – Premier Neurology.

107

many positive actions on the brain. It can increase alertness and well-being, help concentration, improve mood and limit depression.[184]

CONCLUSION

As long as our brain is a mystery, the universe, the reflection of the structure of the brain will also be a mystery.[185]

A plant-based diet improves clarity and focus. Many people who switch to this diet report improved mental clarity and focus and increased energy levels. Perhaps, this is due to the fact that this diet is typically low in processed foods and added sugars which can contribute to brain fog and fatigue.

Plant foods are high in antioxidants and phytochemicals, which generally help to repair damage and decrease inflammation in brain cells. Further, plant foods can help restore balance to neurotransmitters. Many people suffering from depression have elevated levels of an enzyme called monoamine oxidase.

You need to examine some of the ingredients in a plant diet. Leafy greens such as kale, collards and broccoli are rich in brain-healthy nutrients like vitamin K, lutein, foliate and beta carotene. Studies suggest these plant-based foods may help to slow cognitive decline. Foods typical in a vegan diet, such as leafy greens, fermented foods and even dark chocolate have been found to lower levels of cortisol, the stress hormone, in the blood. This helps to combat the stresses of daily lives which can ultimately reduce depression and anxiety. The main brain foods are:

(a) Green, leafy vegetables.
(b) Fatty fish.
(c) Berries of different types
(d) tea and coffee
(e) Walnuts.

These are the same foods that protect your heart and blood vessels.[186] Whereas medication is tailored generally for each ailment, the same plant food is suitable for almost all ailments.

End

---

[184] https://pubmed.ncbi.nlm.nig.gov Effects of coffee/caffeine on brain health and disease.
[185] https://faculty.washington.edu Neuroscience for Kids – Brain Quotes
[186] 6 Mar. 2021. https://www.health.harvard.edu Foods linked to better brainpower.

CHAPTER 9

EFFECT OF SUGAR (CARBS & GLUCOSE)

"I strongly believe that it is better not to eat sugar at all."

John Yudkin

Sugar is an essential component of food, but excess sugar is inappropriate and unhelpful in your diet. Excessive sugar and refined carbohydrate-intake are the main causes of poor health and chronic diseases.

Eating too much of added sugar can have many negative health effects. Excessive sweetened foods and beverages can lead to weight gain, blood sugar problems, and an increased risk of heart disease, among other serious conditions.[187]

EXCESSIVE SUGAR

Excessive sugar consumption has been implicated in causing obesity, metabolic disorders, diabetes, cardiovascular disease (CVD), cancer depression and cognitive impairment.[188] Hidden side effects of sugar are:

- Sugar makes your organ fat.
- It can lead to heart disease.
- It plays havoc with cholesterol levels.
- It is linked to Alzheimer's disease.
- It turns people into an addict.
- It disables your appetite control.
- It can make people go into depression.[189]

Too much added sugar can be one of the greatest threats to cardiovascular disease. Sugar has a bittersweet reputation when it comes to health. It occurs naturally in all foods that contain carbohydrates, such as fruits and vegetables, grains, and dairy. Eating whole foods that contain natural sugar is okay. Plant foods also have high amounts of fibre, essential minerals, and antioxidants, and dairy foods contain protein and calcium. As the body digest these foods slowly, the sugar therein provides a steady supply of energy to the cells of the body. A high intake of fruits, vegetables, and whole grains also has been shown to reduce the risk of chronic diseases, such as diabetes, heart disease and some cancers.

---

[187] 26 Sept. 2022. https://www.healthline.com 11 Reasons Why Too Much Sugar Is Bad for You – Healthline.

[188] 10 Feb 2023. https://www.ncbi.nim.nih.gov The Impact of Free Sugar on Human Health – A Narrative Review NCBI.

[189] https://www.hcf.com.au 7 Hidden side effects of sugar HCF.

Added Sugar

This is sugar that is added to manufactured products either to increase flavour or to extend shelf life. The main sources of such sugar are these:

- Fizzy drinks.
- Flavoured yogurts.
- Breakfast cereals.
- Cookies, cakes, biscuits, candy and chocolate.
- Most processed foods.

These sugars are added at home, eating places or food manufacturers. Sugars in honey, syrup, nectars, and unsweetened fruit juices, vegetable juices, concentrates and smoothies are free sugars. Sugars in these foods occur naturally but count as free sugars. Free sugars include added sugars.

In consequence, we consume too much added sugar. An adult male person takes in an average of 24 teaspoons of added sugar daily, according to the National Cancer Institute. That is equal to 384 calories. As you increase your added sugar intake so is the risk for heart disease. This is according to Dr Hu in JAMA Internal Medicine. Over time, this can lead to greater accumulation of fat, which may in turn cause a fatty liver disease, a contributor to diabetes, which raises the risk for heart disease.

Other issues arising from too much of added sugar are high blood pressure and an increase in chronic inflammation. Both of these are pathological pathways to heart disease. This sugar in beverages also contributes to weight gain by tricking the body into turning off its appetite-control system as liquid calories are not as satisfying as calories from solid foods. This is the reason why it is easier to add more calories to their regular diet when consuming sugary drinks.

The effects of added sugar intake are these:

- High blood pressure.
- Inflammation.
- Weight gain, causing many people to become obese.
- Diabetes, particularly type 2.
- Fatty liver disease.
- Various metabolic syndromes.

The above are linked to an increased risk for heart attack and stroke, according to Dr Hu. Diets containing large amounts of sugar and saturated fat can lead to even the risk of kidney and liver diseases. In addition to naturally occurring sugars, added sugars (as already seen above) are known as the main culprits leading to the development of diet-related poor health. Too much sugar can contribute to people having too many calories, which can lead to weight gain (as noted above) and can also cause tooth decay.

Sugar found naturally in milk, fruit and vegetables does not count as free sugars. Therefore, you do not need to cut down on these. However, they are included in the total sugar found on food labels.

In the US, the main sources of excess added sugars in the diet include sugary beverages (such as soft drinks), fructose syrups and sugary snacks. The food you least expect would have some sugar in it. Even some toothpastes taste a little sweet. Some manufacturers use artificial sweeteners.

It is important to note that artificial sweeteners are not as healthy a substitute for refined sugar as once believed. There are studies showing that consumption of artificial sugars is associated with obesity, insulin resistance and changes in gut microbiota. Therefore, with a view to promoting wellness, refined and artificial sugars should be avoided or minimised.

Quantity of Sugar to Consume. It is recommended that free sugars added to food or drinks, and sugars found naturally in honey, syrups, and unsweetened fruit and vegetable juices, smoothies and purees should not comprise more than 5% of the energy (calories) you get from food and drink daily. Observe the following:

- Adults should have no more than 30g of free sugars daily (roughly equivalent to 7 sugar cubes).
- Children aged 7 to 10 should have no more than 24g of free sugars daily (6 sugar cubes).
- Children aged 4 to 6 should have no more than 19g of free sugars daily (5 sugar cubes).

There is no guideline limit for children under 4, but it is recommended they avoid sugar-sweetened drinks and food with sugar added to it.

Free sugars are found in foods such as sweets, cakes, biscuits, chocolate, fizzy drinks and juice drinks. These are sugary foods we should cut down on. For example, a can of cola can have as much as 9 cubes of sugar, more than the recommended daily limit for adults. For a healthy, balanced diet, cut down on food and drinks containing free sugars. Tips for cutting down are these:

(a) Instead of sugary fizzy drinks or sugary squash, drink water, low-fat milk, or sugar-free, diet or no-added-sugar drinks. While the amount of sugar in whole and lower-fat milk is the same, choosing lower-fat milk reduces your saturated intake.

(b) Even unsweetened fruit juices and smoothies are sugary, so limit the amount you have to no more than 150ml a day.

(c) If you prefer fizzy drinks, try diluting no-added-sugar squash with sparkling water.

(d) If you take sugar in hot drinks or add sugar to your breakfast cereal, gradually reduce the amount until you cut it out altogether. If you switch to sweetener, be aware that a sweetener may have a toxic element in it.

Labels on Back of Packaging. Look for nutrition labels which can be part of the carbohydrate information. By comparing labels you can choose foods that are lower in sugar.

Front Packaging. Labels can include colour coding to enable you to see at a glance if the food has a high, medium or low amount of sugars. Some labels will display the amount of sugar in the food as a percentage of the RI (reference intakes). RIs are guidelines for the approximate amount of particular nutrients and energy required in a day for a healthy diet.

Weight and Sugar. Sugar can contribute to people having too many calories which can lead to weight gain. This can increase your risk of health problems, such as heart disease, some cancers and diabetes type 2.

For a healthy, balanced diet, you should get most of your calories from other kinds of foods, such as starchy foods (whole grain where possible) and fruits and vegetables. Eat only foods high in free sugars occasionally or not at all. The Eatwell Guide shows how much of what we eat should come from each of the main food groups so as to have a healthy, balanced diet.

Prevalence of Sugar Added to Food. It is not easy to escape sugar. Some foods naturally have sugar, especially fruits. Even without a "sweet tooth" and you are serious in avoiding sugary indulgences, you are still likely consuming a lot of sugar on a daily basis. This is because of the prevalence of added sugar in most foods being consumed. According to a report from the University of North Carolina, the average person consumes some 300 calories from added sugar daily, and 20% of Americans exceed 700 calories from added sugar daily. In addition to many marketable items like pastries and soda, sugar is found in pasta sauces, salad dressings and even healthy snacks such as yogurt.

The prevalence of sugar has a profound effect on one's body. Eliminating the large consumption of sugar will result in a change of your body. Firstly, the body will go through mild withdrawal symptoms. Thereafter, there are several amazing health benefits that occur when a person eliminates sugar from his or her diet. These benefits are:

(a) Your memory will get better.

(b) Any risk from heart problems will be lowered.

(c) Your skin will clear up.

(d) Any weight problem will be solved and your BMI will be reduced. The average daily consumption of sugar consumed is 22 teaspoons. This is about 350 calories daily. Although sugar can be addicted, by stopping its use you can lose weight. After a while you will no longer experience any sugar craving.

Sugar does not work like other more nutritious whole foods. It does not tell the body when it is full. The result is that you continue to consume too many calories and gaining weight.[190] When you substitute sugar with nourishing whole foods, your hormones will naturally regulate your brain; it will send signals to the brain when you have eaten enough.

No More Mood Swings. This is not like coming after quitting sugar as at first cutting off sugar is like it has the opposite effect. The symptom of sugar withdrawal is moodiness. However, once you get rid of the bad habit of sugar, your mood will be much more regulated and you will feel much better.

Your Sleep Will Improve. If you are tossing and turning most of the night, it could be due to eating too much sugar. This can leave you feeling sluggish during the day and in need of a nap. Also, added sugars trigger a release of the hormone, cortisol. This interferes with sleep. A diet full of sugars can also affect how the brain releases melatonin. It regulates sleep-wake cycles. A large sugar intake delays the release of melatonin in the brain. This is essential for the homeostatic control of sleep.

CARBS CONVERTED TO SUGAR

When people eat food containing carbohydrates, the digestive system breaks down the digestible ones into sugar, which enters the blood. As blood sugar levels rise, the pancreas produces insulin, a hormone that prompts cells to absorb blood sugar for energy or storage.[191]

Complex carbohydrates, like whole-grain breads, pastas, and sweet potatoes, are chock-full of vitamins and fibre. It takes the body longer to break these down. This is why they do not have a large effect on the blood sugar levels.[192]

---

[190] According to Megan Gilmore, a certified nutritionist in Kansas City, author of No Excuses Detox: 100 Recipes to Help You Eat Healthy Every Day to Reader's digest

[191] https://www.hsph.harvard.edu Carbohydrates and Blood Sugar The Nutrition Source.

[192] 23 June 2020. https://www.iowadiabetes.com How Certain Carbs Affect Your Blood Sugar – Iowa Diabetes

Within 15 minutes of eating carbs, your body will begin to convert them into glucose, causing your blood sugar to begin its rise. About 90 minutes after a meal, most of the carbs will have broken down, and your blood sugar will be at its highest point according to the University of Maine Extension.[193]

Sugar is a type of carbohydrates found naturally in many of the foods we eat. It can either occur naturally in foods or be added in, and is used by the body for energy. Carbohydrates, on the other hand, can include foods made up of starches, fibre, and sugar. These serve several critical functions that are important for your overall health and are turned into energy in your body. Sugar and other forms of carbohydrates are what the body uses for fuel, and the CDC recommends that 45 to 65% of daily calories come from carbohydrates for most people. But individual needs can vary, and some people may even benefit from a low-carb diet.

While these nutrients are important for good health, consuming too much is also possible, leading to blood sugar spikes and other adverse health effects. Eating too much simple carbs, like candy, syrups and fruit juice concentrate, can cause health issues, including diabetes type 2, heart disease, and other health conditions. Many simple carbs have little nutritional value but can be high in calories. However, eating complex carbohydrates, such as whole grains, legumes, and starchy vegetables, take longer to digest than simple carbs. They lead to fewer glucose spikes. Complex carbs are sometimes referred to as "healthy carbs". They possess many critical functions for the body, including decreased cholesterol and triglyceride levels, enhanced digestive health, and better sugar control. Complex carbs provide the body with energy. They also contain more vitamins and minerals and have other vital nutrients.

Eating complex carbs high in fibre can aid gut health on account of their high prebiotic quantities. They are in foods such as:

- Blueberries.
- Watermelon.
- Garlic.
- Onions.
- Leeks.

Complex carbs can help to support sleep, essential for overall health, and can affect your blood sugar levels. You can include complex carbs in your diet to raise melatonin and to support your night's sleep. In addition, such carbs can provide the brain with a steadier fuel level than simple carbs.

---

[193] https://www.livestrong.comHow to Calculate the Percent of Total Carbohydrates from Sugar livestrong

These foods can also protect brain cells from damage and increase cognitive performance.

DANGER OF CONSUMING TOO MUCH SUGAR

Sugar is just one cause of blood sugar spikes. Eating too much can raise your blood sugar as foods are digested and broken down into glucose that enters the bloodstream. Simple carbs, such as baked goods, candy and fruit juices, cereals, pasta and bread made with white flour are digested more rapidly, leading to rapid spikes in blood sugar. Following a low carb diet is recommended for people with certain conditions, such as diabetes mellitus. Foods that are known to prevent blood sugar from rising are a way to combat sugar spikes.

Foods like non-starchy veggies (such as celery), vinegar, prebiotic-rich foods, leafy greens, legumes and good quality proteins are a few examples of these foods.

Tips to Cut Down on Sugar. Observe the following:

(a) Reduce sugar in all beverages.
(b) Reduce or eliminate sugar in food.
(c) Read nutrition labels on food and the back of packaging.
(d) Check ingredient list on food items.
(e) Reduce high carb foods

Sugar can impact brain function and have other effects:

(a) It can lead to increase sugar cravings.
(b) Your skin can age faster.
(c) It could lead to a blood sugar crash.
(d) You might not use all the calories.
(e) It can increase the risk of chronic diseases.
(f) Tooth decay and sugar.
(g) Dried fruit and your teeth.
(h) Your weight varies according to consumption of sugar.
(h) It can increase stress levels.[194]

Sugar in Foods as Shown in Many Tables

There are 8 tables in Chapter 2 which show the amount of sugar in many foods. For example, a portion of 150 g (5.291 ounces) of white rice contains 10.1 teaspoon of sugar. The higher the glycaemic index (GI) the higher the

---

[194] 29 Jan. 2023 https://www.health.com > nutrition

sugar content. The same portion of basmati rice with a GI of 69 contains also 10.1 teaspoons of sugar. While an egg has zero sugar, a portion of 80 g of cabbage has 0.1 teaspoon of sugar. Boiled potatoes of 150 g have 9.1 teaspoons of sugar. Check out the 8 tables for sugar content in many foods.

Sugar: The No 1 Enemy in American Diets. A large body of research showed that sugar is even worse for your heart than saturated (bad) fat.[195]

CONCLUSION

Sugar in your food comes from different sources. Manufacturers add sugar to many of their products. Many people add sugar to their beverages and breakfast cereals (although already laced with sugar by the manufacturer). Most importantly. sugar is inherent in many foods. Many foods, especially carbs, have varying amounts of sugar. Once you consume those with high sugar content they will spike the sugar in your blood stream within minutes. Consumption of excessive sugar and refined carbohydrate-intake are the main causes of poor health and chronic diseases.

While sugar is important for the body to function properly, excessive sugar is bad. Excess intake of added sugar increases your risk of chronic diseases. It can contribute to high blood pressure, inflammation, weight gain, diabetes, fatty liver disease, and various metabolic syndromes. All of these may be linked to the risk of heart disease and stroke.

Reducing sugar intake lowers specifically the risk of developing overweight and obesity, and in turn in developing diabetes. By eliminating or reducing the use of sugar many people describe noticing some benefits, including more energy, emotional stability and better cognitive functioning. Quitting sugar benefits the skin. Cutting out sugar can reduce depression risk. Dr Robert Lustig and his colleagues of the US think they have produced the "hard and fast data that sugar is toxic irrespective of its calories and irrespective of weight."[196] Sugar: The No 1 Enemy in American Diets. A large body of research showed that sugar is even worse for your heart than saturated (bad) fat.[197]

End

---

[195] 10 Jan. 2022. https://www.lancastergeneralhealth.org Is Sugar or Fat Worse for Your Heart? – Lancaster General Health.
[196] https://time.com Sugar Is Definitely Toxic, a New Study Says - Time
[197] 10 Jan. 2022. https://www.lancastergeneralhealth.org Is Sugar or Fat Worse for Your Heart? – Lancaster General Health.

CHAPTER 10

DIETARY FATS, OIL & HEALTH OUTCOME

"Food manufacturers, from Big Food to corner bakery, came to rely upon hydrogenated oils because they're cheaper than butter and lard."

Nina Teicholz

Nina Teicholz is a champion of high-fat, low-carb eating, but she strongly cautions against getting your fat from vegetable "seed" oils.[198]

Oils and spreads (fats) are a source of energy and provide essential fatty acids (A, C and E). Dietary fat is the fat that comes from food. The body breaks down dietary fats into parts called fatty acids that can enter the bloodstream. The body can also make fatty acids from the carbohydrates in food. It uses fatty acids to make the fats that it needs.[199]Excessive dietary fat intake has been linked to increased risk of obesity. Of all the fats, trans fat is the worst for your health.

HEALTH OUTCOME

Fat is an important part of your diet. Some kinds are healthier than others. You need to consider carefully which to choose and which to avoid. Dietary fat comes from food, as mentioned already. Fats are important as to how your body uses many vitamins. Also, fats play a role in how body cells are made and work.

All dietary fats are not the same. They have different effects on the body. While some are essential, some increase the risk for disease, and some help to prevent disease.

TYPES OF FAT

There are two main types of dietary fats: saturated fats and unsaturated fat. These terms are the chemical makeup of the fatty acids. Most foods have a mix of different kinds of fat. While some have higher level of saturated fats, others have higher levels of unsaturated fats. The main differences are here:

(a) Saturated Fats. These are usually sold solid at room temperature. The most common sources are from meats and dairy products.

---

[198] 18 Oct. 2022. https;//www.doctorkiltz.com What is Nina Teicholz Diet? – Dr Robert Kiltz.
[199] 15 Feb. 2023. https://www.mayoclinic.org Diatery fat: Know which to choose – Mayo Clinic.

(b) **Unsaturated Fats**. These are usually liquid at room temperature. Their sources are mainly vegetable oils, nuts and fish. There are two types of unsaturated fats: monounsaturated and polyunsaturated.

Saturated Fats in Food

The American Dietary Guidelines suggest that less than 10% of calories a day should come from saturated fats, while the American Heart Association advocates a goal of 5 to 6% a day from saturated fats. Foods high in these fats include:

- Foods baked or fried using saturated fats.
- Meats, including beef, lamb, pork as well as poultry, especially with skin.
- Lard.
- Dairy products such as butter and cream.
- Whole or 2% milk.
- Whole-milk cheese or yogurt.
- Oils from coconuts, palm fruits or palm kernels.

Saturated fats can add up quickly in foods that combine many ingredients. In the US diets, the most common sources of saturated fats are sandwiches, burgers, tacos and burritos. These are foods that usually combine meat and dairy products. Baked items with butter, full-fat ice cream and other desserts are also common sources of saturated fats.

Saturated fat tends to raise levels of cholesterol in the blood. Low-density lipoprotein (LDL) is the bad cholesterol. High-density lipoprotein (HDL) is the good cholesterol. Saturated fats raise the levels of both. A high level of LDL in the bloodstream increases the risk of heart and blood vessel disease. Limited evidence suggests that saturated fats and high cholesterol level may be linked to an increased risk of Alzheimer's disease or other diseases that cause dementia.

MONOUNSATURATED FATS IN FOOD (MUFA)

These fats are found in many foods, including red meats and dairy products. About half the fats in these foods are saturated and half monounsaturated. Many plants and plant oils are high in monounsaturated fats but low in saturated fats. Sources of these fats are:

- Oils from olives, peanuts, canola seeds, safflower seeds, and sunflower seeds.
- Avocadoes.

- Pumpkin seeds.
- Sesame seeds.
- Almonds.
- Cashews.
- Peanuts and peanut butter.
- Pecans.

Monounsaturated fats from plants may lower bad cholesterol (LDL) and raise good cholesterol (HDL). They also may improve the control of blood sugar levels. Substituting saturated fats with monounsaturated fats in the diet may lower the level of LDL cholesterol and triglycerides in the blood. Triglycerides are fat cells that circulate in the bloodstream and are stored in the body's fat cells. A high level of triglycerides in the blood raises the risk of diseases of heart and blood vessels. Consuming plant foods high in monounsaturated fats, particularly extra virgin olive oil and tree nuts, may benefit heart health and blood sugar regulation.

POLYUNSATURATED FATS IN FOOD (PUFA)

The 2 categories of these fats are omega-6 fatty acids and omega-3 fatty acids. Sources of omega-6 fatty acids include:

- Corn oil.
- Cottonseed oil.
- Peanut oil.
- Soya bean oil.
- Sunflower oil.

Benefits of a diet high in omega-6 fatty acids, especially when they replace saturated fats, may be linked to:

- Lower bad cholesterol (LDL).
- Lower triglycerides.
- Higher good cholesterol (HDL).
- Better blood sugar control.

Health benefits in omega-3 fatty acids may include:

- Lowering levels of triglycerides in the blood.
- Lowering the risk of heart and blood vessel diseases.

TRANS FATS in Food

These fats are a type of fat that raises LDL cholesterol and lowers HDL cholesterol. There are very small amounts of naturally occurring trans fat in meats and dairy from grazing animals, such as cows, sheep and goats.

But most trans fats are in plant oils that have been chemically changed to be a solid fat. These are called partially hydrogenated oils. At one time, trans fat oils were thought to be a healthy choice to replace saturated fats. In addition, they were inexpensive and had a long shelf life. However, the US Food and Drug Administration determined that artificially created trans fats are "no longer recognised as safe" in foods. They are no longer used in US food production, though other countries may continue to use them.

> "By our most conservative estimate, replacement of partially hydrogenated fat in the US diet with natural unhydrogenated vegetable oils would prevent approximately 30,000 premature coronary deaths per year, and epidemiologic evidence suggests this number is closer to 100,000 premature deaths annually."
>
> The Harvard School of Public Health[200]

TYPES OF DIETARY FATS HEALTH OUTCOMES

The types of dietary fats are already given above. There is strong evidence that consumption of saturated fat (found mostly in animal-based foods) and unsaturated fat (found predominantly in plant-based foods) have divergent effects on health outcomes. In a study of 126,000 health professionals, PUFA and MUFA intake were associated with lower mortality risk.

Replacing saturated fat with carbohydrates from refined starches and added sugars did not change coronary heart disease risk. The source of fat (plant or animal) may also affect health outcomes, even when considering the same type of fat. A recent study suggested that replacing 5% of energy intake from saturated fat, *trans* fat, and refined carbohydrates with MUFA intake from plant sources was associated with lower risk of coronary heart disease, whereas the same substitution with MUFA from animal sources was not beneficial.

In the figure below 4 types of fats are shown. It shows changes in total mortality risk associated with increments of calorie intake from specific types of fat (trans fat, saturated fat, monounsaturated fat and polyunsaturated fat). This information is from the Nurses' Health Study and Health Professionals Follow-Up Study (began in 1986). The objective of the study is to evaluate a series of hypotheses about men's health relating to

---

[200] OAWHealth Articles Healthy Oils, Trans Fats and Natural Health Quotes,

nutritional factors to the incidence of serious illnesses, such as cancer, heart disease, and other vascular diseases.

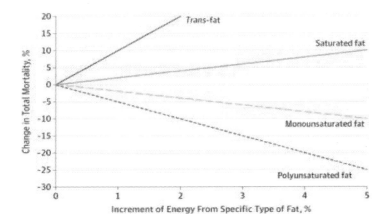

Regulation of Trans Fats. Denmark was the first country in the world to regulate *trans* fats, nearly eliminating them from the Danish food supply. In the 3 years after the regulation was implemented, CVD mortality decreased in the Danish population by 14.2 deaths per 100,000, compared with similar countries without *trans* fat policies.

Between 2007 and 2011, New York State restricted *trans* fat in 11 counties in all public eateries such as restaurants, vending machines and concessions. Three years after implementation, compared with the non restricted counties, the counties with the restriction had an additional 6.2% decline in hospital admissions for myocardial infarction and stroke events, beyond temporal trends.

In 2006, the FDA mandated *trans* fat labelling on all food products, which resulted in many companies reformulating products to reduce *trans* fat content. By June 2018, partially hydrogenated oils, the primary source of artificial dietary *trans* fats, were banned from the US food supply, marking an important step in creating a healthy food environment.

TOXIC NATURE OF SEED OIL

The polyunsaturated fatty acids in industrial seed oils are highly unstable and oxidise easily upon exposure to heat, light and chemical inputs. When industrial seed oils are exposed to these factors, two harmful substances, trans fats and lipid peroxides, are created.[201] Seed oils are known as vegetable oils.

Making Seed Oil Toxic. All industrial seed oils are bad for cooking

---

[201] 19 Feb. 2019. https://chriskresser.com How Industrial Seed Oils Are Making Us Sick – Chris Kresser.

because omega-6 fatty acids, especially linoleic acid, create harmful by-products when they are heated. These deleterious effects occur within minutes of being heated and compound when oils are reheated.[202]

According to leading scientists, cooking with vegetable oils releases high concentration of toxic chemicals known as aldehydes, due to degradation of the fatty acids in oils, which have been linked to diseases, including arthritis, heart disease, dementia and cancer.[203] The more seed oil you consume, the more free radicals will be in your body, resulting in more cellular damage. Once oxidised, omega-6 fats (especially linoleic acid) also produce toxic by-products that have been linked to several chronic diseases such as Alzheimer's, heart disease, and liver disease.[204]

Most Unhealthy Cooking Oils. The worst cooking oils produced industrially are these:

- Canola oil.
- Palm oil.
- Vegetable oil.
- Soybean oil.
- Sunflower oil.
- Coconut oil.
- Margarine.
- Shortening.[205]

In contrast, the healthiest oil to cook with is olive oil. It is versatile, being used in everything from frying to finishing. It is also rich in healthy fats, antioxidants, and polyphenols, all of which have shown protective effects against cancer and liver, heart, and neurodegenerative diseases.[206]

Avoiding Plant Oils for Cooking. Plant oils should be avoided as far as possible.[207]Many persons who have avoided these oils have reversed autoimmune issues, improve acne or heart disease symptoms. Oil can be avoided in cooking. Most evidence shows the benefits of having poly-

---

[202] 15 May 2022. https://www.zeroacre.com Are Seed Oils Toxic? The Latest Research Suggests Yes
[203] https://www.kosterina.com The Toxic Truth about Cook Oils – Kosterina.
[204] 8 May 2022. https://www.zeroacre.com What Are Seed Oils And Should You Avoid Them? - Zero Acre Farms.
[205] https://amscardiology.com Best & Worst Cooking Oils for Your Heart AMS Cardiology.
[206] 4 May 2023. https://www.healthline.com 4 Healthy Cooking Oils (and 4 to Avoid) – Healthline.
[207]There are internet articles stating that industrially produced vegetable oils are bad for health, toxic and killing many people. https://www.healthline.com

unsaturated fats (PUFAs) and mono-unsaturated fats (MUFAs). These are from plants and if used in cooking they contribute 20 to 30% of our diet. Instead of using the industrially-produced oil, you can obtain both of these fats from flax seeds, walnuts and sunflower seeds (which are MUFA rich) and avocados, nut butters and olive (MUFA rich). Fats from these sources are better than from plant-based oils. Remember, industrially produced oils from seeds can make you sick. These oils are marketed as vegetable oils.

Avoid vegetable oil   This oil is toxic

Vegetable Oils to Avoid. In fact, in their natural and unrefined state, fats can be healthy. When possible, Shanahan[208] recommends avoiding or limiting these (hateful eight) oils: corn, canola, cottonseed, soy, safflower, sunflower, grape seed, and rice bran oils. These may lead to inflammation over time.[209]

Inflammatory Oils. Omega-6s are found in oils such as corn, safflower, sunflower, soy and vegetable and products made with those oils. Excess consumption of omega-6s can trigger the body to produce pro-inflammatory chemicals. The American diet tends to be very high in omega-6s.[210]

Oils Not Carcinogenic When Heated. These oils are:

- Extra-virgin, Expeller – or Cold-pressed, Unrefined, Organic Olive Oil (medium heat).
- Organic Ghee (high heat).
- Organic, extra-virgin, Unrefined Coconut Oil (medium heat).
- Organic, expeller – or Cold-pressed Avocado Oil (medium-high heat).
- Refined Safflower Oil (high heat).[211]

---

[208] Dr Cate Shanahan is a board certified family physician and author of *Deep Nutrition and the Fat Burn Fix*

[209] 23 July 2020. https://www.mindbodygreen.com 8 Unhealthy Vegetables Oils To Avoid, According to An MD mindbodygreen.

[210] https://www.arthritis.org Fats and Oils to Avoid – Arthritis Foundation.

[211] 1 Sept. 2016. http://www.badassandhealthy.com The Easy Guide to Cancer-free Cooking Oils Badass + Healthy

A relevant quote on toxic oils is this:

"Industrial seed oil can contribute to heart disease, diabetes, autoimmunity and many more chronic health conditions."

Chris Kresser

OTHER MATTERS RELATING TO OIL

Oils high in polyunsaturated fats are susceptible to oxidation. These are oils both on the shelf and inside your body.[212] Hydrogenated vegetable oils are known to be high in trans fat. This has been associated with various health problems. They are found in certain types of margarine, ice cream, and cookies.

Some vegetable oils appear to be heart friendly. However, some nutritionists are worried about the high levels of omega-6 in certain oils. Currently, there is no evidence that they raise the risk of heart disease.[213] Some people have their doubts.

Olive oil is made by crushing olives and separating the oil from the pulp in a centrifuge. Extra virgin olive oil is 100% natural and high in oxidants. It is known that olive oil is very high in monounsaturated fats and contains vitamin E and K. Extra Virgin olive oil is loaded with antioxidants, some of which have powerful health benefits. Notably, olive oil contains oleic acid and oleocanthal. These 2 nutrients can fight inflammation. This may be the main reason for olive oil's health benefits. Olive oil may be one of the healthiest foods you can consume in the interest of your heart health. It reduces blood pressure and inflammation, protects LDL particles from oxidation, and may help prevent unwanted blood clotting.

Some evidence suggests that olive oil can help fight cancer and Alzheimer's disease. This is not yet confirmed from human studies.

Omega-3 fats are essential fats that come from your diet. They have important benefits for your heart, brain and metabolism.

Omega-6 fats are also essential fats that provide energy for the body. But consume food with more omega-3 than with omega-6. There should be a healthy ratio between them.

Omega-9 fats are nonessential fats that the body can produce, while replacing some saturated fats with omega-9 fats that may benefit your body.

The best sources of omega-3 are from oily fish. Omega-6 and omega-9 are from plant oils, nuts and seeds. A combination of omega 3, 6 and 9 supplements provides optimal ratios of fatty acids. But they are not likely to provide additional benefits compared with omega-3 supplements. Choose

---

[212] Are vegetable and Seed Oils Bad for Your Health? By Kris Gunnars, BSc, 12 Dec. 2019.
[213] Refer to p 187, *Health and Nutrition* by Dr Nat Khublall, 2021, available on Amazon.

omega-3 supplement instead of a combined omega 3-6-9 supplement. If you are buying a combined supplement, accept one with a high concentration of EPA and DHA. (EPA = Eicosapentaenoic acid, and DHA = Docosahexaenoic acid).

An omega-6 to omega-3 ratio that is too high may contribute to excess inflammation in the body, and potentially will raise the risk of various diseases.

Those who ate a pre-industrial diet had an omega-6 to omega-3 ratio of about 4:1 to 1:4, most falling somewhere in between. But the ratio today is16:1. This is bad. This is much higher than what people are genetically adopted to.

The consumption of vegetable oils is high in omega-6. This has increased dramatically in the past 100 years. Scientists believe this may cause serious harm. To reduce omega-6 intake, eliminate processed vegetable oils from your diet, as well as processed foods that contain them.

You can increase the intake of omega-3 fatty acids in your body by using supplements or eating meat from grass-fed animals or obtain it from fish oil.

Olive oil is rich in monounsaturated oleic acid, a fatty acid believed to have many beneficial effects and is a healthy choice for cooking. Extra virgin oil has a lot of antioxidants, some of which have powerful biological effects. Olive oil contains other nutrients that fight inflammation. These include oleic acid as well as the antioxidant oleocanthal.

There are many large studies that demonstrate that those who consume olive oil have a much lower risk of stroke. This is the second biggest killer in developed countries. It is widely known that both observational studies and clinical trials suggest that olive oil, combined with a Mediterranean diet, can reduce your risk of type 2 diabetes. There is evidence that suggests the beneficial effect of olive oil on cancer risk. Further studies are required to confirm this.

While it is known that olive oil can help to reduce joint pain and swelling from rheumatoid arthritis, the beneficial effects can be greatly increased when combined with fish oil.

Finally, extra virgin olive oil has antibacterial properties and has been found to be particularly effective against Helicobacter pylori. There is a bacterium that can cause stomach ulcers and stomach cancer.[214]

CONCLUSION

There are 2 types of fats: saturated and unsaturated. The latter falls under: Monounsaturated Fats (MUFA) and Polyunsaturated Fats (PUFA). MUFA

---

[214] Refer to article by Jeff Nobbs on the internet why vegetables oil is unhealthy: https://www.healthline.com

fats are found in many foods, including red meats and dairy products. About half the fats in these foods are saturated and half monounsaturated. Many plants and plant oils are high in monounsaturated fats but low in saturated fats. PUFA fats fall into 2 groups: they are omega-6 fatty acids and omega-3 fatty acids.

Sources of omega-6 fatty acids include corn oil, cottonseed oil, peanut oil, soya bean oil, and sunflower oil. Sources of omega-3 fatty acids are from fish and other sea food (salmon mackerel, tuna, herring and sardines). The health benefits in omega-3 fatty acids may include: lowering levels of triglycerides in the blood and lowering the risk of heart and blood vessel diseases.

There is also in food what is known as trans fats. These fats are a type of fat that raises LDL (bad) cholesterol and lowers HDL (good) cholesterol. There are very small amounts of naturally occurring trans fat in meats and dairy from grazing animals, such as cows, sheep and goats.

Benefits of a diet high in omega-6 fatty acids, especially when they replace saturated fats, may be linked to: lower bad cholesterol (LDL), lower triglycerides, higher good cholesterol (HDL) and better blood sugar control. However, omega-6 may be far in excess of what is required, and this may be dangerous for health. Omega-6s are found in oils such as corn, safflower, sunflower, soy and vegetable and products made with those oils

There is a wide variety of cooking oils from plant sources, such as olive oil, palm oil, soya bean oil, canola oil (rapeseed oil), corn oil, peanut oil, coconut oil and other vegetable oils, as well as animal-based oils like butter and lard. For people trying to avoid their oil intake, cooking without oil is possible. Oil is not absolutely necessary for cooking.

Eating industrial seed oils raises our omega-6-to-omega-3 fatty acid ratios, with significant consequences for our health. Industrial seed oils are unstable and oxidise easily. They contain harmful additives. They are derived from genetically modified crops.[215]Excess consumption of omega-6s can trigger the body to produce pro-inflammatory chemicals.

The healthiest oil is olive oil. Oils with more monounsaturated fats, such as rapeseed and olive, are also less susceptible to heat. Rapeseed oil and inexpensive olive oil are therefore the best choices for cooking. Be warned that all cooking fats add fat and calories to your diet.

Choose foods with "good" unsaturated fats, limit foods high in saturated fat, and avoid "bad" trans fat.

---

[215] 14 Aug. 2022. https://www.mindbodybasics.com 8 Toxic Seed Oils and What to Know – Dunetz Welness Center

"If optimal health is your goal, then industrial seed oils have no place in your diet."

Chris Kressler

Sugar: The No 1 Enemy in American Diets.

A large body of research showed that sugar is even worse for your heart than saturated (bad) fat.[216]

End

---

[216] 10 Jan. 2022. https://www.lancastergeneralhealth.org Is Sugar or Fat Worse for Your Heart? – Lancaster General Health.

EFFECT OF ULTRA-PROCESSED FOODS (UPF)

"Most UPF is not food. It's an industrially produced edible substance."

Fernanda Rauber

"Do not eat processed food, junk foods, filth, or disease carrying food, animals, or rodents. Some people say of these foods, 'well, it tastes good'. Most of the foods today that statically causes sickness, cancer and disease ALL TASTE GOOD: It is well seasoned and prepared poison."[217]

Unknown

Ultra-processed food is an industrially formulated edible substance derived from natural food or synthesised from other organic compounds. The resulting products are designed to be highly profitable, convenient and hyper palatable, often through food additives such as preservatives, colourings and flavourings.

EXAMPLES OF ULTRA PROCESSED FOODS (UPF)

Examples of ultra-processed foods include ice cream, ham, sausages, crisps, mass-produced bread, breakfast cereals, biscuits, carbonated drinks, fruit-flavoured yogurts, instant soups, and some alcoholic drinks. Such drinks include whiskey, gin and rum.

Unprocessed or minimally processed foods are fruit, vegetables, eggs, meat and grains. Processed culinary ingredients are sugar, salt, butter, lard, oils, and vinegar. Processed foods are freshly made, unpackaged bread, tinned fruits and vegetables, salted nuts, ham, bacon, tinned fish and cheese. Ultra processed are ice cream, ham, sausages, crisps, mass-produced bread, breakfast cereals, biscuits, carbonated drinks, fruit-flavoured yogurts, instant soups, and some alcoholic drinks including whisky, gin, and rum.

Ultra-processed foods are one step ahead of processed food. Most likely they have many added ingredients such as sugar, salt, fat, artificial colours, flavours, preservatives, stabilisers, bulking, foaming, and gelling agents.[218] It is worth understanding in the interest of your health the difference between processed food and ultra-processed food. Eating too much of ultra-processed food may harm you. The definitions between the two may vary.

---

[217] https://www.goodreads.com Processed Food Quotes - Goodreads
[218] 29 May 2023. https://cdhf.ca What are Processed and Ultra-Processed Foods?

The US Department of Agriculture says anything that changes the fundamental nature of an agricultural product – heating, freezing, dicing, juicing – is a processed food. Many can be good for you, such as frozen vegetables, broccoli that has been cut into florets or baby carrots from the supermarkets. Ultra-processed food takes things further. One diet classification system, called NOVA, sums it up as "snacks, drinks, ready meals and many other products created mostly or entirely from substances extracted from foods or derived from food constituents with little if any intact food."

Examples would include packaged chips, soft drinks and candy. "Things that are packaged and pretty much ready to eat with little work at all," according to Kris Etherton, who also said, "things like rice dishes, pasta dishes – all you have to do is to add water and put them in the microwave."

Ultra-processed foods, also called highly processed foods, can be cheap, convenient and tasty. But they may have lots of refined carbohydrates, saturated fats and salt. Although the NOVA system authors assert certain additives may be unsafe, any additives used in food must pass safety tests by the Food and Drug Administration (in US). They also tend to pack a lot of calories into each bite. That means you are likely to eat a lot before you feel full, according to Kris Etherton.[219]

Ultra-processed foods make up half the diet of US adults. This might cause serious health problems. A 2019 study found people given ultra-processed food ate more and gained more weight than people on a diet of minimally processed food. Some studies have linked ultra-processed foods with obesity, high blood pressure (hypertension), cancer and death from all causes. Some of these foods have not been designed with health in mind.[220]

It is really hard not to have any processed foods, let alone ultra-processed foods in your diet. But you can make wise food choices by reading food labels. According to Mozaffarian,[221] good nutrition is more than just counting calories. Food affects our genes, modifies metabolism, altars brain responses and more. Those things together in a powerful manner influence how much we eat, how much we weigh and our overall health. Choose your foods wisely for a healthy outcome.

UPF BAD FOR HEALTH

These foods often contain high levels of saturated fat, salt and sugar. When consumed, there is less room in diets for more nutritious foods. It has been

---

[219] Chair of the American Heart Association's Council on Lifestyle and Cardiometabolic Health.
[220] According to Dr Dariush Mozaffarian, a cardiologist and dean of Tufts University's Friedman School of Nutrition Science and Policy, Boston, USA.
[221] *Ibid.*

suggested that the additives in these foods could be responsible for negative health effects.

The actual processing of the food could also make a difference to how one's body responds to it. For example, studies have shown that when foods such as nuts are eaten whole the body absorbs less of the fat than when the nut is ground down and the oils are realised. Another theory is that diets higher in ultra-processed foods could also affect gut health.

At present, it is difficult to know whether it is something within the foods that is the issue or whether eating a diet high in these foods suggests an overall lifestyle that is linked to poorer health. But bearing in mind the high salt, sugar and saturated fat content of most of these foods, their reduction or cutting down may seem sensible.

Cutting Out Ultra-Processed Foods

It is healthier to return to minimally-processed foods. However, with restricted time and budget, for most people this may not be an option. Although the evidence suggesting that ultra-processed foods are not desirable for health (heart and circulation), it seems to be growing. The research is still not clear that they should be completely excluded. The scientific Advisory Committee on Nutrition (SACN) that reviewed the evidence on processed foods and health in the summer of 2023 was of the view, due to limitations to the research carried out, that caution is still needed with regard to making dietary recommendations.

How to Cut Down on Ultra-Processed Foods (UPF)

Consuming a lot of ultra-processed foods reduces the capacity for healthier foods such as fruit and vegetables, fish, unsaturated oils, pulses, nuts and seeds. Thus, in order to change your diet, try to make some swaps, such as:

1. Instead of flavoured yogurts with added sugar or sweeteners, choose plain yogurt and add your own chopped fresh, frozen or dried fruit for sweetness.
2. Instead of buying sauces or ready meals, cook your favourites in larger amounts at home and freeze the extra in portions to use later.
3. Have porridge in the morning with fruit and nuts rather than sugary low-fibre breakfast cereals.
4. Eat fresh, baked or stewed fruit instead of shop-bought fruit pies or cakes.
5. Eat some nuts rather than biscuits with your afternoon tea.

In the light of nutrition science, manufacturers of UPFs should make changes in the ingredient used with a view to producing healthier foods.

RESEARCH ON UPF AND HEART HEALTH

Many studies have shown that eating higher amounts of UPF is linked to a greater risk of:

- High blood pressure.
- Cardiovascular disease.
- Heart attacks and strokes.
- Early mortality.

There was a study involving 10,000 Australian women over 15 years. It shows that those with the highest amounts of UPF in their diet were 39% more likely to develop hypertension than those with the lowest. A larger analysis looked at 10 studies involving 325,000 men and women. It reveals that those who ate the most UPF were 24% more likely to experience serious heart and circulatory events including heart attacks, strokes and angina. Each 10% rise in daily intake of UPF was linked with a 6% increase in heart disease risk. There are other studies in other countries in recent years that reveal the same bleak result. In Spain in 2019, a study of 19,899 university graduates showed a connection between UPF and risk of early death. People in the highest intake group of UPF were 62% more likely to have died after an average of 10.4 years than people in the low consumption group.

Following the above studies, the recommendation was to adopt a Mediterranean style diet. This includes plenty of minimal or unprocessed foods such as fruit, vegetables, fish, nuts and seeds, beans, lentils and whole grains. Together with regular exercise and no smoking (and vaping), it is beneficial towards lowering the risk of heart and circulatory disease.

Effect of Ultra-Processed Food (UPF)

A study shows that those who ate UPF were 24% more likely to experience serious heart and circulatory events including heart attacks, strokes and angina. Every 10% rise in daily intake of UPF was linked with a 6 % increase in heart disease risk.[222]

HOW BAD IS ULTRA PROCESSED FOOD FOR HEALTH

Such foods include ice cream, ham, sausages, crisps and mass-produced bread and others.

---

[222] https://www.bhf.org.uk Ultra Processed Foodsw: how bad are they for your health? – BHF.

The term "ultra ultra-processed foods" is from the Nova food classification system. It was developed by researchers at the University of Sao Paula in Brazil. The system places food into 4 categories in relation to how much they have been processed during their production:

1. **Unprocessed or Minimally Processed Foods**. They include produce such as fruits, vegetables, milk, fish, pulses, eggs, nuts, and seeds that have no added ingredients and have been little altered from their natural state.

2. **Process Ingredients**. These include foods that are added to other foods rather than eaten by themselves. They include salt, sugar and oils.

3. **Process Foods**. These are made by combining foods from 1 and 2 above. They are altered in a manner normally done at home. They include jam, pickles, tinned fruit and vegetables, homemade breads and cheeses.

4. **Ultra-Processed Foods (UPF)**. They typically have 5 or more ingredients. They tend to have many additives and ingredients that are not typically used in home cooking, such as preservatives, emulsifiers, sweeteners and artificial colours and flavours. The objective in using some of the preservatives, etc is to ensure a long shelf life

Excess consumption of processed food, especially ultra-processed food, can lead to serious health issues, such as obesity, stroke, hypertension, and diabetes. It can also stifle our nutritional intake.[223]

CONCLUSION

A great deal of UPFs are produced industrially by large manufacturers. In this regard you might think of chips, sweets and colourful sugary drinks. But there are some less obvious examples. Items such as breakfast cereals, mass-produced or packaged bread can be considered ultra processed foods.

Although such foods are in great demand by the consuming public, they are not good for health. This being the case they should be consumed in moderation if you cannot live without them.

You might find high fructose corn syrup, inverted sugar, modified starches, hydrogenated oils, and colourings, as well as de-foaming, bulking, and bleaching agents on the food label. These are examples of UPF ingredients.

UPFs are everywhere. They are addictive nutritionally deficient and contain pro-inflammatory ingredients that should be avoided. In order to

---

[223] 4 April 2023. https://www.acko.com The Impact of Processed Foods on Health and How to Make Healthier coices.

avoid these unwanted ingredients, it is better to prepare your own meals at home. This is a way of eating less ultra processed foods.

> "Get people back into the kitchen and combat processed food and fast food."
>
> Andrew Weil

> "Research has shown that even small amounts of processed food alter the chemical balance in our brain and cause negative mood swings along with noticeable dips in energy."
>
> Marilu Henner

> "Processed foods cause inflammation, a source of most chronic illnesses as well as stress."
>
> Kris Carr

Note. This is a chapter on UPF but the information in the charts below on JUNK food is relevant. While the US is No 1, UK is No 4 (though shown as No 2). The other 2 charts show the US and UK rankings on wine drinking and vaping. These charts are from The Daily Mail on 13 Nov. 2023.
From vaping to boozing and even junk food - charts show how Britain really fares vs. the rest of the world

The Organisation for Economic Co-operation and Development (OECD) this week reported that 26 per cent of British women were downing more than six drinks in one go at least once a month. Meanwhile, nearly half British men binged regularly, ranking them third in the world. But alcohol isn't the UK's only vice. Brits also among the biggest vapers (bottom right graph) and junk food addicts (left graph) in the world. Here Mail Online has analysed studies involving up to 188 countries to assess how the UK stacks up against other nations.

End

CHAPTER 12

PROTEIN AND FIBRE

"Protein and fiber are the most ignored nutrients in our diets."

Times of India

To benefit your metabolism, your appetite, and your waistline, snacks need to have protein and fiber."

Brainyquote.com Unknown

"Don't call it heartache when you feel it in every fiber of your being"

Nitya Prakash

The two topics in the chapter are discussed separately. While some people may question whether there is enough protein in a plant-based diet, there is an abundance of fibre in this diet. It is not true that there is no protein in plant-based foods. In fact such foods are the basis for protein in most life forms. The grazing animals obtain their protein from what they eat, mainly grass. Therefore, if you eat plant foods you should get your protein from such foods.

PROTEIN

Protein is an essential nutrient, responsible for multiple functions in your body. It does not only build tissue, cells and muscle, but also responsible for making hormones and anti-bodies. Everyone requires protein in his or her diet. Those who are involved in endurance sports or weight training may benefit from increasing protein intake, as well as factoring it into their training routine at specific times to reap its muscle building benefits.

As people get older they may benefit from consuming more protein as it helps to minimise the muscle loss associated with aging. How much protein you need depends upon your circumstances, but for most people a daily dose of about 0.8 – 1g of protein per 1kg of body weight is recommended. For weight lifters and strength athletes, 1.4 – 2g of protein per kg of body weight per day is recommended. As much as 1.2 – 1.6g of protein per kg of body weight per day is required for endurance athletes. After an exercise, protein is particularly important. This is because muscles need to recover and grow. Some 15 – 25grams are recommended within 30 minutes of exercise as the muscles are particularly receptive to protein synthesis.

PROTEIN FROM A BALANCED DIET

For most people their daily protein requirements are easily attained from a healthy, balanced diet. It is not advisable for adults to consume more than twice the recommended daily intake of protein. This is 55g for an average male and 50g for the average female. This limit is because in the long term consuming too much might lead to health issues, such as an increased risk of osteoporosis and a deterioration of an existing kidney problem. However, some researchers may have different views as other factors may affect the outcome, depending whether the protein is of animal or vegetable origin and how balanced the diet is in terms of both vitamins and minerals.

In the Western diet one of the main issues is that their breakfasts and lunches are usually low in protein and high in carbohydrates but with a protein-packed supper or evening meal. It is advisable to spread protein intake throughout the day.

High-Protein Foods. Protein can be obtained from both plant and animal sources. Listed below are some of the best food sources of protein:

1. **Milk**. Dairy foods are packed with protein and contain bone-building calcium as well. Chocolate milk is a known age-old recovery food after exercise as it contains energy-replenishing carbohydrates and a blend of both slow and fast release whey and casein proteins. Smoothie with fruits and milk can provide the same recovery-boosting effects. The fruits which can be used are cranberry and raspberry.

2 **Eggs**. One medium egg has about 6g of protein in an easily digestible form. A good way to commence the day is to eat an omelette.

3. **Yogurt**. A great-protein rich food is a combination of casein and whey yogurt. As some of the lactose is removed, it may be useful for the lactose intolerant. You can make your own bio-yogurt.

4. **Seafood and Fish**. These are good sources of protein, and they are low in fat. Salmon is packed with heart-healthy omega-3 fatty acids. This can reduce joint stiffness and inflammation. Note that a large fish may have mercury poison. It may be better to go for the small types, such as sardine or herring.

5. **Turkey and Chicken**. You may opt for lean protein from chicken and turkey (white meat).

6. **Soya**. Protein of 52 g and 345 calories are from 100 grams of soya.

7. Nuts and Seeds. Half a cup of dry roasted peanuts contain 17 g of protein. The best high protein nuts and seeds are hemp, pumpkin, peanuts, almonds, sunflower, flax, sesame and chia seeds.

8. Plant-based foods rich in proteins are edamame, lentils, pinto beans chickpeas (19 g per 100 g), mung beans, fava beans, lima beans, green peas

Sources of Plant Protein:

Whole grain bread has about 6 g of protein per slice. Whole grains are also a good source of fibre. It helps to maintain a healthy digestive system and prevent chronic diseases such as CVD and cancer.

Lentils. This is a nutrient-rich diet. The health benefits include protein, fibre and key vitamins.

Quinoa. This could be called a complete protein. All whole plant foods contain the 9 essential amino acids, though some have lower amount than others. Like tofu, quinoa has a large amount of all the essential amino acids plus 8 g of protein per cup. This makes it a really great plant-based protein option.

Tofu contains about 15g. of protein per 4 oz cooked serving. It provides about one-third of the average woman's protein daily requirements. Soy may help prevent chronic diseases, such as cancer, heart disease, and diabetes.[224]

Chia Seeds. These are tiny little nutritional powerhouses: they contain 3.5 g of protein per 2 tablespoons.

Sprouted Wholegrain Bread. One serving has about 15 g of protein.

Hemp seeds provide about 6.5 g of protein per 2 tablespoons. They are easy to toss into smoothies, salads and bowls of food to add a punch of plant-based protein.

Peanut Butter Powder. Standard peanut butter typically has about 190 calories, 16 g of fat and 7 g of protein per serving.

---

[224] https://www.healthline.com The 18 Best Protein Sources for Vegans and Vegetarians – Healthline.

Oats. Oats are regarded as carbohydrates by many but whole rolled oats pack about 11g of protein per cup.

Nutritional Yeast. A 2-tablespoon serving contains 50 calories, 8 g of protein and 1 g of fat.

Amaranth and Quinoa. These provide 8-9 grams of protein per cooked cup (185 grams) and are complete sources of protein, which is uncommon among grains and pseudo cereals. Also, amaranth and quinoa are good sources of complex carbs, fibre, iron, manganese, phosphorus and magnesium.

Proteins for Vegans and Vegetarians. Without meat and dairy, you still need to consume essential amino acids. Vegans can get protein from nuts, peanut butter, seeds, grains, and legumes. Non-animal products like tofu and soy milk also provide protein.[225]

FIBRE

Insoluble fibre is a type of carbohydrate that the body cannot break down and so it passes through the gut into the large intestine (or colon). It is found naturally in plant foods like whole grains, beans, nuts, fruit and vegetables and is sometimes added to foods and drinks. Fibre is made up of the indigestible parts or compounds of plants, which pass relatively unchanged through the stomach and intestines. This is known as insoluble fibre. It is mainly carbohydrate.[226]

There is also soluble fibre which is dissolved in water. It breaks down into a gel-like substance in the colon. It can help improve digestion and lower blood sugar. Foods that are good sources of soluble fibre include apples, bananas, barley, oats and beans.

Source of Fibre

The complex carbohydrates that you find in rice, bread, and pastas provide the body with energy, plus they contain vital vitamins, minerals, and plant compounds. On the other hand, fibre provides no nutrients. It is completely indigestible. But it makes up for it with a lot of other health benefits according to Nichole Dandrea-Russert:[227] "Fibre is important for keeping us regular as most of us know, but it's also the foundation for a healthy gut,"

---

[225] 1 Sept 2011. https://familydoctor.org Vegan Diet: How to Get the Nutrients You Need – familydoctor.org
[226] https://www.betterhealth.vic.gov Dietary fibre – Better Health Channel.
[227] According to Nichole Dandrea-Russert, MS, RDN, and author of *The fibre Effect* (info given to VegNews).

she says. "A healthy gut leads to less acute and chronic inflammation, both in the gut and throughout the body."

Dietary fibre is more than just good at keeping gut microbiomes happy. It has been shown in studies to lower cholesterol and blood pressure, help manage blood sugar, and reduce the risk of Alzheimer's disease and certain forms of cancer. As it helps to feel full, it has an effect on weight management. It even plays a role in hormonal balance and mental health. Also, fibre lowers the levels of cortisol, the stress hormone, in the body.

As already alluded to, there are 2 types of fibre, and each plays a different role. Soluble fibre gels in the intestinal tract and has been shown to lower LDL cholesterol. Further, insoluble fibre adds bulk and speeds the passage of waste through the gut. The other type is fermentable fibre, often referred to as prebiotics. Such fibres are broken down by health-promoting gut bacteria to produce short-chain fatty acids, known as butyrate, acetate, and propionate.[228] They help transport important minerals, like iron, calcium, and magnesium.

Effect of Lack of Fibre

Constipation is the most common symptom of not getting enough fibre, but also it has a sign that you may be dehydrated. Fibre is the foundation of a healthy gut. A lack of fibre can lead to gut dysbiosis. This is an imbalance of bacteria, which can cause short- and long-term inflammation.[229] One could also suffer digestive issues, elevated cholesterol, blood sugar imbalances, mood swings, and other lifestyle diseases

Vegans and vegetarians do not need to worry about getting enough fibre as it is abundant in plant foods. Many sources of fibre are set out below.

Some Details of Fibre Sources

Beans are a great source of fibre. They keep the digestive system running efficiently as they eliminate waste products from the colon. Black beans contain almost 19 g per cup. Beans fall within the category of legumes.

Apples are a high fibre fruit. The fibre is in the skin. This applies to most fruits and vegetables with edible peels, such as pears, plums, peaches, potatoes, parsnips, etc.

Spinach has fibre in fresh or frozen form. It gives your body a decent boost in iron.

Legumes, such as lentils, peas, carob, soybeans, clover, peanuts, alfalfa, and tamarind are stellar sources of fibre. In addition, legumes are

---

[228] According to Nichole Dandrea-Russert
[229] *Ibid.*

excellent source of non-animal based, low fat proteins for vegans and vegetarians.

Whole grains have a lot of fibre. Select the unprocessed grains when choosing bread or pasta. When you keep the healthy part of the whole grain intact you will get the fibre from the content. This applies also for cereals, crackers, popcorn and brown rice.

Broccoli: this coniferous veggie not only lends itself for self-cleansing but also it is super high in vitamins K and C. It contains about 3g per cup.

Flaxseeds are a good supply of both insoluble and soluble types of fibre. Also, it has a heart-healthy source of good fats. Flaxseeds reduce cholesterol and ease the symptoms of menopause.

Carrots are known for boosting eye health. It is particularly high in fibre. A half cup produces about 3 g of fibre.

Chia seeds are ripe in fibre. Sprinkling one ounce in your smoothie or cereal will provide 11g of fibre.

Quinoa is high in beneficial fibre and will provide 6g per cooked cup. It is also high in fibre.

Raspberries are super foods as they are packed with antioxidants, nutrients, and are low in calories. Raspberries are super in fibre content according to the Mayo Clinic producing 8 g per cup. Most berries also contain polyphenols and anthocyanins, which may help fight cancer, reduce inflammation, and reduce the symptoms of arthritis.[230]

Sweet potatoes have healthy benefits including high-fibre content. Ordinary baked potato with the skin contains a source for fibre.

Artichoke is a great source of fibre. Artichoke hearts can be added to salads, pizza or scrambled eggs.

Peas and split peas have a lot of fibre. One cup of green peas boiled accounts for 9 g of fibre. They contain much more than just fibre. Peas also supply vitamin A which may help support healthy skin and eyes, while vitamin K may help to maintain bone health..

Oatmeal can assist in weight loss as it is high in fibre. One cup contains 16.5 g of fibre. Beta-glucan fibre attracts water and increases the viscosity or thickness of digested food. It increases the volume of food in the gut. This slows down digestion and the rate that nutrients are absorbed. This in turn increases satiety.[231] Oatmeal can lower LDL (bad cholesterol). Oatmeal is also high in vitamins, minerals and antioxidants.

Bran cereal or any other cereal has 5g of fibre or more in a serving counts as high fibre.

Brussels sprouts are super healthy; one cup of boiled Brussels sprouts contains about 4 g of fibre. They also help to reduce prostate cancer.

---

[230] According to Everyday Health
[231] According to Health Harvard

Cruciferous vegetables such as broccoli, cauliflower and Brussels sprouts contain a natural chemical that may prevent cancer from growing (according to Men's Health).

Lentils are a great source of fibre. Just one cup of cooked lentils produce as much as 15 g of fibre. Lentils also provide magnesium.[232]. Lentils contain foliate, an essential vitamin for pregnant women, those with liver disease, and people on certain medications, according to Dr Axe.[233]

Avocado is high in monounsaturated fat which is good for the heart. It is packed with fibre. SELF says that just half of an avocado has 15 g of fat.

Popcorn is a great source of fibre. The same applies to butternut squash, cashew nuts, walnuts, almonds, pecans and other nuts. Some nuts have large amounts of fibre than other nuts.

High Fibre and Fluid Diet. This is considered a healthy diet. It is suitable for the entire family. But if constipation is due to Colitis or Crohyn's disease, an increase in fibre consumption could have a detrimental effect. Therefore, it should be discussed with your GP. It is advisable to have a regular meal pattern, ensuring that the entire family is provided with adequate fibre and fluid at every meal. By drinking enough water the stools will be made softer and easy to pass down. Look at the list of high fibre food if it is intended to introduce more high fibre in your diet.

Balanced Diet. Always follow a balanced diet, and introduce high fibre foods gradually to avoid creating any problem. A dietician can help in this regard.

Creating Vegan Food Without Fibre

When whole foods are processed, fibre is often left behind. For example, a lot of vegan cheeses are made from coconut oil extracted from the whole coconut. But while 3 ounces of unprocessed coconut kernel contains 8 grams of fibre, the same amount of coconut oil contains no fibre at all.[234] Despite this lack of fibre in the vegan cheese, you can enjoy it in moderation.

Vegan Food with the Most Fibre. All plant foods contain fibre, but some are better than others. Some vegan sources of fibre to add to your diet are these:

---

[232] According to McKel Hill, MS,RDN, LDN and founder of Nutrition Stripped to Men's Health

[233] See 9 Popular Drugs Linked to Dementiq and Memory Loss. https://draxe.com

[234] *Ibid.*

(a) Legumes.
- Black beans.
- Brown lentils.
- Green and red lentils.
- Kidney beans.
- Split peas.

(b) Navy beans are one of the richest sources of fibre.
(c) Pinto beans are a popular US staple.
(d) Black beans contain good amounts of iron and magnesium.
(e) Other foods that contain fibre are split peas, lentils. Mung beans, adzuki beans and lima beans, among others.

Food Highest in Fibre. Navy and white beans are the most fibre-rich, but all beans are fibre-packed. Any of these is a good choice for your shopping cart; garbanzo, kidney, lima or pinto beans. These make great soups and chillies, and are a flavourful addition to salads.[235]

CONCLUSION

Protein is essential for health. It is needed for growth and repair of body tissues. It is especially important for healthy muscles and bones, particularly for children. Proteins allow for metabolic reactions to take place and coordinates bodily functions. Further, it provides the body with a structural framework. Also, it maintains proper pH[236] and fluid balance.

Good foods for protein are meat, fish, dairy products, eggs, nuts, soya, beans, peas and lentils. Smaller amounts are found in grains and cereals.

Fibre is of 2 types, insoluble and soluble. Insoluble fibre helps speed up food passing in the digestive tract and to prevent constipation. Good sources of insoluble fibre include whole grains, most vegetables, wheat bran and legume. Soluble fibre is dissolved in water. Food that are good sources of soluble fibre include apples, bananas, barley, oats and beans.

Fibre helps regulate the body's use of sugars, helping to keep blood sugar in check. Children and adults need at least 25 to 35 grams daily for good health.

> Chocolate milk has everything you need in a drink: the carbs, the protein, and the electrolytes."
>
> End
>
> BrainyQuote

---

[235] 13 Feb. 2022. https://www.webmd.com The Ultimate High-fiber Grocery List – WebMD.
[236] The letters pH stand for potential hydrogen

CHAPTER 13

FOOD POISONING

"The Centers for Disease Control says that there are 76 million cases of food poisoning every year, 350,000 hospitalisations, and 5,000 deaths. Is that a lot or little? Well, it depends on how you look at it.

Marion Nestle

"The food you eat can be either the safest and most powerful form of medicine or the slowest form of poison."

Ann Wigmore

"As a matter of fact, most cases of food poisoning are never linked back to their source."

Eric Schlosser

WHAT IS FOOD POISONING?

Food poisoning is an ailment caused by consuming contaminated food. In most cases it is not usually serious. Most people recover within a few days without treatment. The likely cause in most cases is that the food is contaminated by bacteria or a virus like campylobacter – most common cause of food poisoning is salmonella.[237] The cause of food poisoning is due to infections with microbes: viruses, bacteria, and parasites. They cause most food poisoning. Harmful chemicals are also responsible for some cases of food poisoning. Microbes can spread to food at any time while the food is being grown, harvested, stored, shipped, or prepared.[238]

Where Bacteria Originate From?

Given the right conditions, millions of bacteria can grow on common, everyday foods. These conditions are:

(a) **Time** – a single bacterium can multiply to over 2 million in as little as 7 hours.

(b) **Warmth** – the "danger zone" temperatures at which bacteria grow best are between 5°C and 63°C.

(c) **Food** – as many other living things, germs need food to grow. High-risk foods that bacteria like best include dairy products, meat, poultry, fish, and shellfish.

---

[237] 29 May 2023. https://www.nhsinform.scot Food poisoning NHS inform.
[238] https://www.niddk.nih.gov Symptoms & Causes of Food Poisoning - NIDDK

(d) **Water** – bacteria need moisture to grow. This includes moisture in "wet" foods such as juicy meats, sandwich fillings, soups, sauces and dressings.

Symptoms of Food Poisoning

Different types of pathogenic bacteria can cause different symptoms. Food poisoning generally presents itself with symptoms such as nausea, vomiting, diarrhoea, abdominal cramping and fever.[239]Some people may experience stomach pain. Your body may experience over 102°F. Vomiting could be so often that you cannot keep liquids down. There could be signs of dehydration, which include not urinating much, a dry mouth and throat, and feeling dizzy when standing up.[240] Less often, food poisoning affects the nervous system and can result in a severe disease. Symptoms may include:

- Blurred or double vision.
- Headache.
- Loss of movement in limbs.
- Problems with swallowing.
- Tingling or numbness of skin.
- Weakness.
- Changes in sound of the voice.

Length of Time to Recover. In most cases, food poisoning will pass within 12 to 48 hours in healthy people. But your length of illness can vary, depending on several factors.

For a healthy adult the chance of getting sick depends on what kind of bacteria, and how many of them, are present in the food. Some people are especially vulnerable to food poisoning, if their immune system is not as effective. These include the very young or elderly, and those who are sick or pregnant. In these cases, lower numbers of bacteria may be enough to cause illness.

Cause. Food poisoning is caused by eating something that has been contaminated with germs. Feeling sick, diarrhoea, vomiting, stomach cramps and a fever are the key symptoms. They usually start within a few days of eating the food that caused the infection.

Most cases can be treated at home by drinking lots of fluids, with symptoms usually passing in a week.

Other Causes. Food poisoning can also be caused by not cooking or reheating food thoroughly, not storing food correctly, leaving it out for too long or eating food after its use by date.

---

[239] 28 August 2017. https://www.usda.gov Are Yiy Sure It Wasn't Food Poisoning? – USDA.
[240] 9 August 2023. https://www.cdc.gov Food Poisoning Symptoms CDC.

Controlling the temperature of food outdoors poses another challenge, as warm weather encourages germs to grow, according to Dr Freestone.[241]

Thoroughly cooking food on a BBQ can also be tricky, raising the risk of consuming bacteria that cause food poisoning.

PREVENTION OF FOOD POISONING

Bearing in mind the right conditions, such as warmth, moisture and time, bacteria can easily grow on food and multiply very rapidly. That is why food that is not properly stored or thoroughly cooked can cause food-borne illnesses.

Steps to Prevent Food Poisoning. These steps are:

(a) Clean – always wash your hands before and after handling and eating food, after using the toilet or playing with pets or animals.

(b) Cook – make sure that food is properly cooked in order to destroy any harmful bacteria that might be present.

(c) Chill – keep food cool in order to prevent bad bacteria from growing; make sure that your refrigerator is at the correct temperature to keep cold foods chilled. Aim to keep the appliance at 5°C or below.

(d) Prevent cross contamination – separate raw and cooked foods during storage and cooking. Never let raw food, eg, raw meat, come into contact with food that is ready to eat.

Prevention. To prevent food poisoning, take appropriate steps when preparing food. Carefully wash your hands often and always before cooking or cleaning. Always wash them again after touching raw meat. Clean dishes and utensils that come into contact with raw meat, poultry, fish or eggs.[242]

> "You need to identify the steps at which contamination can occur – those are the critical control points. You take steps to make sure that it does not happen. And you monitor and evaluate and test to ensure that your system is working properly. And if it is done diligently and faithfully and monitored carefully, then they producing safe food. And no astronaut of whom I am aware has ever gotten food poisoning in outer space."
>
> Marion Nestle

---

[241] Dr Primrose Freestone, University of Leicester (a microbiologist and senior lecturer).
[242] https://medlineplus.gov   Preventing food poisoning: Me4dlinePlus Medical Encyclopedia.

144

Further Causes of food Poisoning

Pathogens such as Salmonella, Campylobacter and E. Coli may be found in food-producing animals. Care in processing, transport, storage, preparing and serving of food is necessary to reduce the risk of contamination.[243]

Ways to Reduce Food Poisoning. Handling food safely is important. Follow these steps:

- Avoid handling food when you are unwell.
- Make sure all food used is fresh and within the use by date.
- Look for signs of potentially unsafe food.
- Raw meats, poultry and seafood should be covered and separated from cooked foods and ready-to-eat foods to avoid cross contamination.[244]

Food Poisoning and Infectious Diseases

For each year the estimate is that as many as 5.5 million people in the UK may suffer from food-borne illnesses. This is 1 in 10 people. Germs are invisible except under a powerful microscope; hence the name micro-organisms or microbes.

Microbes can be grouped according to their different structures. Two common groups of microbes are viruses and bacteria. Not all bacteria are harmful; indeed many are essential for life. The bacteria, viruses and other microbes that cause illness are commonly known as germs.

Germs found in food can lead to food poisoning. This can be dangerous and can lead to death, though rarely. They are very hard to detect as they do not usually affect the taste, appearance or smell of the food. The more bacteria present in food, the more likely you will become ill if you eat the food. Bacteria multiply fast and to do so need moisture, food, warmth and time. The presence or absence of oxygen, salt, sugar and the acidity of surroundings are also important factors. Given the right conditions, one bacterium can multiply to over 4 million in just 8 hours.

Presence of Bacteria. Bacteria are almost everywhere, but they are usually present where a food source is available. It is usual for raw food to come into contact with bacteria. Although most of these bacteria are harmless, some can result in illness. Once you have consumed contaminated food, there is little you can do to prevent food poisoning. Therefore, prevention is the most effective way to stay healthy.

Affected by Food Poisoning. If you have food poisoning, follow these steps:

---

[243] https://www.betterhealth.vic.gov Food poisoning – prevention – Better Health Channel.
[244] 24 May 2022. https://www.qld.gov.au Preventing food poisoning Health and Wellbeing.

(a) Re-hydrate – as you will lose an enormous quantity of fluids during an episode of food poisoning. Drink plenty of liquids. Pregnant women, young children, the elderly and people with serious medical conditions are at an especially high risk. Sip water frequently or other liquids, such as apple juice, broth, bouillon or an isotonic energy drink with electrolytes.

(b) Seek medical assistance – if you are suspicious of food poisoning, contact a health professional.

Report it – if you think you are sick because you bought and ate contaminated food, report it to the local environmental health officer in your region or town.

What You Need to Know

Symptoms of food poisoning are already set out above. Anyone can get food poisoning, but some groups of people are more likely to get sick and to have a more serious illness.

Info graphic: Food Poisoning: Protect Yourself and Your Family.

CONCLUSION

Food poisoning, a food bourne illness, is an infection or irritation of your digestive tract that spreads on account of food and drinks. Most food poisoning is caused by viruses, bacteria and parasites. Also, it can be caused by harmful chemical. The symptoms of food poisoning are these:

- Feeling sick (nausea or vomiting).
- Diarrhoea.
- Stomach cramps.
- High temperature of 38 C (100.4° F) or above.
- Feeling generally unwell.

The symptoms may be experienced within a few days of consuming the food that caused the infection. Sometimes, the symptom may be experienced after a few hours or not for a few weeks.

Recovery time for most people who suffer from food poisoning is from 12 to 48 hours. However, some types can cause serious complications. Death from food poisoning of people who are otherwise healthy is rare in Western countries.[245]

---

[245]https://www.mountsinai.org Food poisoning Information Mount Sinai – New York.

"What's the most humiliating thing? When you take someone to dinner or you cook somebody dinner and they get food poisoning. I mean, how bad do you feel?"

Wendi McLendon-Covey

"Can you imagine the headlines if I gave someone food poisoning? They'd hang me off Tower Bridge by my ballbag!"

Gordon Ramsay

"Worked out regularly for months. Lost no weight. Food poisoning for 3 days. Lost 4 kgs."

Nitya Prakash

End

CHAPTER 14

FOOD TO AVOID

"Eating crappy food isn't a reward – it's a punishment."

Drew Carey

"One cannot think well, love well, sleep well, if one has not dined well."

Brainy Quote Unknown

You cannot put junk food in your body and be healthy. This can cause all sorts of problem, such as diabetes, heart disease, obesity, and strokes. A gardener can usually avoid crappy food by eating healthy food, and the physical work provides him with much exercise that helps towards his mental health.

You can eat all the junk food you want as long as you cook it yourself.[246]

FOODS HIGH IN SALT

Foods to avoid are those high in salt (sodium), such as canned foods, processed meats (eg, lunch meats, sausages, hot dogs, ham), and frozen dinners. Some snack foods and store-bought package toddler foods are high in salt.[247]

Eat all the beans, but put junk foods into the dustbin, not into your stomach. Your stomach is not a dustbin. It requires filling up with healthy stuff, not junk foods. What is contained in junk food is harmful and can lead to serious diseases. It can increase the fat levels in the body. In turn this can lead to cholesterol, blood pressure, heart diseases, obesity and depression.[248]

The following foods should be avoided:

- Soda or sugary soft drinks.
- Sweetened canned fruit.
- Commercially fried foods.
- Energy drinks.
- Refined-grain pretzels.
- Artificial sweeteners.
- Processed deli meats.
- Packaged muffins.

---

[246] https://www.brainyquote.com Junk Food Quotes – Brainy Quote.
[247] https://www.cdc.gov Food and Drinks to Avoid or Limit, Nutrition – CDC/
[248] https://www.vedantu.com Speech on Junk Food for Students in English – Vedantu.

- Cheese in a can.[249]

Many other foods you may want to avoid are these:

- Fruit canned in syrup.
- Vegetable shortening.
- Non-dairy coffee creamer.
- Diet soda.
- Low-fat peanut butter.
- Tilefish which is high in mercury.
- Non-organic strawberries as contaminated with pesticides.
- Salami has more downside than upside as it is a cured meat.
- Juice cocktail as mixed with added sugar.
- Packaged donuts made from refined flour, deep-fried in high trans fats.
- Pre-made dough high in artificial trans fats.
- Packaged butter-flavoured popcorn.
- Instant noodles stripped of fibre and high in sodium.
- Artificial sweeteners as worse than refined sugar.
- Table salt as better to try sea salt or Himalayan salt as stripped of its natural minerals.
- Packaged gelatine as rich with artificial flavourings and sugar.
- Microwaveable rice as often teeming with sodium.
- Energy drinks as packaged with artificial flavourings and sugar.
- Low-fat ice cream as sugar is replaced with sugar alcohols; a large consumption can have a laxative effect.
- The impossible burger with ingredients which are synthetic and nutritionally lacking.
- Cottonseed oil is a refined vegetable oil, genetically modified and highly processed, high in omega-6.
- White rice as it is refined and processed (150 g has 10.1 tpf sugar).
- Sweet tea as the sugar removes the benefit of the tea.
- Pre-made pie crusts as it has hydrogenated oils which can raise LDL and reduce HDL.

Limit Some Foods and Drinks. Limit your consumption of these:

(a) Sugar-sweetened beverages (such as soda, fruit drinks, sports drinks).
(b) Fruit juice should be no more than a small quantity daily.
(c) Refined grains, such as white bread, white rice, white pasta and sweets.

---

[249] 16 Aug. 2022. https://www.eatingwell.com

(d) Baked or fried potatoes.

(e) Red meat such as beef, pork, lamb, and any processed meat, such as salami, ham, bacon and sausage.[250]

FOODS TO AVOID FOR BETTER HEALTH AND LONGEVITY

People should always be careful what they consume especially if their objective is to live to a great old age. Foods to avoid are these:

- Alcohol.
- Coffee (some nutritionists support moderate consumption of coffee).
- Meat.
- Refined sugar.
- White bread, cookies and cake.
- Artificial sweeteners and additives.
- Movie theatre popcorn.[251]
- Highly refined grains (eg. 150 g portion of white rice and basmati rice will have 10.1 teaspoons of sugar).

Not-So-Gut-Friendly Foods. These may raise your risk for diabetes and heart disease:

(a) **Diet Soda**. Artificial sweeteners in zero-calorie drinks may mess with your microbes, according to some researchers.

(b) **Red Meat**. What is bad for your gut can be bad for your heart.

(c) **Processed and refined goods**.[252]

Foods Causing Alzheimer's Risk. These are:

(a) **Red Meats**. Red meat is a source of iron, which is necessary for preventing anaemia.

(b) **Refined Carbohydrates**. A diet rich in starch and sugar also puts older adults at risk.

(c) **High-AGE** Foods.

(d) **Foods** with high cholesterol.

(e) **Gluten**.[253]Many people are gluten intolerant. The most common sources of gluten are all types of bread and baked goods like cakes and cookies.

---

[250] https://www.hsph.harvard.edu Healthy Weight cdheck List Obesity Prevention Source.

[251] https://betterme.world Health and Longevity – BetterMe.

[252] 7 Sept. 2017. https://www.eatingwell.com 3 Foods to Ditch for a Healthy Gut – EatingWell.

[253] 4 May 2023.https://www.homecareassistanceoshkos 5 Foods that Raise the Risk of Alzheimer's Disease – Home Care.

Undigested gluten makes its way to the small intestine. Most people can handle the undigested gluten without any problems. However, for some people it can trigger a severe autoimmune response or other unpleasant symptoms. Such a response is called celiac disease.[254]

Dos and Don'ts to Avoid Food Poison

If you want to avoid getting food poisoning. a microbiologist has shared her must-know guide of dos and don'ts to stop you being struck down with crippling stomach pain, vomiting and diarrhoea. Dr Primrose Freestone, a senior lecturer at the University of Leicester, says she avoids eating in certain settings, such as BBQs and picnics, and never asks for a doggy bag for her leftovers at restaurants.[255]

Despite being seemingly harmless activities, they raise the risk of becoming unwell due to incorrectly prepared food, which can be deadly in severe cases. Here are the tips Freestone shared with The Conversation[256] as in the picture below.

 X denotes food to avoid

Avoid BBQs and Picnics[257]

Moving mealtimes outside for picnics and BBQs is a summer highlight for millions of us. But Dr Freestone warned that the risk of food poisoning skyrockets as soon as food is taken outdoors due to unclean hands, germ-ridden insects and the temperature. She said that she "rarely" eats alfresco.

Washing hands before touching food is vital for avoiding becoming unwell but there are rarely facilities to do so when eating outdoors, she said. While hand sanitisers are better than nothing, they aren't always going to kill germs lurking on your food.

---

[254] https://www.hopkinsmedicine.org What is Gluten and what Does it Do? Johns Hopkins Medicine.

[255] Published 14:47, 29 Sept. 2023, updated 16:11, 29 Sept.2023.

[256] The Conversation https;//theconversation.com

[257] Dr Primrose Freestone, a Senior Lecturer at the University of Leicester, says she avoids eating at certain settings, such as BBQs and picnics, and never asks for a doggy bag for leftovers at restaurants.

Additionally, flies, wasps and ants are in abundance and often swarm when food is being eaten outside, which can spread E coli, and salmonella

CONCLUSION

Some foods are not needed in our diet. Therefore, they can be excluded without any problem. They include chocolate, cakes, biscuits, sugary soft drinks, butter, ghee and ice cream. If you have a fancy for them they should be eaten less often and in smaller amounts. As for beverages, you should go for water, lower-fat milks, lower-sugar or sugar-free drinks, tea and coffee.

"Junk foods" are foods that lack nutrients, vitamins and minerals, and are high in kilojoules (energy), salts, sugars, or fats. The name "junk foods" is appropriately used for certain foods because such foods does not play a role in healthy eating, especially if you eat too much of it.

Whereas healthy food can improve your immune system, maintain the right weight balance, among other benefits, unhealthy food can increase your weight and can have a negative effect in your lifespan.

"Healthy citizens are the greatest asset any country can have."
Winston Churchill

End

KIDNEY HEALTH AND LIVER HEALTH

"I'd like people to know that you can head off kidney disease, maybe prevent a transplant or stop the disease from progressing after detection by doing a simple urine test in the doctor's office."

Sean Elliott

"Old age is when the liver spots show through your gloves."

Phyllis Diller

The health of these two important organs, kidney and liver, are discussed in this chapter. They are vital organs and perform important functions.

Kidneys and Liver Work Together to Stay Alive

The liver removes harmful substances from the body by breaking them to smaller by-products. These by-products leave the liver through bile or blood. By-products in bile are removed from the body through feces while those in the blood are filtered out in the kidneys and removed through the urine.[258]

KIDNEY HEALTH

The kidneys are two bean-shaped organs, each about the size of a fist. They are located just below the rib the rib cage, one on each side of your spine. Healthy kidneys filter about a half cup of blood every minute, removing wastes and extra water which passes as urine.[259] Kidneys also regulate blood pressure and levels of water, salt, and minerals in the body.

CHRONIC KIDNEY DISEASE (CKD

Living with kidney disease, especially during the later stages, can be challenging. To overcome this challenge you have to be positive. Here is a quote from Melanie Litt:

"For anyone dealing with an illness or another difficult situation, positivity is the key to getting through it. To me, being able to go to work and live a life that is as normal as possible is wonderful

---

[258] 6 Sept. 2023. https://liverfoundation.org Understanding Your Liver, Location, function, and Complexity.
[259] https://www.niddk.nih.gov Your Kidneys & How They Work - NIDDK

because it's something I really didn't think I would get to do. There's always something to be thankful."[260]

A chronic kidney disease (CKD) cannot always be prevented but you can take steps to reduce the chances of developing the condition.

Ten Common Bad Habits. These may have an adverse effect on your kidney:

- Overusing painkillers.
- High salt intake.
- Drinking inadequate water.
- Not sleeping enough.
- Eating too much meat.
- Consuming too much sugar.
- Smoking.
- Drinking too much alcohol.
- Following a sedentary lifestyle.
- Working out too much (exercise).

Kidney Disease and Build-Up of Acid. A kidney disease can cause a build up of acid in your blood. This can worsen the disease. Eating no animal-based foods can lower the acid load with less stress on your kidneys. Plant-based foods that are not highly processed have phytates.[261] Phytates (phytic acid) in whole grains, seeds, legumes, and some nuts can decrease the absorption of iron, zinc, magnesium, and calcium. Saponins in legumes and whole grains can interfere with normal nutrient absorption. Tannins in tea, coffee, and legumes can decrease iron absorption.[262] Phytates is a salt or ester of phytic acid, occurring in plants, especially cereal grains, capable of forming insoluble complexes with calcium, zinc, iron and other nutrients and interfering with their absorption by the body.

Eating more plant-based foods such as vegetables and grains instead of animal-based foods, such as red meat, may help prevent and slow the progression of chronic kidney disease (CKD), type 2 diabetes, high blood pressure and heart disease.[263]

---

[260] Melanie Litt was a focal segmental glomerulosclerosis (FSGS) and peritoneal dialysis patient.
[261] 18 Aug. 2018. https://www.kidney.org What is a Plant-Based Diet, and Is It Good for Your Kidneys?
[262] https://www.hsph.harvard.edu Are anti-nutrients harmful? The Nutrition Source Harvard T.H. Chan.
[263] https://www.kidney.org Plant-based Diets and Kidney Health, National Kidney Foundation.

Healthiest Diet for Your Kidney. The DASH diet is recommended. This is a dietary pattern promoted by the US-based National Heart, Lung, and Blood Institute to prevent and control hypertension. The diet is rich in fruits, vegetables, whole grains, and low in fat dairy foods.

Managing Underlying Conditions. If you have a long-term condition that could lead to CKD, such as diabetes or high blood pressure, it is important to manage it carefully. Note the following:

Smoking. If you are a smoker quit immediately. This course will improve your general health and reduce the risk of more serious conditions.

Healthy Diet. A healthy, balanced diet can reduce your risk of kidney disease by keeping your blood pressure and cholesterol at a healthy level. A balanced diet is discussed later. Also, note the DASH diet above.

DIALYSIS FOR KIDNEY

If your kidneys are not working properly, because you have advanced chronic kidney disease, the kidneys may not be able to clean the blood. Waste products and fluid can build up to dangerous levels in your blood.[264] Dialysis is a treatment for people whose kidneys are failing. In such a failure, your kidneys do not filter blood they are intended for. Wastes and toxins build up in your bloodstream as a result. Dialysis does the work of the kidneys by removing waste products and excess fluid from the blood.[265]

The most common causes of kidney failure are diabetes and high blood pressure. Kidney failure happens when 85-90% of kidney function is gone. GFR falls below 15.[266] GFR is for glomerular filtration rate which is a test used to check how well the kidneys are working. Specifically, it estimates how much blood passes through the glomeruli each minute.[267]

Presently, someone can be on dialysis for many years. Many patients lead long and fulfilling lives for as much as 20 or more years. This depends on many factors such as age, gender, other health problems, and how well a treatment plan is followed. People who perform best on dialysis actively work with their care team (doctor, nurse, social worker, dietician, and family and friends). This ensures the treatment plan fits their lifestyle and life goals.

---

[264] https://www.nhs.uk Dialysis - NHS
[265] 18 Aug. 2021. https://myclevelandclinic.org Dialysis: Types, How It Works, Procedure & Side Effects.
[266] https://www.kidney.org Key points: About Dialysis for Kidney Failure.
[267] https://www.ucsfhealth.org Glomerular filtration rate – UCSFHealth.

Natural Treatment as an Alternative to Dialysis. This dispenses with the following:

- Need for painful dialysis.
- Need for transplant without any side effects.

Kidney Transplant. This is surgery to place a healthy donor's kidney into your body. A working transplanted kidney does a better job filtering wastes and keeping the patient healthy than dialysis, but it is still not a cure.[268]

Treatment without Transplant or Dialysis. This alternative involves medical management to enable the patient to live comfortably and do some activities. This management uses medicine and kidney-friendly eating to lower the symptoms of kidney disease and assist the patient to feel better.[269]

Rebuild Kidney Function by Balanced Diet. If you have kidney disease, a well-balanced diet is your super food. It can help to make any meal you prepare super. To prepare such a meal, these foods are relevant:

- Pomegranates. They are sweet and tart fruits high in antioxidants.
- Avocado.
- Tofu.
- Low phosphorus cheese.
- Milk alternatives.
- Healthy oils and fats.
- Fish (avoid the big ones which usually have a lot of mercury).
- Spices.[270]

PLANT-BASED DIET AND KIDNEY HEALTH

Eating more plant-based foods such as vegetables and grains is better for your health than animal-based foods, eg. red meat. Making a switch from animal products may help prevent and slow the progression of a chronic kidney disease, diabetes type 2, high blood pressure, and heart disease, among other diseases.

Healthy Diet for the Kidney. Eat these:

1. Plenty of fruit and vegetables. Aim for at least 5 portions daily.

---

[268] https://www.niddk.nih.gov Choosing a Treatment for Kidney Failure - NIDDK
[269] https://www.kidneyfund.org Treatment for kidney failure
[270] https://www.kidney.org Superfoods – National Kidney Foundation.

2. Eat meals that include starchy foods, such as potatoes, wholegrain bread, rice and pasta.
3. Eat some dairy or dairy alternatives.
4. Eat some beans or pulses, fish, eggs, or meals as a source of protein.
5. Consume low levels of saturated fat, salt and sugar.

The Benefits of Plant-Based Diets on Kidney Health

Many studies show that eating whole grains, nuts, fruits and vegetables is one of the most important ways to keep your kidneys healthy. Note these:

(a) The right foods help to keep you healthy and fight chronic disease.
(b) Plant-based diets help to prevent kidney disease for people with type 2 diabetes.
(c) There are 10 common habits that may harm your kidneys:

- Overusing painkillers.
- Abusing the salt shaker.
- Eating processed foods.
- Not drinking enough water.
- Missing out on sleep.
- Eating too much meat.
- Eating too many foods high in sugar.
- Lighting up (smoking).
- Drinking alcohol in excess.
- Sitting for long periods could cause kidney disease.

(d) Plant-based v animal-based diets: the jury is in!

A suitable diet is one that is rich in fruits, vegetables, low-fat dairy products, whole gains, fish, poultry, beans, seeds, and nuts. It is low in salt and sodium, added sugars and sweets, fats and red meat.[271]

Food to Help to Repair Kidneys. When you are suffering from a kidney disease, a well-balanced diet is your super food and it can help to make any meal you prepare super! The foods are already set out earlier to rebuild your kidney.

Plant Helps Kidney to Function. Triphala is an excellent herb to improve natural function of the kidney. It works towards strengthening the liver and

---

[271] https://www.kidney.org The DASH Diet – National Kidney Foundation.

kidneys. These are the organs responsible for removing toxins from the body.[272]

Repair Kidneys Naturally. There are 6 natural ways to help keep your kidneys functioning at their best. They are:

- Eat plenty of fresh fruits and vegetables to boost your kidney health.
- Drink enough water to hydrate your kidneys (6 to eight 8-ounce glasses of water daily).
- Keep sodium levels below 2,300 mg per day.
- Exercise regularly.
- Do not eat processed foods and sugary drinks, which can damage your kidneys.[273]

Best Breakfast for Kidney Disease. Whole foods not overly processed are generally good for a kidney-friendly breakfast. Consider these:

- Whole grain cereal, bagel, bread, or English muffin.
- Oatmeal.
- Fresh fruit such as a bowl or cut strawberries, sliced cucumber, or diced bell peppers.
- Plant-based choices like almond milk, peanut butter and chia seeds.[274]

Best Plant-Based Protein for Kidney. Just focus on plant-based around minimally processed protein choices. These are soy foods, whole grains, nuts, seeds, beans, and lentils. These are better options for kidney health than highly processed faux meats or frozen dinners.[275]

A Guide to Plant-Based Diets

Starting a plant-based diet does not mean that you need to become a vegetarian and cut all sources of animal protein from your diet.

- What is a plant-based diet, and is it good for your kidneys?
- The Beginner's Guide to starting a plant-based diet.

---

[272] 12 March 2023. https://hindustantimes.com
[273] 14 Feb. 2023. https://cura4u.com Six Natural Ways to Improve Kidney Health – Cura4U.
[274] https://www.freseniuskkidneycare.com 5 Simple and Nutritional Kidney – Friendly Breakfasts.
[275] 14 Aug. 2023. https://www.health.com Plant-Based Protein May Reduce Risk of Chronic Kidney disease – Health.

- Plant-based diet or vegetarian diet – what is the difference?
- How to stock a plant-based pantry.
- Myths and misconceptions about plant-based diets.

The Role of Plant-Based Diets for Patients With Kidney Disease

With guidance from a registered dietician nutritionist (RDN), a carefully planned plant-based diet may be helpful in the setting of kidney disease, depending on a patient's specific needs. Note the following:

- How much to eat is based on your stage of the kidney disease?
- Breaking down dietary protein: what is it?
- Maintaining a vegetarian diet with kidney disease.
- Plant protein may be associated with reduced mortality in chronic kidney disease patients.

How to Prevent and Reverse Kidney Disease

Dr John Mcdougall of the US explains the importance of eating a plant-based diet and avoiding animal products in order to prevent and reverse kidney disease.[276] He has a few YouTube videos and he organises programmes towards helping people with this disease.

Want an Easy Way to Start Eating Less Meat?

Start by going meatless every Monday of every week, and get regular tips and recipes by following a Meatless Monday. Gradually do likewise on another day. Improve on this as time progresses.

 Importance of the kidney/

LIVER HEALTH

The liver is an organ with many functions. The two main responsibilities in the process of digestion are to make and secrete bile and to process and purify the blood containing newly absorbed nutrients that are coming from the small intestine.[277]

---

[276] This doctor is involved in a 12-day Mcdougall Program. Check if it is right for you.
[277] https://www.uofmhealth.org Your Digestive System Michigan Medicine.

Liver and its Functions

The liver is the largest solid organ in the body. It removes toxins from the body's blood supply, maintains healthy blood sugar levels, regulates blood clotting, and performs hundreds of other vital functions. It is located beneath the rib cage in the right upper abdomen.[278] The 5 main functions of the liver are:

- Filtration.
- Digestion.
- Metabolism and detoxification.
- Protein synthesis.
- Storage of vitamins and minerals.[279]

Advice for Your Liver

Weight loss can play an important part in helping to reduce liver fat. Towards this objective, eat a balanced diet. Avoid high calorie meals, saturated fat, refined carbohydrates (such as white bread, white rice and regular pasta) and sugars. Do not eat raw or undercooked shellfish.[280]

Fight Liver Disease

Thirteen steps to follow to maintain a healthy liver. They are:

- Maintain a healthy weight.
- Eat a balanced diet.
- Exercise regularly.
- Avoid toxins. Limit direct contact with toxins from cleaning and aerosol products, insecticides, chemicals, and additives. When you use aerosols, make sure the room is ventilated, and wear a mask. Do not smoke.
- Use alcohol responsibly, if you have to.
- Avoid the use of illicit drugs.
- Avoid contaminated needles. Unsafe injection practices, though rare, may occur in a hospital setting, and would need immediate follow up. Use only clean needles for tattoos and body piercing.

---

[278] https://columbiasurgery.org Liver Functions, Location, Anatomy and Disease Columbia Surgery.

[279] 16 Oct. 2019. https://www.letsgetchecked.com What are the functions of the Liver? 5 Main Roles.

[280] 24 June 2021. https://liverfoundation.org 13 Ways to a Healthy Liver – American Liver Foundation.

- Seek medical care if you are exposed to blood.
- Do not share personal hygiene items, such as razors, toothbrushes and nail clippers. They can carry microscopic levels of blood or other body fluids that may be contaminated.
- Practise safe sex. Avoid unprotective sex or sex with multiple partners. It can increase your risk of hepatitis B and hepatitis C.
- Wash your hands thoroughly immediately after using the bathroom, after changing a diaper and before preparing and eating food.
- Follow directions on all medications.
- Get yourself vaccinated. There are vaccines for hepatitis A and hepatitis B, but there is none against the hepatitis C virus.

Ensure you have a healthy weight. This is a good way to reduce your risk of developing liver disease. If you are already overweight, try to reduce your weight slowly. This is the best approach. Eat a healthier and more balanced diet and be more physically active. This can help in keeping off or reducing the weight.[281]

Signs and Symptoms of Liver Disease. They may include:

- Skin and eyes that appear yellowish (jaundice).
- Abdominal pain and swelling.
- Swelling in the legs and ankles.
- Itchy skin.
- Dark urine.
- Pale stool.
- Chronic fatigue.
- Nausea or vomiting.[282]

Signs of a Fatty Liver (Symptoms of NAFLD). The signs are these:

(a) A dull or aching pain in the top right of the tummy (over the lower right side of the ribs).
(b) Fatigue (extreme tiredness).
(c) Unexplained weight loss.
(d) Weakness.[283]

---

[281] https://www.britishlivertrust.org.uk Looking after your liver – British Liver Trust.
[282] 21 June 2023. https://www.mayoclinic.org Liver problems – Symptoms and causes – Mayo Clinic.
[283] 29 May 2023. https://www.nhsinform.scot Non – alcoholic fatty liver disease (NAFLD) NHS inform

FOODS FOR LIVER REPAIR

The best foods to eat for your liver are these:

(a) **Coffee.** It is one of the best beverages you can drink to promote liver health. People who drink a few cups of coffee daily may be less likely to get liver diseases including cancer and scarring (fibrosis, cirrhosis). It might even slow those conditions in some people who suffer from them. You can choose filtered, instant, or expresso. They all seem to work. Although helpful, coffee cannot take the place of a balanced diet, a healthy weight, plenty of water, and regular exercise for a healthy liver.

(b) **Tea**. You can drink tea for liver detox. NutraLiver tea supports liver health, liver detox and more. Green tea is also good.

(c) **Grapefruit**. Citrus fruits stimulate the liver. They help to turn toxic materials into substances that can be absorbed by water. As a grapefruit contains naringin and naringenin, it is especially good as these 2 ingredients in it are antioxidants that reduce inflammation to protect liver from injury.

(d) **Berries.** Many dark berries, including blueberries, cranberries, and raspberries, contain antioxidants known as polyphenols, which may protect the liver from damage.

(e) **Grapes**. They are full of nourishment for your liver. Dark, red or purple grapes, in particular, are powerhouses for this major organ, on account of their rich antioxidant content.

(f) **Prickly Pear**. Its betalains have anti-inflammatory properties that may help reduce inflammation in the liver. A lowering of inflammation levels can contribute to better liver health and its function.

(g) **Beetroot Juice**. It is high in fibre, antioxidants and essential minerals. Beet juice is one of the best homemade remedies for fatty liver. Its nutrients help to detoxify the liver and will improve the processes of fat elimination.[284]

(h) **Cruciferous Vegetables**. Together with cauliflower, Brussels sprouts and mustard greens are good for your liver. Their fibre supports liver health.

---

[284] 17 Au8g 2023. https://www.frontiersin.org Comparing effects of beetroot juice and Mediterranean diet on liver enzymes.

In addition, they contain antioxidants and phytochemicals that may help prevent liver cancer.[285]

(i) **Oatmeal.** The beta-glucans from oats may help to reduce liver fat of mice. This could also help to protect the liver. There is no research as yet to confirm this benefit to humans. Oatmeal is associated with a reduced risk of NAFLD-related diseases. Oatmeal may help reduce triglyceride levels.

(j) **Garlic**. Present in garlic is the mineral known as selenium. It can cleanse the liver. Also, it can trigger liver enzymes, and naturally flush out the toxins from your body. Further, it can cleanse the arteries, and help to get rid of liver toxins.

(k) **Apples** contain a chemical called pectin that naturally detoxifies the body, including the liver.

(l) **Prickly pear**.[286] It deals with liver problems on account its antioxidant qualities that may prevent inflammation and oxidative stress.

According to World Liver Day, carrots, turmeric, and garlic will keep your organ healthy.

Improve Liver Health. Observe and being involved in these:

(a) Maintain a healthy weight.
(b) Eat a balanced diet.
(c) Exercise regularly.
(d) Avoid toxins.
(e) Use alcohol responsibly and do not start if you are off it.
(f) Avoid the use of illicit drugs.
(g) Avoid contaminated needles.
(h) Seek medical assistance if you are exposed to blood.[287]

Be Kind to Your Liver

Your liver is all that and more according to Saleh Alqahtani.[288] As the

[285] 18 Aug. 2022 https://www.goodrx.com The 8 Foods that are Super Healthy for Your Liver GoodRx.
[286] https://www.medicalnewstoday.com The 12 Best Foods and Drinks for Liver Health – Medical News Today.
[287] 24 June 2021. https://www.liverfoundation.org 13 Ways to a Healthy Liver – American Liver Foundation.
[288] Director of Clinical Liver Research for John Hopkins Medicine.

second largest organ in your body, your liver has some 500 critical jobs. "Your liver removes all toxins, clears medication from your body and metabolises (breaks down) all your food," says Alqahtani. It also adjusts cholesterol levels, builds proteins and makes bile, which helps you absorb fats, stores sugar for when you really need it and regulates hormone levels. Quite a lot in deed is done by the liver "in a days work".

WHAT COULD POSSIBLY GO WRONG?

The minute your liver malfunctions, there would not be much else in your mind. Cirrhosis, in which liver cells are replaced with scar tissue, can prevent your liver from doing its critical jobs. The same applies to non-alcoholic fatty liver disease. The growing epidemic among overweight and obese people can lead to cirrhosis. If your liver no longer works, toxins would accumulate, you could not digest your food and medications would never leave your body, according to Alqahtani. In fact you cannot survive a week without your liver. Ways how to avoid liver disease are these:

1. Be careful about alcohol consumption (reduce quantity or do not start).
2. Wash any produce and stay clear of toxins.
3. Prevent hepatitis A, B and C by:
>   (a) Being vaccinated
>   (b) Practise safe sex
>   (c) Wash your hands as Hepatitis A is spread by contact with contaminated food or water.
4. Look out for medications and herbs as 20% of liver injury in the US is caused by supplements.
5. Exercise regularly and eat a healthy diet. Avoid a fatty liver disease by avoiding obesity. A plant-based diet can help enormously in this regard.

Vitamins for the Liver

Vitamins for the liver are A, C, D and E. Vitamin B can benefit liver function in several ways, including reversing liver inflammation. Many B vitamins, including B12 and folic acid, can improve liver health in people with fatty liver disease.[289]

Impact of Alcohol on the Liver

The use of alcohol can have a significant impact on the liver, and long-term

---

[289] 5 Feb. 2023. https://driphydration.com Top 8 Vitamins and Supplements for Liver Health Drip Hydration Mobile IV.

alcohol misuse is one of the leading causes of liver disease. The liver plays a role in processing alcohol and detoxifying harmful substances from the body. But excessive alcohol consumption can overwhelm the liver's ability to perform its functions effectively. The result is that the liver can suffer from various conditions, including fatty liver, alcohol-related cirrhosis, liver failure and cancer. The adverse effects of alcohol can include:

(a) Fatty liver characterised by the accumulation of fat in liver cells. This condition is reversible if you quit alcohol. A continuation can progress to more severe conditions.

(b) Alcoholic hepatitis is characterised by inflammation and liver cell damage. Symptoms may include stomach pain, jaundice, fatigue, and liver enlargement. A recovery can result on a discontinuation of alcohol. However, continued drinking can cause further complications.

(c) Alcoholic cirrhosis is caused by long-term persistent liver damage. Healthy liver tissue is supplanted by scar tissue, impairing liver function. The resultant symptoms include jaundice, stomach pain, fluid retention, fatigue, and liver failure. Cirrhosis is irreversible, and a liver transplant may be the only treatment option that can optimise a person's chances of survival. Do what is necessary to avoid reaching this stage.

(d) Hepatocellular carcinoma, also known as liver cancer, could result from alcoholic abuse. Having alcohol-related cirrhosis substantially increases the risk of developing this condition.

Not every person who drinks heavily will develop the above conditions. Susceptibility to these conditions by different individuals varies. It depends on many factors. The intensity and duration of alcohol use, genetic predispositions, overall health, and nutritional status also play a role.

PLANT-BASED DIET FOR KIDNEY AND LIVER HEALTH

Concentrate on eating more plant-based foods. These are vegetables and grains in the place of mainly animal-based foods, particularly red meat. Their avoidance may help prevent and slow the progression of chronic kidney disease, type 2 diabetes, high blood pressure and heart disease.[290]

The DASH diet is a healthy diet for liver and kidney. It is rich in fruits, vegetables, low-fat dairy products, whole grains, fish, poultry, beans, seeds, and nuts. It is low in salt and sodium, added sugars and sweets, fat

---

[290] https://www.kidney.org Plant-Based diets and Kidney Health National Kidney Foundation.

and red meats.[291] As already mentioned, the DASH diet is a dietary pattern promoted by the US-based National Heart, Lung, and Blood Institute to prevent and control hypertension. It is rich in fruits, vegetables, whole grains, and low-fat dairy foods.

Vegan diets improve liver function in patients with non-alcoholic fatty liver disease (NAFLD).[292]

Kidneys and Liver Work Together to Stay Alive

The liver removes harmful substances from the body often by breaking them down to smaller by-products. These by-products leave the liver through bile or blood. By-products in bile are removed from the body through feces while those in the blood are filtered out in the kidneys and removed through the urine.

CONCLUSION

Your kidneys primary function is to filter your blood. They also remove waste and balance your body's fluids. Common kidney conditions include disease, infections and cysts.[293] Diabetes is the most common cause of kidney disease. Also, heart disease and obesity can contribute to the damage that causes kidneys to fail. Without dialysis or a kidney transplant, kidney failure is fatal. Some people can live up to 30 years on dialysis, though the average life expectancy is 5 to 10 years. With appropriate treatment, in some cases, the kidneys can go back completely to normal.

The liver helps your body to digest food, store energy, and remove poisons. Liver diseases caused by viruses are hepatitis A, B and C. Also, liver diseases can be caused by drugs, poisons or too much alcohol. After some scarring tissue, your liver can repair or even regenerate itself. Damage from liver disease can often be reversed with a well-managed treatment plan. People with cirrhosis in Class A have the best prognosis, with a life expectancy of 15 to 20 years.

Plant-based diets can help both kidney and liver patients. The DASH diet is a healthy diet for liver and kidney. It is rich in fruits and vegetables.

> "I require something so horrifically alcoholic that it makes livers tremble with fear and run for their lives when its name is mentioned."
>
> Mira Grant

End

[291] https://www.kidney.org The DASH Diet – National Kidney Foundation.
[292] 9 Feb. 2021. https://www.pcrm.org Vegan diets Improve Liver Function.
[293] 17 May 2022. https://my.clevelandclinic.org Kidneys: Location, Anatomy, Function & Health – Cleveland Clinic

CHAPTER 16

HYDRATION (WATER & OTHER LIQUIDS)

"Water is the only drink for a wise man."

Unknown

"Thousands have lived without love, not one without water"

H. Auden

"Granted it's just a guess at age 63, but I feel 'longevity' comes from: sleep, hydration, exercise, and to never stop dreaming."

Gary Fitchett

Drinking enough water daily is crucial for many reasons: to regulate body temperature, keep joints regulated, prevent infections, deliver nutrients to cells, and keep organs functioning properly. Being properly hydrated also improves sleep quality, cognition, and mood.[294] Your body needs to be hydrated to function at its best. In the absence of enough liquid in your body, essential functions like circulation do not perform as smoothly and your organs will be lacking necessary nutrients. This result is less efficient performance. Also, mood dehydration can affect your mood.[295]

Hydration is Important

Your body depends on water to survive. Every cell, tissue, and organ in your body needs water to work properly. For example, your body uses water to maintain its temperature, remove waste, and lubricate your joints. Good hydration is important for overall good health.[296]

What Drinks Can Hydrate You. They are:

- Water.
- Milk.
- Fruit infused water.
- Fruit juice.
- Watermelon.

---

[294] 28 Sept. 2017. https://www.hsph.harvard.edu The importance of hydration – Harvard T.H. Chan School of Public Health.

[295] https://www.hhs.texas.gov Importance of Hydration – Texas Health and Human Services.

[296] 3 May 2023.https://familydoctor.org Hydration: Why It's So Important – familydoctor.org.

- Sports drinks.
- Tea and coffee.
- Coconut water.[297]

Benefits of Proper Hydration. They are:

(a) Improved brain performance. Even mild hydration, as little as 2% fluid loss, can affect memory, mood, concentration and reaction time.
(b) Digestive harmony.
(c) More energy.
(d) Weight loss management.
(e) Decrease joint pain.
(f) Better temperature regulation.
(g) Kidney stone prevention.
(h) Healthier heart.[298]

Dehydration. Signs of dehydration are visible in your urine. Dark and strong smelling urine is a clear sign that you need to consume more fluids. You will be thirsty, you may have a headache and you will be constipated. You may feel dizzy or lightheaded. You will feel foggy brained and sluggish, and will constantly crave for snacks and sugar.[299]

If you are lacking enough water, hard stools and constipation could be common side effects, in addition to abdominal pain and cramps. Dull skin will show up. Dehydration shows up on your face. It is in the form of dry, ashy skin that seems less radiant, plump and elastic.[300]

Best Drinks for Hydration. They are:

(a) Water. This is one of the best drinks to fight dehydration.
(b) Electrolyte, Infused Water. What is better than water?
(c) Pedialyte.
(d) Gaytorade.
(e) Homemade Electrolyte, rich drink.
(f) Watermelon.

---

[297] 13 Sept. 2023. https://www.tasteofhome.com The Best and Worst Drinks to Keep You Hydrated.
[298] 23 Sept. 2021. https://www.ncoa.org Discover 10 Big Benefits of Staying Hydrated – National Council on Aging.
[299] 24 May 2018. https://www.chicagohealthandwellness.com Warning Signs Your Body Drastically Needs Water – Chicago Health.
[300] 19 May 2020. https://www.henryford.com 6 Side Effects of not Drinking Enough Water Henry Ford Health – Detroit, Mi.

(g) Coconut Water.[301]

WATER

Drinking naturally filtered spring water is one of the most beneficial things you can do to your body. With all the beverages available in the shops and cafes, water seems to take a back seat. However, the health benefits of drinking water cannot be underestimated. One's body comprises some 70% of water. Almost all of the body's functions to operate at their optimum levels rely on water. This is because:

- Water helps to transport vital nutrients and oxygen into your cells.
- Water moisturises the air in your lungs.
- Water aids your metabolism.
- Water helps your organs to absorb nutrients.
- Water helps to detoxify your body.

While you body comprises some 70% of water, the figure for you brain is around 90%. If you are not delivering enough water to the brain, it will slow down. The result is that you will become dehydrated and will experience fatigue. This may trigger headaches or even migraines, constipation, irregular blood pressure and even kidney problems.

On average, most people urinate around 1.5 litres daily with an additional litre of fluid lost in breathing and sweating. A failure to replace the 2.5 litres will cause your body to become dehydrated.

About 20% of your water comes from food, so the rule of thumb is to drink 2 litres daily. This depends on what you do. While this figure is OK for an office worker, a person who is heavily involved in sports will need more water. Note the following:

- Water helps in losing weight. It breaks down fat cells faster and it contains nil calories.
- Water hydrates your brain, reducing headaches and back pain.
- Water increases skin elasticity, hydrates your skin and flushes toxins out of your body.
- Water increases your productivity by making you more alert and focussed at your work.
- Water raises your metabolism and helps with digestion.
- Water hydrates joints and muscles which reduces the likelihood of cramps and sprains.

---

[301] 2 Oct. 2018. https://www.epicurious.com The 7 Best Drinks for Dehydration – Epicurious.

- Water makes you feel healthy, refreshed, clear-headed and possibly happier.

To conclude, water is healthy and is a cheap choice to keep you hydrated. But other drinks can also count towards your fluid. So much for water, now other drinks (liquids).

OTHER LIQUIDS

For hydration, other liquids can be a substitute for water. Some people hardly drink water. They rely on hot and cold drinks, including alcoholic drinks. Be that as it may, water is the best.

Alcoholic Drinks.

If you are seeking liquids for hydration, alcohol should be eliminated from your list of beverages. Alcoholic functions as a diuretic, meaning it makes you urinate more, leaving less fluid in your blood and potentially leading to dehydration.[302] A vodka water or vodka soda is probably your best bet if hydration is a goal while drinking. This choice is great as you are drinking water at the same time as the alcohol, so you have to focus as much on rehydrating between drinks.[303]

In general, drinks with higher alcohol content, spirits such as vodka, gin, whiskey and rum, are higher on the spectrum of alcohol content, making them more dehydrating per ounce than alcohols such as beer and wine.[304]

As a substitute for water intake for wellness, alcoholic drinks, such as beers, can be used. However, people should be careful in not becoming addictive to alcohol, especially spirits and wine. Although a daily unit of alcoholic drinks is advocated, it is not recommended if you have not started.

Negative Effects of Alcohol

Alcoholic beverages may also have negative health impacts. Furthermore, emerging research suggests that higher alcohol intake may be associated with hypertension and cardiovascular disease.

Long-term excessive alcohol use also has a tremendous impact on the health of major organ systems, leading to cognitive decline and mental

---

[302] 22 Feb 2022. https://www.everydayhealth,com Does alcohol Count as fluid? – Everyday Health.

[303] 14 June 2021. https://www.yourroutine.com Q Guide to Staying Hydrated While Drinking Alcohol.

[304] 8 June 2022. https://www.birdsall-law.com What Alcohol dehydrates You the Most? – Birdsall Obear & Associates

health problems, and increasing the risk of stroke and liver failure. Alcohol consumption affects the kidney by producing a diuretic effect, which promotes water loss through urine and inhibits vasopressin, a hormone which can cause dehydration in some cases based on percentage and volume of alcohol.

Coffee and Tea

Coffee. There are conflicting claims about the risks and benefits of caffeinated beverages, specifically coffee and tea. When consumed in moderation, coffee and tea pose little to no health risks for healthy individuals. Contrary to common belief, moderate consumption of coffee does not produce a dehydrating effect. While coffee consumption can produce a slight diuretic effect, this is not significant enough to be of concern in healthy individuals who drink less than two cups per day. Studies have found that consuming as much as four cups of coffee in a day does not produce significant dehydration. But be careful about the caffeine in the coffee and to a lesser extent in tea. Green tea is probably better than ordinary tea.

According to Hu (possibly of Harvard), moderate coffee intake (2 – 5 cups daily) is linked to a lower likelihood of type 2 diabetes, heart disease, liver and endometrial cancers, Parkinson's disease, and depression. Drinking coffee can reduce the risk of early death.[305]

Excessive caffeine can lead to unpleasant side-effects. Too much caffeine, either over the course of the day or in one large dose (like in some energy drinks), can sometimes cause unwanted side effects. These could include anxiety, restlessness, an irregular heartbeat, headaches or insomnia.[306]

Tea. The consumption of tea is of even less concern. Regular consumption of black, green, oolong[307] or white tea has been associated with reduced risk of stroke, diabetes type 2 and heart disease. That said, it is important to be careful that daily cups of tea or coffee do not become vessels for excess sugar, fat and calories through the addition of syrups, sweeteners and creamers. Drinking large amounts of tea might cause side effects due to the caffeine content, as in coffee. Drinking very high amounts of black tea containing more than 10 grams of caffeine is likely to be unsafe.[308]

---

[305] https://www.hsph.harvard.edu Is coffee good or bad for your health.

[306] 4 May 2021. https://www.bupa.co.uk How Caffeine affects your body – Bupa UK.

[307] Oolong tea is made from the Camella sinensis plant. Its dried leaves and leaf buds are used to make several different teas, including black and green teas. Oolong tea is fermented for longer than green tea, but less than black tea. It contains caffeine. It affects thinking and alertness.

[308] https://www.webmd.com BLACK TEA – Uses, Side Effects and More.

Green tea is a better choice if the preference is to drink tea. It is healthier than black tea. Green tea contains higher levels of natural antioxidants in the form of EGCG. This is a form of polyphenols that help limit free radical damage to the cells in the body, reduce inflammation, and protect against heart disease.[309]

Hand-in-hand with a proper diet, water intake and hydration play an important role in wellness. Water intake is essential for homeostasis and the continuation of metabolic functions.

Adequate water intake can vary depending on age, gender, activity level and pre-existing conditions. General guidelines recommend that adult men consume about 13 cups of water and adult women about 9 cups of water per day. For all individuals, hydration needs generally increase during and following any physical exercise. For women, this need increases during pregnancy and breastfeeding.

Many beverage companies make sensational claims about the ability of their beverages to compete with water as a source of hydration. Everything from sweetened electrolyte drinks to coconut water and even soda has been peddled at some point as a worthy substitute for water. Consider, however, that such drinks may provide more electrolytes than plain water, or might contain unnecessary calories and added sugars, or may have artificial sweeteners. This could be dangerous as some may be toxic.

Infused water is a healthy and tasty alternative to plain water and flavoured drinks. Infused fresh water can be made by placing sliced citrus or herbs in a receptacle of water and allowing the flavour to dissipate. This is an excellent method for unenthusiastic water drinkers to make hydration more feasible.

Fruit Juice or Soda

Sugar-laden drinks such as carbonated soft drinks and fruit juices pose a large risk for general health. The CDC recommends that drinks sweetened with sugar be avoided, if not eliminated. This is because their regular consumption is associated with the development of obesity; type 2 diabetes; kidney, liver and cardiovascular diseases; as well as dental problems.

Fruit juices that do not contain added sugars (100% juice beverages) may be consumed in small amounts from time to time, but consumers should be aware that sugar from the fruit still spikes blood glucose just as sugar from other sources.

Fruit Juices High in Sugar. All fruit juice, whether it is apple, orange, grape or a fancy blend such as peach-mango-blueberry, is high in sugar. An

---

[309] https://www.sipsby.com Black Tea vs. Green Tea Sips by.

eight-ounce serving of juice and cola both contain about 30 grams of sugar on average. That is almost 8 teaspoons of sugar.

Sugar-Laden Drinks. These drinks include, soda, pop, cola, tonic, fruit punch, lemonade, sweetened powdered drinks, as well as sports and energy drinks.[310]

The Healthiest Types of Juice. These are:

- Tomato.
- Beet.
- Apple.
- Prune.
- Pomegranate.
- Acai berry.
- Orange. This is a classic breakfast staple juice around the world and well known for its nutritional properties.
- Grapefruit. This juice is a tart drink that many people enjoy.[311]

It is always better to eat the whole fruit as by squeezing the fruit for the juice removes the fibre.

Best Veggie Juice for Seniors. They are:

- Zesty Carrot Juice.
- Green Cucumber Juice.
- Elderly Care: Bright Red Beetroot Juice.
- Elderly Care: Celery Juice.[312]

Not all seniors love eating because it may be too hard to chew. When they stop eating, they no longer get the necessary nutrients to remain healthy.

MILK

Milk is a natural source of fluid. Specifically, it contains about 87% water, making it a natural choice for a hydrating drink. Not only does dairy milk

---

[310] https://www.hsph.harvard.edu Sugary Drinks The Nutrition Source.
[311] 24 Oct. 2019. https://www.healthline.com The 9 Healthiest types of Juice – Healthline.
[312] https://avivainhomecare.com Elderly Care: Best Veggie Juice For Seniors – Aviva In-Home Care.

contain water naturally, it also contains hydrogen-supporting electrolytes and sugars in the mix. This helps to retain the water therein.[313]

A few US doctors have argued that the human specie is the only specie in the world who continue to drink milk after they have been weaned from their mother's milk. Some say that drinking another mammal's milk is unnecessary, unnatural, even unhealthy. As the only animal to drink the milk of other species, humans have an unusual relationship with the white stuff. Most other animals are weaned off milk in infancy..[314]

Dairy (Milk)

Milk is a good source of calcium and nutrients, but there is no biological reason why humans require it from another species after weaning. However, drinking cow's milk is common. The ability to digest the lactose in this milk is known as "lactose persistence", though some people lack this ability after being weaned from their mothers' milk.[315] Today, the place of dairy in a balanced diet is increasingly being questioned. This is partly attributable to intensive farming practices and the environmental cost by the dairy industry. The human health benefit is also being re-evaluated.

There is no direct link between milk consumption and the reduction in the risk of bone fracture, according to some studies. Some studies indicate that fracture of bones and premature mortality are more prevalent where people consume more milk. Sugar found in milk tends to induce oxidative stress and chronic inflammation.[316] The latter is linked to heart disease, cancer, bone and muscle loss.

Also, dairy is linked to increased rates of prostate, breast and ovarian cancer, according to some studies, but colorectal cancer appears to be less with dairy consumption. Other serious bowel conditions could be adversely affected by dairy. The bacterium in milk releases a molecule that prevents blood cells from killing E.coli. It is the same bacterium that is responsible for the development of Type 1 diabetes.

The recent Canadian Dietary Guidelines have removed diary products entirely from their dietary recommendations. Also, as already mentioned,

---

[313] 31 May 2023. https://www.organicvalley.coop What Is This About Cow's Milk Hydrating Better than Water.

[314] 25 May 2019. https://www.bbc.com Is it better to drink cow's milk or a dairy-free alternative? – BBC Future.

[315] A study in 2017 indicates that the global prevalence of lactose intolerance due to lack of lactose activity is 68%. Those affected by consuming dairy products suffer from diarrhoea, bloating, cramps, nausea or headaches.

[316] What causes inflammation are trans fat, animal fats, high fat diet, stress, smoking, sleep deprivation, obesity, excessive calorie intake, sugar sweetened drinks, high sodium diet, low fibre consumption and excessive alcohol

many people in some advanced countries are rejecting diary for environmental reasons.

You do not need to rely on calcium from dairy products as plants are an excellent source for it. Calcium is important for healthy bones and teeth, in addition to other roles for regulating metabolism, muscle function, a normal blood flow, nerve transmission and the release of hormones. Some 99% of the body's calcium is stored in the bones and teeth. The daily intake of calcium is shown in the table below.

Table Showing Calcium Requirement

Age Range in Years	Daily Intake of Calcium
1 – 3	350 mg
4 – 6	450 mg
7 – 10	550 mg
11 – 18	800 – 1,000 mg
19 – 64 & over	700 mg[317]

Most fruits and vegetables have been shown to provide calcium and to increase bone health and density. Some vegetables contain oxalates, which is an organic compound that makes it hard for your body to absorb the calcium. Your body may only absorb 5% found in high-oxalate vegetables, such as spinach, rhubarb and Swiss chard. Boiling them has the effect of reducing the oxalate levels by 30 to 80%, though it diminishes nutrients like vitamin C. Brussels sprouts, kale, okra and broccoli are particularly rich in calcium and low in oxalate. Plants containing calcium include lentils, peas, beans, watercress, cabbage, tahini, cauliflower, broccoli, bok choi, kale, collard greens, soy-based foods, calcium fortified plant milk, cereals and juices, various types of nuts, seaweed, fresh and dried fruits and seeds.

PLANT DRINKS (SUBSTITUTES FOR DAIRY MILK)

These drinks are not really milk in the true sense of the word, though plant substitutes for milk. The most environmentally friendly to produce are soy and oat milks, while almond milk and rice milk require much water to produce. Half the quantity of water is used to produce the equivalent quantity of cow's milk. There are many plant milks to choose from what is available, either sweetened or unsweetened. The list comprises:

(a) **Soy Milk**. It is made from soya beans and is very nutritious as cow's milk. It is a good source of protein and calcium and can be fortified with additional vitamins and minerals. It has a similar consistency as cows' milk. It can be used in tea, coffee, cereals, or for cooking and baking.

---

[317] https://www.nhs.uk Calcium, Vitamins, and minerals – NHS.

(b) **Oat Milk**. It is a creamy texture with much fibre. Some brands are fortified with additional vitamins and minerals including calcium, iodine, and vitamin D. It is very good for added fibre and a good choice for reducing environmental impact. It is suitable for cereal, tea and coffee, and cream in cooking.

(c) **Almond Milk**. It is made like oat milk (soaking and blending) from whole almonds in water. Its high vitamin E is good for skin health and immunity. It can be used for breakfast cereals and porridge as it has a creamy and nutty texture. Its protein level is less than that in soy and oat milk.

(d) **Coconut Milk**. This is quite different from the tinned version as it is made from blended grated coconut in hot water and separating the water content. The fat level can be high and it tends to have a higher sugar content compared with other plant-based milks. It is good for cooking and baking.

(e) **Hazelnut Milk**. It is made from roasted Hazel nuts which are soaked and blended with water to produce rich-flavoured milk. Its calcium level is high and so is foliate. It can be used for tea, coffee and cooking.

(f) **Hemp Milk**. It is made by blending hemp seeds with water. It is a good source of calcium, omega 3 and omega 6 fatty acids, while being low in saturated fat. The texture is thin with a nutty taste. It can be used in porridge or with granola. It is allergen-friendly milk, suitable for children.

(g) **Pea (Split Peas) Milk**. It is made by grinding yellow split peas into a flour, then separating the starch and protein and mixing with water. This milk has a taste similar to other plant-based milks. It has much protein and sometimes supplemented with DHA, an important omega-3 fatty acid.

(h) **Rice Milk**. Milled rice and water are used to produce it. It is naturally sweet, contains no saturated fat and low in calories. It is somewhat not a good source for protein or calcium, unless these have been added. Look out for added sugars.

(i) **Cashew Milk**. It is produced like almond milk by using cashew nuts. It is rich in vitamin E and has fewer calories. Sometimes it is fortified with additional vitamins, such as vitamin D. It can be used for coffee and lattes on account of its thick texture.

Plant-powered beverages (alternatives to dairy milk)

Various plant milks

Doctors Supporting Plant-Based Diets.[318] The doctors below have devoted their lives to medical research, nutrition and optimal living:

(a) Neal Barnard. A plant-based powerhouse.

(b) Colin Campbell (The China Study) 86 years young.

(c) Caldwell Esselstyn.

(d) Dean and Dr Ayesha Sherzai.

(e) Garth Davis.

(f) Michael Klaper.

(g) Deen Ornish (you can look at his YouTube videos).

Pictures of many doctors are shown in Chapter 7 and a table listing many is in Chapter 19. These doctors embrace a plant-based diet which they acquired mainly on their own, rather than being wholly thought at medical schools. In addition, many other doctors are following this diet themselves and some of them advocate it to their patients for a healthy lifestyle.

In addition to the doctors in the pictures, there are many more that support a plant-based diet. But many who pass through med schools have no proper clue as to this diet, and they may not be showing an interest.

---

[318] 7 Plant-Based Doctors You Should Be Following - Oops Vegan 22 April 2021.
https://oopsvegan.com › blog › vegan-plant-based-doctors

CONCLUSION

Hydration is the process of replacing water in the body. This is usually done by drinking water, eating foods that have high water content, and drinking other fluids. We can get liquid for hydration from various sources such as water and other drinks (teas, coffee, fruit juices, squash and milk.

The key is to drink regularly during the day at least 6 to 8 mugs. If you are active, or if the weather is particularly hot, there is a greater likelihood that you will become dehydrated. Being dehydrated is when your body is lacking water levels necessary to function optimally.

The best hydration drinks are water, milk, fruit infused water, fruit juice, watermelon, sports drinks, tea and coffee, coconut water. Anything liquid that is consumed goes to hydration.

While all beverages restored hydration status equally, it has been found that milk may be more effective than water or sports drinks at maintaining normal hydration status after exercise. This is due likely to milk's electrolyte content and energy density.[319]

"Nothing will benefit human health and increase the chances for survival of life on Earth as much as the evolution to vegetarian diet."
Albert Einstein

"Pure water is the world's first and foremost medicine."
Leaniumps
End

---

[319]https://gonnaneedmilk.com Hydrates Betten Than Water GonnaNeedMilk

CHAPTER 17

POSITIVE THINKING AND IMMUNE SYSTEM

"Why expert say a good mood can lead to good health."
Unknown

One minute of anger weakens the immune system for 4 to 5 hours.
One minute of laughter boosts the immune system for 24 hours."
Unknown

"All that we are is the result of what we have thought. The mind is everything. What we think, we become."
Buddha

Multiple studies show that positive thinking improves the body's ability to fight disease. Medical schools globally now accept that the body's response to stress can suppress parts of the immune system and, over the long term, lead to damaging levels of inflammation.[320] The cells in your body react to everything that your mind says. Negativity brings down your immune system.

"Once you replace negative thoughts with positive ones, you'll start having positive results."
Willie Nelson

HOW TO BOOST IMMUNE SYSTEM

"Positive thinking will let you do everything better than negative thinking will."
Zig Zigler

Consistent with this quote on positive thinking, a positive attitude can boost your overall wellness. But positive thinking can also have a particularly powerful effect on your immune system. In a study, researchers found that an influx of negative emotions led to weaker immune response to a flu vaccine.[321]

A healthy immune system is important for overall health. Research

---

[320] https://dailygreatness.co 4 Powerful Health Benefits of Positive Thinking Daily Greatness USA.
[321] 15 Feb. 2021. https://www.thecrossingsatriverview.com Benefits of a positive Attitude – The Crossings at Riverview.

has shown that being happier may help keep your immune system strong. This may help reduce your risk of developing colds and chest infections.[322]

Positive Attitude and Your Immune System

Most importantly, a positive mindset can help reduce cortisol. Cortisol, the primary stress hormone, increases sugar, also called glucose, in the blood stream, enhances the brain's use of glucose and increases the availability of substances in the body that repair tissues.[323] Cortisol is the main stress hormone required in a healthy stress response. It can cause changes to the whole body but is usually most obvious in the immune and digestive systems.[324]

Be Optimistic to Improve your Immune System. Being optimistic is associated with biological risk factors such as lower blood sugar and cholesterol. In addition, that positive thinking may boost your immunity and reduce your chances of infection and risk of cancer.[325]

Positive thinking for healing has also been shown to have a positive impact on depression, pain, resilience, and coping skills. Research indicates that it also reduces the risk of many physical ailments such as cardiovascular disease.[326]

Happiness for Immunity Boost. When your mood is elevated, so is your immune system also. Experiments offer strong evidence that happy people are less likely to get sick or will experience symptoms that are less severe when exposed to anything contagious such as the common cold. [327]

Other Ways to Strengthen the Immune System. Some additional ways to adopt to strengthen the immune system are these:

- Eating well
- Being physically active
- Maintaining a healthy weight
- Getting enough sleep

---

[322] 27 Aug. 2017. https://www.healthline.com How Being Happy Makes You Healthier.
[323] https://www.mayoclinic.org Chronic stress puts your health at risk – Mayo Clinic.
[324] https://www.fusionhealth.com.au Manage your mindset for immune health – Fusion Health.
[325] 5 March 2020. https://www.heartandstroke.ca How optimism benefits your health Heart and Stroke Foundation.
[326] 18 April 2022. https://www.fairviewrehab.com Positive Thinking For Healing – Chase Away Your Illness.
[327] 7 Feb 2019. https://www.jerseysbest.com Happy people are healthier. These 10 ways show it is far from fiction.

- Not smoking
- Avoiding excessive alcohol use.[328]

Positive Thinking and Life Span. Studies show that how you perceive aging and your life as a whole affects longevity. A 2019 study found that positive thinking can result in an 11-15% longer life span and a stronger likelihood of living to age 85 or older.[329]

Ways to Boost Immune System. Here are 7 ways to fight off possible infections by boosting your immune system:

- Establish (or continue) an exercise routine.
- Minimise stress.
- Maintain an adequate amount of sleep.
- Drink less alcohol (if you are already a drinker).
- Vaccinate against infections.
- Stop smoking/vaping (if you indulge in them).
- Support a healthy immune system.[330]

Effect of Negative Emotions. Poorly-managed negative emotions are not good for your health. Negative attitudes and feelings of helplessness and hopelessness can create chronic stress. This upsets the body's hormone balance, depletes the brain chemicals required for happiness, and damages the immune system. [331]

> "Negativity brings down your immune system."
>
> Unknown

Stress and the Immune Function

> "Every negative belief weakens the partnership between the mind and body."
>
> Deepak Chopra, MD

Sadness and Immune System. Depression increases your risk of a number of diseases and other conditions by, for example, increasing levels of stress hormones such as cortisol or adrenaline. As already alluded to earlier,

---

[328] https://www.cdc.gov Six Tips to Enhance Immunity DNPAO – CDC.

[329] 4 Feb. 2020. https://www.verywellmind.com How Positive Thinking Can Help You Live Longer – VeryWell Mind.

[330] 17 March 2020. https://www.orlandohealth.com 7 Ways to Boost Your Immune system – Orlando Health.

[331] https://www.takingcharge.csh.umn.edu How Do Thoughts and emotions Affect Health?

depression can affect the immune system, making it harder for your body to fight infection.[332] You need a positive attitude to heal yourself from within.

"Natural forces within us are the true healers of disease."

Hippocrates

"Healing the world begins with healing yourself."

Anthon St. Marten

THE HEALING MECHANISM

The adopted self-healing mechanism is inspired by the human immune system.[333] Your lifestyle should be consistent in maintaining a healthy body. There are six healthier ways that can help your immune system[334] by ensuring:

(a) good hygiene (the first line of defence);
(b) vaccination (to prevent serious infections);
(c) food safety (avoid serious food poisoning);
(d) healthy travel (check if you need any immunisation);
(e) clean water (do not consume unhealthy water and food); and
(f) safe sex (avoid sex if it is not safe).

Our immune system is essential for survival, and without it our bodies would be at peril from bacteria, viruses, parasites and other dangers. It is this immune system that keeps people healthy as they navigate through a sea of pathogens (a pathogen is bacterium or a virus).

THE BODY'S IMMUNE SYSTEM

"No doctor has ever healed anyone of anything in the history of the world. The human immune system heals and that's the only thing that heals."

Bob Wright

"If you want to have a healthy immune system, you need to laugh often, view life with a positive eye, and put yourself in a relaxed state of mind on a regular basis."

Michael T. Murray, ND

---

[332] 27 Sept 2022. https://www.webmd.com How Depression Affects Your Body - WebMD
[333] Human immune system inspired architecture for self-healing https://ieeexplore.ieee.org
[334] Harvard Health Publishing https://www.health.harvard.edu

The immune system is the body's natural defence system.[335] It does not reside in one single part of the body. Rather, it comprises a network of cells, molecules, tissues, and organs working together to protect the body. Each of these elements plays a key role in how the immune system works. The immune system functions as a whole, and this is crucial in not only preventing infection or disease, including cancer, but also performs the task, as appropriate, in getting rid of diseases.

The body's powerful immune system can protect against cancer, and is capable of eliminating tumours that have been formed. What is known as immunotherapy is a class of treatments that taps into the power of the immune system. By doing so, immunotherapy can enable the immune system to target and potentially cure all types of cancer, ultimately saving more lives. However, this treatment has not been widely successful on every cancer patient.[336]

There are two branches of the immune system, the innate immune system and the adaptive immune system. The former provides a general defence against common pathogens, which are bacteria, virus, or disease-causing microorganism. This is why it is also known as the nonspecific immune system. On the other hand, the adaptive immune system targets specific threats and learns how to launch precise responses against viruses or bacteria with which the body has already come into contact. The components of the immune system together provide both types of protection.

Cells of the Immune System

There are different cells in the immune system. They work together to fight infections and disease. Each type of cell plays an important role in identifying, marking, and destroying harmful cells that enter or develop in the body. These cells are set out below.[337]

(a) What are known as the **B cells** release antibodies to defend against harmful, invading cells. Each such cell is programmed to make one specific type of antibody. For example, one B cell might be responsible for making antibodies to defend against the common cold virus. Tumour-reactive antibodies can bind to cancer cells, disrupting their activity as well as stimulating immune responses against them.

---

[335] Defences Against Infection – Infections – MSD Manual https://www.msdmanuals.com
[336] The late Dr Raghunandan Nery, PhD, DSc, DSc, a cancer scientist, was aware of the enigma in biology with regard to a cure for cancer. Refer to his book, *Cancer: An Enigma in Biology and Society*. The author knew Dr Nery personally since childhood.
[337] The Immune System and Primary Immunodeficiency https://primaryimmune.org

(b) The **CD4⁺helper T cells** render "help" signals to other immune cells (as in (c) below) to better direct their response to ensure that they destroy harmful cells expeditiously and efficiently as possible. These cells also communicate with those cells under (a) above in producing antibodies.

(c) The **CD8⁺killer T cells** eliminate numerous virus-infected cells in the body every day and can also directly target and destroy cancer cells.

(d) The **Dendritic cells** absorb foreign or cancerous cells and present their proteins on their surfaces. This is how other immune cells can better recognise and then destroy the harmful cells.

(e) The **Macrophages** are known as the "big eaters" of the immune system. As such, they engulf and destroy bacteria and other harmful cells. As in those cells under (d) above, they present antigens to other cells of the immune system to identify and destroy them.

(d) Finally, the **Regulatory T cells** provide a system of checks and balances to ensure that the immune system does not overreact. A chronic immune overreaction is known as an autoimmune disease.

The Molecules of the Immune System

Antibodies are proteins that bind to specific markers. They are known as antigens on harmful invaders, such as germs, viruses, or tumour cells. Antibodies also mark these harmful cells for destruction. The attack and destruction are carried out by other immune system cells.

Cytokines are messenger molecules which enable immune cells working together by coordinating the proper immune response to any given invader, infection, or tumour.[338]

Tissues and Organs of the Immune System

An intricate system of tissues and organs collaborate to protect the body from harmful cells and fight against disease, including cancer. Such tissues and organs, bone marrow, lymph nodes, the skin, the spleen, and the thymus

---

[338] Targeting the "Cytokine Storm" for therapeutic Benefit. F:\
https:\www.ncbi.nlm.nih.gov › articles › PMC3592351
https://www.ncbi.nlm.nih.gov › articles › PMC3592351

gland provide a broad framework in which the individual components of the immune system develop and operate.

Bone Marrow. This is a soft, sponge-like material. It is within the bone and is a crucial part of the immune system. It contains immature cells that either divide to form stem cells or mature into red blood cells, white blood cells and platelets.

Lymph Nodes. These are small glands and are located throughout the body to filter out viruses, bacteria, and cancer cells. They are then eliminated by specialised white blood cells.

The largest organ is the **skin** and serves as a protective barrier against pathogens and toxins. It also possesses its own immune cells and lymphatic vessels.

To the left of the stomach is the **spleen,** an organ that filters blood and provides storage for platelets and white blood cells. This organ is also the site where key immune cells multiply to fight invasive, foreign cells.

What is known as the **thymus gland** is a small gland located in the upper chest, beneath the breastbone. It provides a place for key immune cells to mature into cells which can fight infection and cancer.

THE IMMUNE SYSTEM AND IMMUNOTHERAPY

Each element within the immune system performs an important function in the body's ability to protect against disease and harmful pathogens. Everything works in such a manner to fight against many types of cancer through treatments like immunotherapy.[339]

On the whole, the immune system does a remarkable job of defending against disease-causing microorganisms. However, it sometimes fails when a germ invades your body successfully and makes you sick.

What to do to Boost Your Immune System

The ability to boost your immune system has proved elusive for many reasons. The system is not a single entity. Therefore, to function well, it requires balance and harmony. There are still many imponderables yet to be resolved by research into the immune response.

It is known that studies are exploring the effects of diet, exercise, age, psychological stress and other factors in respect of the immune response. Meanwhile, a healthy lifestyle makes some sense as it is likely to assist the immune function, not to mention other proven health benefits.

---

[339] Learn more about why immunotherapy research matters and how the Cancer Research Institute's innovative approach has shaped the progress of cancer treatments.

Choose a Healthy Lifestyle. This is the single best step to take naturally in helping your immune system to work properly. To enable your body parts, including your immune system, function better when protected from environmental assaults and bolstered by healthy-living strategies, observe these essential requirements:

(a) Avoid smoking and over indulgence in alcohol above the prescribed limits.
(b) Ensure you eat a diet high in vegetables and fruits.
(c) Exercise regularly and maintain a healthy weight.
(d) Sleep adequately about 7 to 8 hours daily.
(e) Observe proper hygiene to avoid infection, such as washing your hands frequently, among other things.
(f) Avoid or minimise stress and avoid being hateful to others regardless of the circumstances. When you extend love to everyone, it rebounds back with tremendous force.
(g) Most importantly, in the light of the Covid-19 pandemic, take all recommended vaccines to ensure your immune system can stave off infections before it is too late.

Immune System and Age. As people age over the years, the ability of their immune system becomes less dependable. What this means is that the immune response capability is reduced. Therefore, an older person is amenable to more infections and cancers. As life expectancy has been significantly extended, especially in the West, there are more age-related conditions. As you live longer, try to avoid an unhealthy state of your body. It makes no sense to live longer if you cannot live in a healthy state.

A commensurate reduction in immune response to infections has been demonstrated by the response of older people to vaccines. For example, studies on influenza vaccines have shown that for elderly people over age 65, the vaccine is less effective when compared to healthy children over the age of 2. However, in spite of the reduction in efficacy, the elderly does enjoy some immune response from vaccinations for both influenza and *S. pneumoniae*. Thus, the level of sickness and death has significantly been lowered compared with no vaccination.

Connection Between Nutrition and Immunity in the Elderly. There is some positive connection between nutrition and immunity in the elderly. Surprisingly, a form of malnutrition of the elderly is common even in affluent countries as older people tend to eat less and often have less of a variety in their diets. Perhaps, a dietary supplement may help to maintain a healthier immune system.

Diet and Your Immune System

186

Proper diet plays an important part in maintaining a healthy lifestyle. A healthy immune system needs good, regular nourishment. It has long been known that people who live in poverty and are usually malnourished are more prone to infectious diseases. It is not yet known what particular dietary factors are responsible for this. Is it due to processed foods, high intake of sugar or some other factor? Scientists are still unable to understand what adversely affects the immune function.

Perhaps any immune deficiency is attributable to a lack of all micronutrient needs in your diet. Some people who do not like to eat vegetables may take a daily dose of a multivitamin. However, it is not advisable taking a mega dose of a single vitamin as a larger amount is not necessarily better. But it is always better to have your nutrients from food.

Herbs and Supplements to Improve Immunity

There are various claims that certain herbal preparations help to "support immunity" or otherwise boost the health of your immune system. While some preparations tend to alter some components of the immune function, scientists claim that there is lack of evidence that they actually increase immunity for the better protection against infection and disease.

Many people around the world believe in boosting the immune system by the use of herbs. This has been the foundation of Ayurveda since time immemorial. Some victims of disease, such as cancers, who have been given up by their doctors that nothing more can be done for them, have turned to herbs and surprisingly have been cured. A notable case is a Brazilian medical doctor (psychiatrist) who returned from the USA to his home country and after six months was completely cured by herbs from his dreaded pancreatic cancer. The name of the doctor is Jose and is discussed later in this chapter. Some people who avoided western medication have been cured by herbs.

There is a close link of a relationship between the mind and the body, as mentioned already. Stress is a function of your mind and it has an effect on your immune system. Thus, a serious stress can impair your immune system in providing protection against maladies in your body. Many maladies, such as stomach upset and even heart disease, are linked to the effects of emotional stress. Scientists are actively studying the relationship between stress and immune function.

The effect of stress varies from person to person. People behave differently in the same situation. Thus, it is difficult for scientists to determine how much stress different people experienced in a given situation. A person's subjective impression of the amount of stress cannot be measured. What can be measured are the things that have some bearing on stress, such as the number of times the heart beats each minute, but at the same time what is measured may reflect other unknown factors.

187

Other Factors. There may be other factors which have an effect on the immune system. Canadian researchers have reviewed many medical studies on the subject and conducted some themselves and conclude that moderate cold exposure has no detrimental effect on the human immune system..

Another important factor that supports your immune system is regular exercise. This is the pillar of a healthy lifestyle. It improves cardiovascular health, reduces hypertension and body weight and protects you against many other diseases. As in the case of a healthy diet, regular exercise can contribute to good health and, therefore, your immunity against diseases.

Immunotherapy and Cancer

A cancer treatment to help your immune system to fight cancer is immunotherapy. As such, it helps your body to fight diseases. It is made up of white blood cells and organs and tissues of the lymph system. It is a type of biological therapy, and as such is a type of treatment that uses substances made from living organisms to treat cancer.[340]

While there are no guarantees that any cancer treatment will work for everyone, immunotherapy has many potential benefits. It improves the long-term survival rate of many types of cancer. It destroys multiple tumor types and can prevent tumours from returning in many cases.[341]

How the Immune System Fights Cancer. The immune system detects and destroys abnormal cells. As such, most likely it prevents the growth of many cancers. This includes immune cells which are found in and around tumours. Such cells known as tumour-infiltrating lymphocytes (TILs) are a sign that the immune system is responding to the tumour. Victims of cancers whose tumours **contain** TILs may do better than people whose tumours do not contain them. Although the immune system can either prevent or retard the cancer growth, cancer sometimes avoid destruction by the immune system:

(a) There are genetic changes which make them less visible to the immune system.
(b) They have surface proteins which turn off the immune cells.
(c) They change the normal cells surrounding the tumour to interfere with how the immune system responds to the cancer cells.

Types of Immunotherapy. The types used to treat cancer include:

---

[340] https://www.cancer.gov > types > im... 24 Sep 2019 Immunotherapy for Cancer – National Cancer Institute.
[341] 6 Sept. 2022. https://clevelandclinic.org Immunotherapy: Side Effects, Risks & Benefits - Cleveland Clinic.

188

(a) The immune checkpoint inhibitors which block the immune checkpoints which are a normal part of the immune system. They keep the immune responses from being too strong.

(b) The T-cell transfer therapy is a treatment that boosts the natural ability of your T-cells to fight cancer. In such a treatment, the immune cells are taken from your tumour.

(c) Monoclonal antibodies, which are immune system proteins created in the lab, are intended to bind to specific targets on cancer cells. Some of them mark cancer cells to enable a better destruction by the immune system.

(d) Treatment vaccines work against cancer by boosting your immune system's response to cancer cells. Such vaccines are different from those that help prevent disease.

(e) The immune system modulators enhance the body's immune response against cancer. While some of these agents affect specific parts of the immune system, others affect the immune system in a more general way.

Cancers Treated with Immunotherapy

Immunotherapy involves stimulating the body's natural defences to fight cancer.[342] This biological therapy is an evolving and promising cancer treatment, though it has not yet proved very successful. It works by stimulating the immune system. It is already being used to tackle certain cancers, and some forms are available in the UK on the NHS.

This type of drugs has been approved to treat many types of cancer, though not yet being widely used as surgery, chemotherapy, or radiation therapy.

Like other drugs, immunotherapy can cause many serious side effects. The side effects are greater when it has been revved-up to act against the cancer as it also acts against healthy cells and tissues. Different types of immunotherapy may be administered in different ways, to include:

(a) Intravenously by going directly into a vein.
(b) Oral in the form of pills or capsules.
(c) In the form of a cream that you rub onto your skin (tropical). This can be used for very early skin cancer.
(d) Intravesical by inserting it directly into the bladder.

---

[342] Immunotherapy: Cancer Treatment, CAR T-Cell Therapy, types
https://my.clevelandclinic.org

Immunotherapy may be received in a doctor's clinic or in the outpatient unit of a hospital. There is no need to be admitted into the hospital for a night stay. How often you receive the treatment depends on:

(a) The type of cancer and how advanced it is.
(b) What type of immunotherapy you are given.
(c) How your body reacts to treatment.

You could be given treatment every day, week, or month, or for some types may be administered in cycles. Certain periods will be followed by rest to allow your body a chance to recover, respond to the immunotherapy, and build new healthy cells. Your doctor will check whether the treatment is working. You will be asked about how you feel and tests and scans will be carried out. The tests will measure the size of your tumour and the doctor will look for changes in your blood work. Only a small number of people who receive the treatment will respond positively. This is a relatively new type of treatment and a prediction as to how patients will respond is not possible at this stage of research.[343]

How Immunotherapy Make You Feel? Some of the most common side effects associated with this treatment may include but are not limited to: chills, constipation, coughing, decreased appetite, diarrhoea, fatigue, fever and flu-like symptoms, headache, infusion related reaction or injection site pain, itching, localised rashes and/or blisters.[344] The mere number of such side effects may deter a cancer patient from undergoing this treatment.

Breast Cancer

Most women with early-stage breast cancer can avoid toxic chemotherapy. "This is an area in which the technology is moving so quickly that things that seem impractical at the moment in very few years' time may well be deliverable." A woman has been completely cured of breast cancer.[345] This was after doctors tweaked her immune system. This treatment destroyed the tumours that had spread through her body. As such, the treatment succeeded after all other conventional treatments had failed. It marks the first successful application of T-cell immunotherapy for late-stage breast cancer.

---

[343] NCI's list of cancer clinical trials includes all NCI-supported clinical trials that are taking place across the United States and Canada, including the NIH Clinical Center in Bethesda, MD.
[344] https://www.cancerresearch.org Immunotherapy Side Effects Cancer Research Institute.
[345] Study shows one patient's advanced breast cancer has been cured. https://breastcancernow.org

Although the technique is still in its early days, scientists have welcomed its potential as a future treatment for cancers that have resisted all other forms of therapy. Immunotherapy has resulted in effective new treatments being made available for melanoma and kidney cancers.

Tumour Spread to Liver. After several chemotherapy sessions had failed to kill cancer tumours, which had begun to spread to a female engineer, the cutting-edge treatment of immunotherapy was selected. Before this treatment, doctors had given her three years to live. For over two years now she has been declared free of cancer.

Immunotherapy Stopped "Untreatable" Prostate Cancer

Men with otherwise untreatable prostate cancer could halt its spread and survive longer by undergoing immunotherapy treatment, as shown in a trial. A major trial of an immunotherapy drug has shown it can be effective in some men with advanced prostate cancer.[346] The men had stopped responding to previous treatment options. Immunotherapy uses one's own immune systems to recognise and attack cancer cells.

Immunotherapy is already being used as a standard treatment for some cancers, such as melanomas, and is being tested on many others. Some highlights are:

(a) Immunotherapy drug prolongs life of some cancer patients.
(b) Prostate cancer drug is hailed as a big deal.
(c) About 50% of patients survive "untreatable cancer".

Some men with prostate cancer respond to the drug pembrolzumab and their tumours actually shrink or disappear altogether. Although this is a very small number, some of the men gained many years of life.[347] A further 19% of cancer patients experienced some evidence of improvement. Most patients in the study lived on average for 8 months on the drug.

Prostate cancer is the most common cancer for men in the UK. Around 47,000 are diagnosed each year and this number has been rising over the last 10 years. This is probably attributable to the population getting older, and more people are being tested for PSA. Some 30% of men with advanced or stage 4 prostate cancer survive for 5 years or more after diagnosis

"This is an illustrative case report that highlights, once again, the power of immunotherapy," said Dr Tom Misteli, director of the NCI's Centre for Cancer Research.

---

[346] BBC News 28 Nov 2019.
[347] According to the Journal of Clinical Oncology.

HEALING OR CURING FROM WITHIN

> "Switch your mentality from 'I'm broken and helpless' to 'I'm growing and healing' and watch how your life changes, for the better."
>
> averstu.com

The body is capable of curing itself by its own immune system.[348] In this regard, healing may be referred to as "an inside job".[349]

Emotions, Mind and Spirit

What is meant by "an inside job" is that the body contains the mechanism for curing itself; it already has "the most essential components to healing, such as life force, harmony, regeneration, and repair". These do not come from others but from within. The mind is a very powerful healing tool and is inherent in every person as of right. Healing is a process within the body; nothing new is added to your body or mind and nothing is taken out.[350] The entire process of healing "involves a greater experience of oneness, wholeness, and reconnection with all aspects of your being."[351]

Many people who have been given up by medical doctors that nothing can be done for them in finding a cure have made a remarkable recovery. This was due to the power of the mind to heal the body. After experiencing a health problem and, regardless of the finest medical care, many patients got sicker and died. However, many other patients who had life-threatening terminal diseases returned from the prospect of death to enjoy a long, healthy useful life. Cases like these are downplayed by those likely to lose financially, notably medical doctors and the drug barons. They still maintain that drugs, radiation and surgery to remove cancers are the determining factors for recovery of one's health. It is beyond belief by them that healing occurs from within. It is contrary to their years of training at medical schools.

Use of Herbs to Kill Cancer

An herb used in traditional medicine in Middle East countries may help fight pancreatic cancer. It is an extract from **nigella sativa seed** oil that

---

[348] Refer to Healing from Within: The Keys to Curing Chronic Illnesses Through the Mind-Body Connection by Nathaniel Altman.

[349] According to Donald M. Epstein, author of *The Twelve Stages of Healing and Healing Myth, Healing Magic.*

[350] Dr Paul Epstein in his essay "There is no Cure for Healing"

[351] *Ibid.*

blocked pancreatic cancer cell growth. The extract kills cells by enhancing programmed cell death. [352]

The Story of the Brazilian Psychiatrist

Earlier in this chapter mention was alluded to the remarkable recovery of Jose, a Brazilian psychiatrist from a terminal illness. He was working in the US when he was diagnosed with pancreatic cancer. After some treatment, his oncologists at a major Boston hospital had suggested surgery but he refused. He returned to Brazil and, after confirmation by Brazilian doctors of what had been diagnosed in the US, Jose refused surgery, radiation and chemotherapy. He was aware, being a doctor himself, that these drugs would kill him. He decided that he would avoid all western drugs and surgery. Instead, he decided to retreat to the countryside and embarked on a holistic path to mind-body healing. This involved himself in a great deal of spiritual and psychological work and in using local healing plants. Everything he was involved in resulted in changes in behaviour, attitude and diet. In consequence together they had a positive impact on his health.

Six months later, Jose returned to the Brazilian hospital where he had been earlier reconfirmed of his stage 4 pancreatic cancer. To his oncologists' utter amazement, after tests and a CT scan, Jose was told his cancer had completely disappeared. They could not believe the total transformation, as they knew that people with such a cancer would not live for more than six months. They refused to accept a complete remission in the absence of western medicine. They were happy for Jose who lived for another 8 years but died from a heart attack rather than from cancer. In keeping with the belief in their system of medicine, they concluded that they probably made a serious error in their diagnosis and for them to accept that he did not have cancer to start with. It is inconceivable for them to accept a complete recovery from pancreatic cancer by means of herbs.

The Case of Marisa Harris of New York

There is also the case of Marisa Harris who survived stage 4 pancreatic cancer for over 21 years, though her oncologist who treated her died some 8 years ago. When she was first diagnosed, she was given a mere 6 months to live.[353]

---

[352] Traditional Herbal Medicine Kills Pancreatic cancer Cells
https://www.sciencedaily.com

[353] Reimagining the Possible to Survive Stage IV Pancreatic Cancer – Marisa Harris.

Marisa Harris (a 21-year stage 4 cancer survivor)

As a cancer coach, Marisa uses her experience to help guide patients and give them the tools to pursue vibrant health and well-being. Note these points:

(a) She was given a poor prognosis after being diagnosed with stage 4 pancreatic cancer.
(b) She focused on positivity.
(c) She found a doctor who combined minimum chemo with complementary treatments.
(d) Now as a long-term survivor she helps others.
(e) In the spring of 2018 she already survived for 20 years.

Marisa had a long history of gastrointestinal problems, so any time she had stomach aches and back aches, she thought it was just her sensitive GI tract. But after a horseback riding accident she noticed a hard swelling in her groin. After some tests, she was diagnosed with stage 4 pancreatic cancer and was given 6 months to live. Most people with stage 4 do not live for more than a few months.

Changing How She Thought. She was told nothing could be done after being diagnosed with stage 4 pancreatic cancer. This was life-changing for her. She had spent most of her lifetime asking this question: "Why do some people manage or navigate more successfully through the worst circumstances – what do they bring to those situations?" She decided to implement what she could to live happier and possibly longer. She turned her attention to people who live longer than the odds or even survive. Her research studies on many articles became the basis of her healing programme.

Finding a Brilliant Oncologist. So, her first step was to find a brilliant, impeccably trained oncologist who believed in the possibility that she could get well again. Thinking positively her own healing, she decided to have a team of experts, headed by that oncologist, who understood the factors that may contribute to getting well and staying well. She was referred to Dr Mitchell Gaynor who practised integrated oncology. This oncologist believed that patients needed to include changes on the physical, mental, emotional and spiritual realms. This doctor ran his own support group and, regardless of being his patient, people are accepted in his group, which included chanting and Tibetan bowls. At his group, she met people who were exercising, even running, while in stage IV. By meeting his other patients, who were so filled with life, led Marisa to choose him as her oncologist. The quality of their experience was a very important factor in her decision.

Extensive Family History of Cancer. Those included her mother, father, sisters, uncles, and both grandmothers who had died of cancer. She under went genetic testing and she found she carried the BRCA2 gene.

She did not start chemotherapy right away. The other oncologists she had seen were adamant that chemotherapy would at most give her a couple of extra months, but she would be as sick as a dog!

She told her oncologist that she wanted to try his non-medical interventions first. He agreed. Dr. Gaynor changed her diet, put her on supplements and some prescription medications, recommended a trainer to teach her exercises to complement her running, and recommended a cancer therapist to deal with fears around her diagnosis and unresolved trauma from the past. Her tumour markers dropped, and she was physically, mentally, and emotionally feeling better, though the CT scans showed no improvement. He persuaded her to do chemotherapy, saying that he felt that without it the cancer would spread to her brain. She had chemotherapy for seven months. He prescribed supplements and drugs to bolster her immune system, to alleviate some of the side effects and to destroy cancer cells.

She continued eating foods that were good for the body, and taking supplements that strengthened her immune system. She underwent acupuncture to minimize or eradicate the side effects such as nausea and neuropathy. It took a while for the treatments to show results but she was feeling positive.

After the treatment ended, she had regular follow-ups and had CT scans every eight weeks for 10 years. To avoid effect from radiation she switched to MRIs. She also had blood work every three months for tumour markers. Years later, because of continuing concerns about other cancers, she had genetic testing for a second time. This time the test was done at a bigger lab, and she found out that she carried the BRCA1 mutation. She began to see her oncologist every 6 months for various scans and she had blood work every four months.

The Power Within. Once she started changing her diet and doing the other things Dr Gaynor recommended, she felt empowered and confident. She was focusing on her quality of life, not just the quantity of life, and was not willing to hear negativity from anyone.

She decided that after being recovered she would never have another unhappy day. Later, she realised that in some ways the hardest work in the world is to think and act in a way that is congruent with what people would really love to think, feel and do. She deepened her spiritual connections with her husband and religion and she continued to focus on the positivity. This process of thinking, feeling, and acting in a way that supports what people most want is a lifelong commitment.

A Positive Life. The minute she started feeling more hopeful she started sharing her experience with anyone facing a life-ending diagnosis. She became a certified master integrative coach, a cancer coach, and certified in mind-body medicine, and a resilience practitioner. These steps and more were to help guide and serve people going through what may seem like hopeless odds. Serving others is one of the most uplifting things people can do.

It is important to educate the medical community to use everyday terms so lay people can understand. And people must ask questions when they do not understand. Even more important, the medical community should be reminded of the essential power of people's minds to impact the qualitative experience and the quantitative experience. She would advise patients to choose doctors and healing professionals that have a positive attitude, that see patients as partners in the process of healing, and share information with each other so that they can best serve the whole person. Do not try to do this alone. Be part of a support group.

MIND-BODY HEALING

"Let go of every thought that isn't pushing your mind in a positive direction."

averstu.com

Mind-body healing is nothing new. It has been practised for ages. The human body contains energies and it vibrates at different frequencies, encompassing physical, mental, emotional and spiritual aspects.[354] Mind-body practices are techniques that are designed to embrace the mind's positive impact on the body. These techniques include behavioural, psychological, social, expressive and spiritual approaches. This is not a new idea but may seem unfamiliar to some people in the West where the mind and the body have been traditionally taken as distinct entities over several centuries. But this is rapidly changing in the light of links between the mind and body as observed in scientific research.[355] Your mind and body are powerful allies. How you think can affect how you feel, and vice versa.[356]

---

[354] Ancient Indian Energy Healing: Practices for Physical, Mental and Emotional Well-Being. Can be checked out on the internet.
[355] [355] Mind-Body Therapies https://www.takingcharge.csh.umn.edu
[356] Mind-Body Wellness https://www.uofohealth.org

The Body Can Perform Optimally

The body can perform optimally if the laws of nature are observed. These laws involve breathing of pure air, eating natural food, drinking chemical-free water, and avoiding toxic medication, smoking, alcohol, using inorganic body and household products. Most importantly, you should avoid being exposed to electromagnetic pollution and even thinking of negative thoughts. Energy imbalances in our body will lead to disease.

Holistic View of Healing

Look at yourself as more than the physical body. People's emotions, thoughts, attitudes and spirituality play an essential part in healing. Based on a medical opinion, you will be told that there is one cause of your disease and a single cure for it. However, under the holistic approach, there is a mind-body connection.

> "The worst disease in the world is hate. And the cure for hate is love."
>
> India Arie

There is an interplay involving the physical, emotional, mental and physical aspects of our being, not to mention our relationship with the environment. A technical term has come into use; it is psychoneuroimmunology which links the mind, the brain and the immune system, and how they communicate with one another. Scientists have confirmed that our minds and feelings have something to do with our health.[357] The major findings of psychoneuroimmunology for understanding mind-body healing are summarised here:[358]

(a) Mind-directed, cell-enhancing chemicals communicate directly with the immune system.
(b) Mental attitude and mood can alter the course of disease.
(c) The mind can direct changes in the body.
(d) The immune system is weakened by stress-related hormones.
(e) Chemicals made by the immune system communicate with the brain.
(f) The brain communicates with the immune system, and the immune system talks to the brain.

---

[357]Refer to the research of Candace B. Pert, PhD., research professor in the Department of Physiology and Biophysics at Georgetown University Medical Center in Washington, DC.
[358] Sara Shannon *Good Health in a Toxic Environment*, Time Warner Quick Reads, 1995.

Connection Between Mind and Body. The above discoveries show the connection between the mind and body, and how life's situations can affect our immune response. There is fear, hopelessness, and the feeling that nothing works, they are linked to the production of neurochemicals. Thus, they can lower the immune response and promote the aging process. On the other hand, positive feelings will have the opposite effect and will strengthen the immune system, slow down the aging process and protect you from cancer and other viruses.

Effect of Different Thoughts and Emotions. This effect may have a temporary impact on health, but guard against chronic, repeated, and habitual thought and emotional patterns as they can have a far more profound, long-term impact on our well-being. Whatever is the thought process, this effect underlies the power of the mind to heal the body. Always think positively rather than harbouring feelings of fear, hopelessness, worry, and worthlessness. Everyone affects our body-mind system. Negative thoughts and hatred of others must be eliminated; you are your mind. When you say you have no control over your life, such a thought is linked to a number of diseases which could be very serious, such as **cancer** and heart disease.

How to Adopt to Stresses

There is always some stress in life whatever you are involved in. What should be borne in mind are not necessarily the stresses in life that lead to disease but how you adopt to such stresses.[359] People learn from their young days how to adopt in different situations, and they tend to look at the problem through these old perspectives. However, those who are rigid in their perspectives often find it far more difficult to adjust to changing events as time progresses. To avoid serious problems, it is better to adapt oneself to every situation in seeking practical solutions. Never accept a feeling of hopelessness. Instead of taking appropriate measures for action to change the situation, some people accept what they are confronted with. This acceptance leads them to fear and paralysis.

Never Accept Nothing Can be Done

An illness should never be viewed as a punishment. Instead, a disease can be seen as a failure in the alignment of the physical, emotional, mental, and

---

[359] Hans Selye, MD (1907-1982) and other researchers. Selye was the founder of the stress theory – NCBI – NIH. He was the first to identify stress as underpinning the nonspecific signs and symptoms of illness.

spiritual aspects of our being. This is in the context of the holistic mind body healing process.

Symptoms of disease are the means by which information is given that something is wrong and that something has to be done to right the situation. Obviously, something needs to be done for the better. Lifestyle habits that may have contributed to one's health problem should be examined. Sometimes, if you are sensitive to the symptoms emanating from your body, you may be able to deal with the problem before it becomes serious. Cancer can play a transformative role resulting in major changes in thinking and lifestyle. Thinking in terms of fear often result in more suffering. On the other hand, knowledge and hope may lead to healing. In this regard, mind-body healing could lead to inner alignment and harmony. A positive attitude is fundamental for a change.

You should eliminate from your mind childhood hurts, if any, and other negative thoughts of the past. Summarised below from a book[360] are the traits that some AIDS' survivors have in common, some of which are similar to long-term cancer survivors. Many of these traits apply to those who are from all serious illnesses, life-threatening or not. These traits include the following:

(a) A sense of personal responsibility for their health and a sense that they can influence it.
(b) A sense of purpose in life.
(c) A new meaning in life following from the illness itself.
(d) Previously mastered a life-threatening illness or other life crisis.
(e) Accepted the reality of their diagnosis, yet refusing to believe that it is a death sentence.
(f) An ability to communicate their concerns to others, including concerns regarding the illness itself.
(g) Being assertive and having the ability to say no.
(h) The ability to withdraw from involvements and to nurture themselves.
(i) Being sensitive to their body and its needs.

Other Common Traits

Some traits among long-term AIDS survivors in respect of the healing power of the mind are addressed in a book[361] in which ten points in particular stand out. They are summarised here:

1. These survivors had expectations of favourable results in respect of their situation.

---

[360] *Living in Hope* by Cindy Mikluscak-Cooper, R.N. and Emmett E. Miller, M.D.

[361] By Scott J. Gregory, *A Holistic Protocol for the Immune System.*

2. They took charge of their healing and assumed control of decisions that vitally affected their lives.

3. They learned to laugh by developing a sense of humour.

4. They were able to develop compassion toward others.

5. They were patient in their expectations knowing that they could not be healed overnight.

6. They developed a stronger self-image by changing their attitudes about themselves.

7. They understood that there was no one thing that could cure them and sought a combination of life-reinforcing factors and modalities.

8. They had no fear of death—or life.

9. They learnt the importance of prevention and treatment.

10. They were fighters against their plight.

Self-Nurturing

Self-nurturing is taking care of yourself. Some people place themselves at the bottom in a list of priorities. This could result in a burnout, exhaustion and/or resentment. You can decide how to prioritise in a less painful manner and in relation to self-nurturing. With a view to helping yourself be more positive and joyful; this can be regarded as self-nurturing.[362]

Healing Power of the Mind and Self Nurturing

Accept the healing power of the mind. The environment created may differ from person to person. It involves both the emotional being and the mental being. A few ideas are set out under different sub-headings below. They offer a few ideas that can enhance self-nurturing on emotional, mental, and even spiritual levels.

Nurturing the Emotional Self. Emotions play an important role in health and disease. Positive feelings strengthen the immune system Negative, repressed, or distorted emotions can decrease immune response leading to a variety of health problems. Therefore, it is imperative to cultivate your emotional well-being. Your emotions should try to nourish and guide you towards good health. What can help is to have a support system from relatives and friends. Do not accept feelings of anger, frustration and sadness. Be positive and cultivate joy and affection for everyone, even your enemy.

Do Not Block Emotions. Those that are blocked are harmful, and any long-term repression could lead to a number of common diseases, such as cancer,

---

[362] Taking Care of You: 25 Great Ways to Self-Nurture http://wingsfortheheart.com

heart attack and stroke. To avoid these dreaded and other afflictions people should reclaim their body mind connection by cultivating good emotions, and avoid at all costs destructive emotions. A pertinent quote is relevant:[363]

> "I believe all emotions are healthy, because emotions are what unite the mind and the body. Anger, fear, and sadness, the so-called negative emotions, are as healthy as peace, courage and joy. To repress these emotions and not let them flow freely is to set up disintegrity in the system, causing it to act at cross-purposes rather than as a unified whole. The stress this creates, which takes the form of blockages and insufficient flow of peptide signals to maintain function at a cellular level, is what sets up the weakened conditions that can lead to disease. All honest emotions are positive emotions."

There are many mind-body healing techniques. They include meditation, dynamic exercise, or different forms of body-oriented modalities. These include bioenergetics, network chiropractic, zero balancing, and other mind body healing techniques. All emotions can be accepted and channelled into positive areas of expression. Laughter at intervals may be good as suggested in a book.[364] For example, a person suffering from a life-threatening disease recovered from laughter prompted by watching Marx Brothers movies and old *Candid Camera* television shows.

Forget old emotional feuds. Go out of your way to be friendly with others, including your age-long enemies. Apologise and ask for forgiveness from those you have wronged.

Nurturing the Mind. Today, a lot of information could cause damage in different ways. Avoid gossip, sensationalism and negative, fear-producing ideas. These are all negative traits. Their effect could inhibit people's mind body connection and healing capacity.

There are many negative reports regarding death and disease in many countries.[365] News reports and media articles often focus on agents that cause cancer, tuberculosis, AIDS, and a myriad of other diseases. You have a choice to a certain extent of whether to listen to them. The negative information can be reduced through your powers of discernment and discrimination.

Common Negative Image. While humans may be genetically predisposed to certain health problems, this does not necessarily mean that they will

---

[363] Candace B. Pert, PhD, *Molecules of Emotion*, eBook and paperback, 1999.
[364] Norman Cousins, *Anatomy of an Illness*, W.W. Norton & Co., 1979. This is the first book by a patient that spoke of taking charge of our own health.
[365] Presently there is a daily report of killing by the army in Myanmar (Burma) after their military suppression of a legally elected government.

result as symptoms in your case. The body changes over every five to ten years. Every cell in the body is in the process of dying and being replaced constantly. Your future health is dependent on your mind on how you live, eat, and think at the present time. Avoid negative beliefs and myths that affect the healing process. Concentrate on what contributes to the healing power of the mind.

Breakthrough Book.[366] This book focuses on these:

(a) social myths -"healing means understanding what went wrong or who did what to me";
(b) biomedical myths - "healing takes time";
(c) religious myths - "disease is a punishment for my sins"; and
(d) new-age myths - "I must understand my feelings to heal".

The author of the book suggests alternative ways to help people reclaim their innate ability to heal. He wrote an interesting passage in respect of mythology in this quote:[367]

> "Every culture sleeps within its own mythology. If we wish to awaken from our sleep, we must be willing to evaluate the way we are programmed to experience our world, our circumstances, and ourselves. Then we may choose our own stories of the world we live in, and the way in which we will live in it. When we awaken from our sleep and question the stories given to us by our authority figures, we may choose to continue with those stories, or we can create new stories that work even better for us. Choosing our own stories can be a liberating, life-transforming, and empowering experience."

According to the author (Dr Epstein) of the above quote "healing means understanding what went wrong or who did what to me". He further says under religious myths "disease is a punishment for my sins" and he states under new-age myths "I must understand my feelings to heal." He suggests alternative ways to help people to reclaim their innate ability to heal.
occur.

By being involved in self-nurturing on the emotional and mental levels, the goal of spiritual nurturing is a natural result. There is a connection among them. Spiritual healings support you being grounded in

---

[366] *Healing Myths, Healing Magic* by Dr Donald Epstein.
[367] Dr Donald Epstein, *Healing Myths, Healing Magic*.

your body, releasing unwanted energies, and getting your own energy flowing so you can heal yourself.[368]

Spiritual Nurturing. Despite belief in spirituality not generally supported by health professionals, it can be the foundation for deep healing. Whatever may be the label, spirituality penetrates into people's inner being. This connection creates a sense of harmony and alignment with regard to various aspects. As such, it supports the healing process.

Mind Body Healing Technique: Creative Visualisation

There are numerous publications on the technique of mind, body healing. Positive visualisation can be adapted according to individual needs as set in three different images on:

(a) Problem or pain or disease, or the diseased part of the body.
(b) Positive force eliminating this problem.
(c) The body being rebuilt to perfect health, then seeing the body move through life with ease and energy.

A positive visualisation can have literal images, symbolic images relating to treatment, or abstract images. One universal image is a source of bright, white healing light; people can imagine it shining around (and through) every aspect of their being.[369]

CONCLUSION

> "The body's immune system is like any other system of the body. Each of them has their vital function for the human host."
>
> Anthony S. Fauci

The immune system in the body is essential for survival. It is the body's natural defence system. The different cells in the immune system play an important role in identifying, marking and destroying harmful cells that enter or develop in the body.

The immune system defends against disease-causing microorganisms. But it could fail when a germ invades the body to cause an ailment. A healthy lifestyle can assist the immune system. Various things can be done, such as avoid smoking and eat a healthy diet. Herbs and supplements can be

---

[368] For further reading refer to *10 Ways to Nurture your Spiritual Life* by Dr Depak Chopra, MD.
[369] Refer to How to Use Visualisation Techniques to Speed up Healing. See also How to Use Visualisation to Heal Physically or Emotionally – Gaiam.

used to improve immunity. You can help by avoiding stress and refrain from negative thoughts of others.

Immunotherapy can be used to treat cancer. Different types of this treatment can be administered in different ways for various cancers. It has many side effects. So far, it is not very successful.

The body being healed from within is an important aspect of the immune system. The body is capable of healing itself. Complementary to this is emotion, mind and spirit. Mention is made of a Brazilian doctor and Ms Marisa Harris of New York. Together with the power of the mind, certain herbs can be used to kill the cancer, though not generally accepted by the science as possible.

The mind-body healing technique has been in use for generations. This technique is designed to enhance the mind's positive impact on the body. It includes behavioural, psychological, social, expressive and spiritual approaches. How you think you can affect how you feel. There is also what is known as the holistic approach to healing. This includes a mind-body connection. This is known as psychoneuroimmonunology which links the mind, the brain and the immune system to communicate with each other.

When faced with health challenges, you can often feel overwhelmed and highly stressed. In this regard, integrative medicine may be relevant in addressing the full range of physical, emotional, mental, spiritual, social and environmental influences that affect health.

Integrative medicine involves a holistic approach. It encompasses an array of scientific disciplines to promote healing, coping and relaxation. All these are intended to complement the standard of care. It is not to replace conventional medicine but to enhance medical treatment, help to reduce side effects and pain and enhance the immune system.

"Every act of kindness on your part is a boost to your own immune system."

Marianne Williamson

"You will face many defeats in life, but never let yourself be defeated."

Maya Angelou

End

CHAPTER 18

NUTRITION GENERALLY

"The doctor of the future will no longer treat the human frame with drugs, but rather will cure and prevent disease with nutrition."

Thomas Edison

"Our food should be our medicine and our medicine should be our food."

Hippocrates

"Don't eat anything your great-great grandfather wouldn't recognize as food. There are a great many food-like items in the supermarket your ancestors wouldn't recognize as food (Go-Gurt?[370] Breakfast-cereal bars? Non-dairy creamer? Stay away from these."

Michael Pollan

"When diet is wrong, medicine is of no use."

Unknown

IINTRDOCTION TO NUTRITION

The 7 major classes of nutrients are carbohydrates. They are fats, fibre, minerals, proteins, vitamins, and water. These nutrients can be grouped as either macronutrients or micronutrients. Carbohydrates, fats, and protein are macronutrients, and they provide energy.[371] Water is essential for life but it has no nutrient.

Micronutrients are essential dietary elements required by organisms in varying quantities. They orchestrate many physiological functions to maintain health. These nutrients are vitamins and minerals needed in small quantities. Their deficie4ncy can lead to health problems on account of malnutrition. There are 4 main kinds of micronutrients required in your diet:

(a) Water-soluble vitamins B and C that dissolve in water.
(b) Fat-soluble vitamins that dissolve in fat and they are vitamins A, D, E and K.
(c) Micronutrients are essential nutrients. They are calcium, magnesium, sodium, and potassium.

---

[370] Yoplait Go-Gurt is a healthy snack made with live and active yogurt cultures.
[371] https://en.m.wikipedia.org Human Nutrition – Wikipedia.

(d) Trace minerals that include iron, manganese, copper, zinc and selenium. They are critical for muscle health, nervous system function and to repair damage to cells.

Nutrition involves the processes by which an animal or plant takes in and utilises food substances. Essential nutrients include protein, carbohydrate, fat, vitamins, minerals and electrolytes. Normally, the daily intake is 85% from fat and carbohydrates and 15% from protein.[372]

Good nutrition and physical activity can help maintain a healthy weight. But the benefits of a good nutrition are more than just weight. It can help to prevent the risk of some diseases, including heart disease, diabetes, stroke, some cancers and osteoporosis.[373]

Nutrition is a process by which living beings (animal, human or plant) take in and utilise food substances. Humans get their nutrition mainly through chewing and swallowing, and the amount required varies by age, size and the state of the body, which in some cases could be affected by disease.

Nutrition is essential for good health, growth, development and wellbeing. A healthy diet helps to prevent illness, improving one's quality of life and lifespan. A person's intake of nutrition will influence his body mass index (BMI) which is an indicator of his nutritional status as regards height and weight.

BMI = kg/m^2 where kg is a person's weight in kilograms and m^2 is height in metres squared. An adult's BMI of 25.0 or more is overweight, while a healthy range is 18.5 to 24.9. A high figure is indicative of excessive fat while a low value indicates insufficiency. Thus, your BMI can be used as a diagnostic tool for over or under nutrition. A BMI of 30 is indicative of obesity. The waist circumference should be used together with the BMI calculation as the former is a better indication of health risk than BMI. A BMI calculation for a child or an adolescent must be compared against age and gender percentile charts, usually done by a physician.

As already mentioned, a waist circumference is a better indication of health risk. Fat around the belly, irrespective of body size, could result in the development of obesity-related health conditions.

Fat predominantly deposited around the hips and buttocks do not appear to have the same risk. Men, in particular, often deposit weight in the waist region. Body fat could trigger risks in respect of diabetes, hypertension, high cholesterol and cardiovascular disease.

---

[372] Introduction to Nutrition https://healthengine.com.au
[373] The Importance of Good Nutrition https://www.tuftsmedicalcarepreferred.org

Height and Weight Guide Chart

The following weight (in lbs) and height (imperial) chart uses BMI tables from the National Institute of Health to determine how much a person's weight should be for their height. For each height, 4 categories of weight are given.

Height	Weight			
	Healthy range	Overweight	Obesity	Severe obesity
4ft 10″ (58″)	91 to 115	119 to 138	143 to 186	191 to 258.
4ft 11″ (59″)	94 to 119 .	124 to 143.	148 to 193.	198 to 267.
5ft (60″)	97 to 123 .	128 to 148	153 to 199.	204 to 276.
5ft 1″ (61″)	100 to 127.	132 to 153 .	158 to 206.	211 to 285.
5ft 2″ (62″)	104 to 131.	136 to 158	164 to 213.	218 to 295.
5ft 3″ (63″)	107 to 135.	141 to 163	169 to 220.	225 to 304.
5ft 4″ (64″)	110 to 140.	145 to 169.	174 to 227.	232 to 314.
5ft 5″ (65″)	114 to 144	150 to 174.	180 to 234.	240 to 324.
5ft 6″ (66″)	118 to 148	155 to 179	186 to 241.	247 to 334.
5ft 7″ (67″)	121 to 153	159 to 185.	191 to 249.	255 to 344.
5ft 8″ (68″)	125 to 158	164 to 190	197 to 256	262 to 354

5ft 9" (69")	128 to 162	169 to 196	203 to 263	270 to 365
5ft 10" (70")	132 to 167	174 to 202	209 to 271	278 to 376
5ft 11" (71")	136 to 172	179 to 208	215 to 279	286 to 386
6ft (72")	140 to 177 lbs.	184 to 213 lbs.	221 to 287 lbs.	294 to 397 lbs.
6ft 1" (73")	144 to 182	189 to 219	227 to 295	302 to 408
6ft 2" (74")	148 to 186	194 to 225	233 to 303	311 to 420
6ft 3" (75")	152 to 192	200 to 232	240 to 311	319 to 431
6ft 4" (76")	156 to 197	205 to 238	246 to 320	328 to 443
BMI	19 to 24	25 to 29	30 to 39	40 to 54

Waist Circumference and Health Risks

Both men and women should try to maintain a healthy waist circumference. Irrespective of your height or body mass index (BMI), you should try to lose weight if your waist is:

(a) For men 94 cm (37 in) or more.
(b) For women 80 cm (31.5 in) or more.

You are at very high risk of some serious health conditions if your waist is:

(a) For men 102 cm (40 in) or more.
(b) For women 88 cm (34.5 in) or more.

Risks associated for men and women in respect of waist circumference are set out in this table:

Table of Waist Size

Nature of Risk	Men	Women
Increased risk	94 cm	80 cm
Substantial increased risk	102 cm	88 cm

To reduce your risk, try to reduce your weight. This can be done by making lifestyle changes. Be aware of what you eat, be physically active, avoid smoking and avoid saturated fat. Malnutrition may develop if there is an imbalance between your nutritional intake and requirement. There could be over nutrition or under nutrition. The former is common in male.

Related Health Risks. Dietary factors result in many leading causes of death. These relate to coronary type-2 diabetes, heart disease, stroke and some types of cancers.

Food/Nutrient Requirements

"How long will it be before we realise the simple truth that the health of every individual depends upon his nutritional status."

Dr Royal Lee

The nutrients in food requirement can be described as the chemical components and are under six broad categories: proteins, carbohydrates, fats, vitamins, minerals and water. The last is technically not a nutrient, though essential for the absorption of nutrients, which render various functions. These are energy provision to maintain the important processes of digestion, breathing, growth and development.[374]

How much energy you require is dependent on your age, the size of your body and the nature of your activity. If your intake is equal to how much you expend, then you are in balance. Any excess energy is converted into body fat and in consequence weight gain. The opposite scenario is a weight loss. Therefore, to maintain a stable weight, the calories consumed through food must not exceed what is used up through metabolic processes. The average intake of calories for men and women are 2800 kcal and 1800 kcal per day respectively. There will be some variation on account of body size and activity.

Protein. This is important to maintain the body as the tissues and organs in the body are made up of protein and protein compounds. The building blocks of protein are called amino acids. The protein for adults is about 0.75 g/kg body weight per day. The highest protein is from animal products. The

---

[374] Refer to Human Nutrition – Kimball's Biology Pages https://www.biology-.info

next highest is from legumes (beans), cereals (rice, wheat, corn) and roots. Protein from meat, eggs, fish and milk contains all the essential amino acids. What is derived from plants is devoid of one or two essential amino acids. But a combination of plant-based protein can be of equal value to animal protein. A mixture of beans and rice will supply all the essential amino acids. Protein needs to be consumed daily as it cannot be stored in the body. It is not recommended to consume too much protein as it results in increased calcium excretion via the urine. This causes osteoporosis.

Carbohydrates. These can be classified as monosaccharide, disaccharide and polysaccharide (e.g., starch, fibre). Carbs must be reduced to the simplest form of glucose by digestion so that they can be absorbed by your body. Carbs should make up at least 55% of total energy intake. The brain depends primarily on glucose for its energy; it requires about 100 g/day of glucose for fuel. Occasionally, when there are less carbs, the body can compensate by using alternative energy by burning fatty acids.

Fatty Oils. Healthy fats are an important part of a healthy diet. They are discussed in Chapter 10 in relation to saturated fat, polyunsaturated fat, (MUFA) monounsaturated fat (MUFA) and trans fat. According to Harvard Medical School, fat supports many body functions such as vitamin and mineral absorption, blood clotting, building cells, and muscle movement. Although fat is high in calories, those calories are an important energy source for your body. The recommendation is that 20 to 35% of calories should come from fat,[375] but the World Health Organization suggests keeping it under 30% of your calories. Including healthy fats in your diet can help you to balance your blood sugar, decrease your risk of heart disease and type-2 diabetes, and improve your brain function. They are also powerful anti-inflammatory, and they may lower your risk of arthritis, cancer, and Alzheimer's disease. The most famous unsaturated fats are omega-3 and omega-6 fatty acids. You can find these healthy fats in nuts, seeds, fish, and vegetable oils (like olive, avocado, and flaxseed). Coconut oil provides plant-based fats in the form of medium-chain triglycerides which impart health benefits like faster utilisation by organs as fuel and appetite control. You should avoid trans fats and limit your consumption of saturated animal-based fats like butter, cheese, red meat, and ice cream.

The worst cooking oils are canola oil, palm oil, vegetable oil, soya bean oil, sunflower oil, coconut oil, margarine, shortening, and butter. There are a few articles on the internet stating that seed oil is toxic.

---

[375] The Dietary Guidelines for Americans Trusted Source.

The healthiest cooking oil is extra virgin olive oil, avocado oil, safflower, grape seed oil, and sesame oil.[376]

VITAMINS

There are various types of vitamins. They constitute a group of nutrients required in small quantities. As in the case of amino and fatty acids, likewise most vitamins cannot be made in the body but must be obtained from dietary sources. Only vitamin D can be made by the body if exposed to sunshine. The essential vitamins are divided into two groups. These are water soluble and fat soluble. Those in the first group can dissolve in water (thiamine, riboflavin, niacin, vitamin C, folic acid) and cannot be stored in the body and, therefore, need to be consumed every day. On the other hand, fat soluble vitamins (A, D, E, and K) can dissolve in a fat medium. These 4 vitamins are taken in while consuming fat-containing foods. Vitamins are essential to human health; they are essential for the growth and development of the body, such as in forming connective tissue and creating hormones.[377]

(a) Vitamin A is derived from carotene and affects vision, reproduction, and the formation and maintenance of skin, mucous membranes, bones and teeth. Any lack of it results in night blindness. Vitamin A is from either carotene or by absorbing ready-made vitamin A from plant-eating organisms. Carotene is found in leafy vegetables and yellow-orange fruit and vegetables. Other sources of pre-formed vitamin A are found in butter, milk, cheese, egg yolk, liver, and fish-liver oil.

(b) Vitamin B complex is a mixture of eight essential vitamins required to enhance immune and nervous system function, and promote cell growth and division. The elderly, alcoholics, pregnant or lactating women are likely or prone to suffer from vitamin B deficiency.

(c) Vitamin B1 (thiamine) acts as a catalyst in carbohydrate metabolism, and its deficiency causes beriberi. Such a vitamin deficiency disorder is characterised by muscular weakness, swelling of the heart and leg cramps. In severe cases, the beriberi may lead to heart failure. The sources of thiamine are organ meats (liver, heart, and kidney), brewer's yeast, lean meats, eggs, leafy green vegetables, whole or enriched cereals, wheat germ, berries, nuts, and legumes.

---

[376] https://amscardiology.com Best & worst Cooking Oils for Your Heart. AMS Cardiology.
[377] Vitamins: what are they, and what do they do? https://www.medicalnewstoday.com

(d) Vitamin B2 (riboflavin) acts as a coenzyme in the metabolism of carbohydrates, fats, and respiratory proteins. The best sources are liver, milk, meat, dark green vegetables, whole grain and enriched cereals, pasta, bread and mushrooms.

(e) Vitamin B6 (pyroxidine) is necessary for the absorption and metabolism of amino acids. It also has some function in the body's use of fats and in the formation of red blood cells. The best sources are from whole grains, cereals, bread, liver, avocados, spinach, green beans and bananas.

(f) Folic acid (vitamin B9 or folacin) is a coenzyme needed for forming body protein and haemoglobin. Any deficiency is associated with neural tube defects. The sources are from organ meats, leafy green vegetables, legumes, nuts, whole grains and brewer's yeast. Folic acid is lost in foods stored at room temperature and during cooking.

MINERALS

These are essential as they act as cofactors of enzymes. Some of the minerals necessary for health are:

(a) Calcium which is a very important mineral in the diet, especially for women during menopause. The most important function of calcium is to build and help maintain strong bones. It can prevent the onset of osteoporosis and reduce bone loss and fragility. It is involved in blood clotting. Vitamin D deficiency can result in calcium deficiency.

(b) Iron in food exists as haem and non-haem iron. The former is found in red meat and is relatively well absorbed (20–30%), while non-haem iron is found mostly in cereals, pulses, certain vegetables (e.g., spinach) and eggs, and is generally less well absorbed.

(c) Zinc represents only 0.003% of the human body, but is essential for synthesising protein, DNA and RNA. It is required for growth in life, and its sources include meats, oysters and other seafood, milk, and egg yolk.

Water. Although water provides no nutrition by itself, it is very important to sustain life. Water is discussed in the Chapter 16 in relation to Hydration.

> "One of the biggest tragedies of human civilization is the precedents of chemical therapy over nutrition. It's a substitution of artificial therapy over nature, of poisons over food, in which we are feeding people poisons trying to correct the reactions of starvation.
> Dr Royal Lee

Need for Balanced Diet

"Diet is the essential key to all successful healing. Without a proper balanced diet, the effectiveness of herbal treatment is very limited."

Michael Tierra

This is discussed in Chapter 4 on Balanced Diet.

Nutrients in the body are critically important in sufficient amounts and in the right proportions.[378] Without a balanced nutrition, your body is more prone to disease, infection, fatigue and low performance. Children who do not get enough healthy foods may face growth and developmental problems, poor academic performance and frequent infections.

A variety of foods must be consumed to attain a balanced diet, as different foods contain different nutrients in varying amounts.[379] A healthy diet can comprise both plant and animal types. Plant food is made up mainly of fruits and vegetables, grains, potatoes, and cereals. Animal products should include moderate amounts of items like milk, fish, lean red meat and poultry. Too much of meat is not good for health. Fats and oils[380] should not normally exceed 30% of one's energy, and of this saturated fat should be less than 10%. Rich sources of animal protein comprise lean red meat, poultry and fish, eggs and dairy foods. Dairy foods are also rich in calcium. Vegetarians can obtain their sources of protein from legumes, such as lentils, peanuts, kidney beans, grains, soya products, various nuts and seeds.[381]

CONCLUSION

The body requires a good nutrition from a balanced diet. With such a diet adequate physical exercise an optimum weight can be maintained. The greater the height the higher the weight which can be determined from a chart in the chapter or it can be individually calculated.

Adequate nutrients for your body depend on your age, body size and the nature of your activity. Weight maintenance depends on calorie intake. The body also requires proteins which can be obtained from different sources to support body tissues and organs, as carbs are responsible for the calorie intake.

---

[378] Balanced Diet: What is it and How to Achieve it – Healthline
https://www.healthline.com > health

[379] The importance has been stressed by Nutrition Australia by encouraging 30 different foods daily. This may not be attained by many people around the world.

[380] Vegetable oil is basically seed oil. Refer to Chapter 12 for its deleterious effect.

[381] The Australian Nutrition Foundation Inc (Nutrition Australia) has created its own food pyramid which can be viewed on the internet.

Also, your body needs fatty oils as healthy fats are important for a healthy diet. But too much of saturated fat could increase the bad (LDL) cholesterol level and triglyceride in the blood. Polyunsaturated fatty acids are essential for the body from which can be obtained omega-3 and omega-6, but there must be a proper ratio between these two. Your total fat intake is limited to 30% of your energy intake. Together, saturated fat and trans fat should be less than 10%. Other fat consumed should consist of monounsaturated fat. Seed oils which are sold as vegetable oils make people sick according to many internet articles and YouTube videos.

The body requires various types of vitamins and minerals. Except for vitamin D, which is made by the body when exposed to sunshine, all the vitamins, including vitamin D can be obtained from diet. In particular, vitamins A, B, C, and K are taken in food. Ensure that your body has enough vitamin B12. Minerals are calcium, iron and zinc consumed in food. Although water has no nutrient, it is important for life and hydration. There is a need for a balanced diet.

"The doctors of the future will no longer treat the human frame with drugs, but rather will cure and prevent disease with nutrition."
Thomas Edison

"The main weapons in the prevention and treatment of disease and human carelessness will probably always be food and exercise."
Dr Blake F. Donaldson, Strong Medicine

"First, nutrition is the master key to human health. Second, what most of us think of as proper nutrition – isn't
T. Colin Campbell
End

CHAPTER 19

VEGETABLES AND FRUITS

"Nothing will benefit human health and increase the chances for survival of life on earth as much as the evolution to a vegetarian diet."

Albert Einstein

"My aim is to ensure that my patients heal themselves, and they don't need any doctor."

Dr Rupa Shah

EMBRACING PLANT BASED FOOD TO BE HEALTHY

"Vegans following a whole food diet [without supplements] had a borderline supply of vitamin B12, Folic acid, vitamin B6, TSH, iron metabolism, and the blood count was in the normal range. Vegans taking dietary supplements demonstrated satisfactory overall results. An ingestion of sundried mushrooms can contribute to the supply of vitamin D."

Clin. Lab. 2014; 60: 2039-2050

In the interest of your health, start with your diet and manage your weight to what is consistent with your height. Focusing on whole foods from plant sources can have a profound influence on various aspects pertaining to health. A plant-based diet can:

(a) reduce body weight;
(b) reduce your blood pressure and risk of heart disease,
(c) avoid or reduce the risk of cancer and diabetes; and
(d) contribute to a better and sustainable environment.

Those who have been accustomed to eating a lot of meat and dairy as their primary nutrition sources will have to make a positive effort to change. This change can be done gradually. Dr Reshma Shah is a plant-based diet advocate and co-author of "*Nourish: The Definitive Plant-Based Nutrition Guide for Families*". It includes how to have more plants in your diet and the benefits this can provide for both you and the planet.[382]

---

[382] In addition to Dr Reshma Shah's suggestions on plant-based diet, refer also to "The Plant Power Doctor – a simple prescription for a healthier you" by Dr Gemma Newman. There are many other books and YouTube videos on this diet. Relevant authors are Dr

Nutrients and Protein in Plant-Based Diets

Some vegetarian diets, including total vegetarian or vegan diets, "are healthful, nutritionally adequate, and may provide health benefits in the prevention and treatment of certain diseases."[383] It has been reported that well-planned vegetarian diets are suitable for individuals in all life stages, including pregnancy, lactation, infancy, childhood, adolescence, and also for athletes.[384] Some key nutrients which strict vegans and vegetarians should bear in mind are vitamin B12, iron, calcium, iodine, omega-3 fatty acids and vitamin D. However, there is nothing of much concern as all can be obtained through plant-based foods, including fortified plant-based milks, fresh fruits and vegetables or supplements if needed.

Plant foods contain the 9 essential amino acids required to make up the proteins the body requires. Many foods like soy, beans, nuts, seeds and non-dairy milk products have proteins comparable to what is obtained from animal foods. Protein is not of any concern if you consume a wide variety of foods up to your calories requirement. You can enjoy your plant diets of various dishes from around the world as are available in the supermarkets.

Adopting a plant-based diet does not mean subsisting on boring, tasteless food. Dr Shah enjoys incorporating flavourful, varied dishes from around the world, including Ethiopia, Thailand and her native India.

Embark on Your New Diet Possibly in Stages

You can start gradually in cutting down on animal and dairy products and/or not eating them on certain days in the week.

Start Small. You can have only plant-based food on a certain day in the week. You can look for simple recipe from books to prepare your meal plan. You can try different recipe each time until you arrive at a simple and delicious recipe. Like this, you will be able to identify many dishes which you can add to your weekly diets. Such dishes can include steaming or roasting different types of colourful vegetables or blending them in quick and easy soups. You can increase the number of days in the week gradually when you do not eat animal and dairy products.

Reduce Quantity of None Plant-Based Foods. Another method of transferring to a plant-based diet is to gradually reducing one and increasing the size of the other. Instead of a full serving of a meat diet or full serving of roast chicken, try a mixture with stir-fry vegetables or you can add slices of

---

Deen Ornish, Dr Neal Barnard, Dr Mark Hyam, Dr William Li and Dr Jason Fong, to name a few.

[383] According to the American Dietetic Association.

[384] *Ibid.*

chicken to a bowl of salad. In the course of a few weeks your palate and mindset will have adjusted to lesser amounts of animal food. Occasionally, you can replace a dish of animal-based diet completely with a plant-based diet. You can have your proteins from tofu, seitan, beans or lentils.

Eating Out. You can examine a restaurant menu before and ahead of ordering your meal. In this way you can arrive with a plan as to what to order. You can request the vegan options and ask for substitutions and omissions. In the light of more and more people today choosing a vegetarian lifestyle, many restaurants try to accommodate the requirements of this lifestyle.

Flexibility to Accommodate Family Members. Some family members may continue with their usual diet. This situation requires some flexibility. Your family members may support you in converting to a plant-based diet even though they have not yet committed themselves to this change. What is important is the need for discussion to arrive at a compromise so that some dishes can be shared.

Eat Enough Filling Food. If you concentrate only on lettuce and vegetables, you may still feel hungry and unfilled. To avoid this feeling, you need to consume some fibre-rich whole grains, plant-based proteins and healthy fats. Substitute meat with plant-based foods like seitan and veggie burgers and food from other whole grain items. These will satisfy your otherwise craving for your favourite meat-based comfort food.

Be prepared properly to embrace your new lifestyle. Compassion is required in a family. It takes time to enjoy the different flavours and textures you discover in your plant-based diet

Doctors Supporting Plant Foods

The doctors in the below table are some of the main ones who support plant food.

Table of Some Doctors Supporting Plant-Based Diets, etc

Doctors	Advice, etc
Dean Ornish, MD	Diet & lifestyle change to treat & prevent heart disease. Eat well, move well, stress less and love well
Brooke Goldner, MD from Texas, USA	Suffered from lupus, recovered by eliminating certain diet & processed foods. Going vegan helped her to kick lupus. After obtaining her MD she coaches people with chronic disease

217

Michael Greger, MD	As a vegan doctor he gave evidence in a case in which Oprah Winfrey was sued for saying that meat was unsafe. His grandmother at the age of 65 was sent home to die from end-stage heart disease. Another doctor took her on and after 3 weeks she got rid of her wheelchair & walked for 10 miles daily, and living for 31 years by changing her diet
Joel Kahn, MD	Plant-based diet is the most powerful source of preventative medicine in the planet
Gareth Davis, MD	As a powerful vegan doctor, he gives talks on diet & health implications. He changed his own unhealthy state by changing his diet.
Alan Gold Hamer, DDC	He is against all oils, sugar and salt in addition to just following whole plant-based foods
Pamela Popper, PhD	From being very sick in her younger days, then adopting plant-based diet rendered her transformation so much that she made it a priority in a forward movement
Doug Lisle, PhD	Follows and advocating a vegan diet
Robert Ostfield, MD, MSc	Our western toxic diet is the No 1 cause of the increasing epidemic in heart disease. Elsewhere people who consumed more plant-based diets have better health
Ellsworth Wareham, MD (lived up to 104 years)	From carrying out surgeries he learnt that patients who had a plant-based diet had cleaner arteries. Therefore, he himself changed 50 years ago to a fully plant-based diet
Mathew Lederman, MD & Alona Pulde, MD	Advocated lifestyle change in reversing disease by developing a programme used by patients in the documentary "Forks over Knives"
Shobha & Arjun Rayapudi, MDs	They introduced plant-based lifestyles unheard of some years ago in Newfoundland, Canada
Terry Wahl, MD, Professor of Medicine	She conducts trial and testing on the effect of diet and lifestyle to treat multiple sclerosis from which she herself fully

	recovered
Neal Barnard, MD	Several ways to reverse Type-2 diabetes
Michael Klaper, MD	The Standard US diet is killing us. He was on whole-plant food for 45 years. Living on this diet (low in sugar, fat, salt & oils) is the best thing you can do for your health
David Unwin (a UK doctor in Liverpool)	How to eat a vegetarian or vegan low carb diet
Colin Campbell, MD	There are virtually no nutrients in animal-based foods that are not better provided by plants. Plant foods have dramatically more antioxidants, fibre & minerals
Caldwell Esselstyn, MD	You can reverse heart disease with a plant-based diet
Dean & Ayesha Sherazi, MDs	They work to illuminate the steps to long term brain health
Mark Hyam, MD. He has many You Tube videos	He advocates how to maintain optimum health and well-being and claims there is a big myth behind heart disease and what actually caused it. He supports plant-based diets.
Angela Fitch, MD	Fasting can help patients lose weight

American doctor and physician Dr Mark Hyam has some of his most favourite spices and the main properties of those spices in his Instagram page. Look at Dr Mark Hyam's list of his favourite spices (Image Credit source: Pixabay). All those ingredients are present in our kitchen, which is a treasure trove of anti-bacterial properties to anti-inflammatory, anti-oxidant, and anti-cancer properties.[385] He says there is no need to go to the pharmacy for anti-bacterial and anti-inflammatory medicine as such "medicines" are in your kitchen. They are spices you use for cooking.

WHOLE FOOD PLAND-BASED (WFPB) DIET

This type of diet focuses on whole foods.[386]There is a large number of foods which come under WFPB diet. Included here are:

(a) Fruits of various kinds: apples, bananas, grapes, grapefruit, lemons, limes, oranges, berries (including blackberries, blueberries, raspberries and

---

[385] https://www.newsncr.com/.../no-need-to-go-to-the.../
[386] Refer to "The Plant Power Doctor – A simple prescription for your healthier life" by Dr Gemma Newman.

strawberries), mangoes, avocados, peaches, plums, melons of different types, papaya, tomatoes and pears, among others.

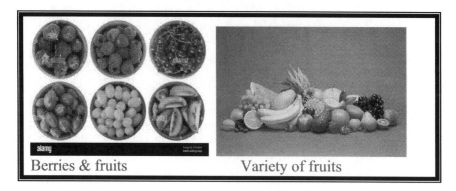

Berries & fruits   Variety of fruits

(b) Wholegrains such as brown rice, whole-wheat pasta, cereals, crackers, quinoa, barley, oats, whole-wheat bread, other starchy foods in their whole form, amaranth, millet, buckwheat, and popcorn, among others.

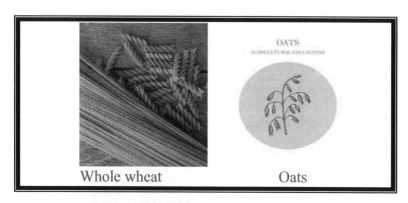

Whole wheat   Oats

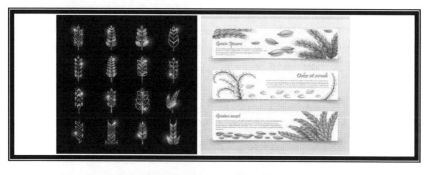

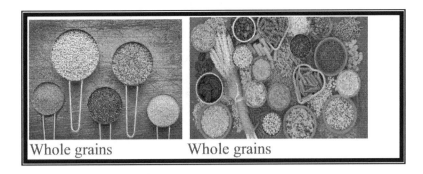

Whole grains   Whole grains

(c) Vegetables of various kinds include: broccoli, kale, cucumber, celery, spinach, onions, corn, peppers, peas, broad beans, lettuce, radishes, turnips, sweet potatoes, beetroot, pumpkins, cauliflower, parsnips, sprouts, Swiss chard, bok choy artichokes, among others.

Variety of vegetables   Variety of vegetables

(d) Beans and legumes include: chickpeas, adzuki beans, black-eyed beans, lentils of different colours, split peas, kidney beans, mung beans, white beans, , peanuts, soya beans, tofu, tempeh, runner beans, haircut beans, among others

Coloured beans   Different dried legumes

(e) Nuts and seeds of many kinds: flax seeds, Brazil nuts, almonds, cashew nuts, hazelnuts, macadamia nuts, pistachio nuts, pecans, walnuts, sesame seeds, chia seeds, sunflower seeds, pumpkin seeds, among others.

Nuts & seeds   Nuts & seeds

(f) Herbs, spices and other seasoning include turmeric, cinnamon, oregano, ginger, garlic, bay leaves, parsley, mint, mustard, garam masala, curry powder, chilli powder, cardamom, cloves, coriander, cacao, fennel, cumin, paprika, nutmeg, basil, vanilla, lemongrass, and mint, among many others.

Herbs & spices   Indian spices

(g) Alternatives to dairy include unsweetened plant milks such as soy, oat, almond, pea, hemp, rice and yoghurts. This is discussed in the Chapter 16 on Hydration.

(h) Some supplements may be necessary for vitamin B12 which is essential. In the USA, the RDA is 4-7mcg, but some experts believe that adults can benefit from 4-7mcg of vitamin D for optimal B12 status and a supplement of 500-1000mcg daily for the over 65. In the UK, guidelines state that adults only need about 1.5mcg of B12 daily. In the case of vitamin D, if you are not exposed to the sun, you can get it from brown mushrooms and fortified foods, such as plant milks and cereals. Other supplements you can get from algae oil (fish get it from algae), flax seeds. Iodine can be obtained from seaweed and fortified foods, selenium notably from Brazil nuts, and zinc from a balanced diet of pulses such as baked beans and oats.

(i) As mentioned in Chapter 10 on Dietary Fats, plant oils should be avoided as far as possible.[387]Many persons who have avoided oils have reversed

---

[387]There are internet articles stating that industrially produced vegetable oils are bad for health, toxic and killing many people. A few on seed oil state there is no evidence for this.

autoimmune issues, improve acne or heart disease symptoms. Oil can be avoided in cooking. Most evidence shows the benefits of having poly-unsaturated fats (PUFAs) and mono-unsaturated fats (MUFAs). These are from plants and if used in cooking they contribute 20 to 30% of our diet. Instead of using the industrially-produced oil, you can obtain both of these fats from flax seeds, walnuts and sunflower seeds (which are MUFA rich) and avocados, nut butters and olive (MUFA rich). Fats from these sources are better than from plant-based oils. Remember, industrially produced oils from seeds can make you sick. These oils are known and marketed as vegetable oils.

Avoid vegetable oil   This oil is toxic

WHOLE FOOD PLANT-BASED (WFPB)FOODS AND FAMILIES

The family in a household can be involved in a WFPB as it is suitable for all ages.[388] It is never too early or too late to make the switch. Even a pregnant person can start the diet. The NHS in the UK recommends an extra 200 calories in the last 3 months of pregnancy, bearing in mind that a pregnant woman will require more protein and more folic acid. These are available in fruit, veggies, pulse and whole grains. In addition, appropriate levels of vitamin D (600UI daily), choline (450mg daily), iodine (220mcg daily) and calcium (1,200mg daily) are required for the growth and brain development of a baby. Perhaps detailed information can be obtained at your medical clinic and from your doctor. In this regard, details can be obtained with regard to amounts of protein, calcium, vitamin D, vitamin B12, iodine, iron, and omega-3 fatty acids.

Likewise, in the course of breastfeeding you can continue with your WFPB diets and follow your healthcare professionals for any special advice.

Growing children need to watch their weight. Today one in five are overweight or obese in the US. Obesity rates are higher in the poorer population. However, a well-planned WFPB diet can reduce the obesity and the risk of developing heart disease, diabetes and cancer. An advantage of a WFPB diet is that it fights against asthma, allergies and other recurrent infections in childhood.

---

[388]According to the Academy of Nutrition and Dietetics (formerly the American Dietetic Association) and the British Dietetic Association.

Sometimes it may take some time for fussy kids to adapt to a new taste. Therefore, choose what food to serve, and they will decide how much they eat. A way forward is to involve your children in food preparation.

For older people, they will decide when to start on this diet and how aggressively they will go into it. They are intelligent to know that there is no point living to an old age without being healthy. They can optimize their health as they advance in years by being active (including involvement in some physical exercises) among other things of interest to them. The chronic diseases can be avoided by combining a quality diet with exercise, adequate sleep and avoiding stress. They will ensure you live better for longer. Also, a WFPB diet can slow down aging.

Treating chronic conditions with medication may interfere with your ability to eat, digestion, nutrient absorption and hydration. In addition, factors like fatigue, depression and loneliness may have some effect on food choices. To a certain extent this state can be avoided or reduced if a healthy diet was adopted before the arrival of frailty and old age. If you encounter any struggle with food consumption, you may seek the assistance of a dietician. In this regard, you may benefit from the advice of a healthcare professional.

EXCLUSION FROM WFPB DIET

Excluded from whole food plant-based (WFPB) diet are:

(a) Dairy products.

(b) Meats of all types, poultry, eggs and all types of fish and fish sauce.

(c) Most importantly, refined grains such as pasta, white bread, white rice and refined flour are excluded. Wheat is fully refined by removing the bran and germ to create a finer texture. Some brown bread is actually white bread coloured with molasses or other ingredient to give the appearance of wholemeal.

| Refined cereals | White flour (bread) |

Refer to Chapter 4 for various tables showing extent of sugar in various foods. White bread of 30 g contains 3.7 teaspoons of table sugar.

(d) Highly processed, high fat, high sodium and high sugar foods.

Bad food choices

(e) Sugary drinks, including sodas, energy drinks and fruit juices.

Avoid sugary soft drinks & Other sugary drinks (squash)

If you suffer from certain ailments, you can try to recover by switching to a plant-based diet. Check whether there is any improvement. Even those who are healthy can choose to stay healthy by adopting a plant-based diet, either partially or preferably fully, especially as you add on the years. It is never too late.

By eating less of the above products in preference to a plant-based diet, your taste bud will be adjusted accordingly. By substituting highly processed foods with whole foods (fruits, vegetables, whole grains and legumes), your taste buds will reset to accommodate the change and it can happen relatively quickly.

Some cruciferous vegetables are bitter, but a repeated exposure to them can change the proteins in the saliva. This will make the bitter foods more palatable and in the course of time you will no longer experience the bitter taste.

CHOOSE FOODS WITH DIFFERENT COLOURS (Go for the Rainbow)

Choose your foods to reflect different colours. Look for plants and whole foods with a variety of colours like the rainbow:

| 6 rainbow coloured foods | Foods of many colours |

(a) Red. In this category are red peppers, tomatoes, red cabbage, watermelon, grapefruit, radishes, rhubarb, raspberries, red onions, red potatoes, cherries, cranberries, and pomegranates.

(b) White. Included here are cauliflower, garlic, white beans, white mushrooms, parsnips, seeds, onions, shallots and perhaps chickpeas.

(c) Blue/purple. Included in this category are blueberries, blackberries, plums, olives, purple carrots, prunes, aubergines, and raisins.

(d) Yellow. Items in this colour are lemons, sweet corn, yellow peppers, ginger root, and summer squash.

(e) Orange. This colour includes sweet potatoes, carrots, turmeric root, butternut squash, orange peppers, grapefruit, mangoes, peaches, papaya, satsumas, nectarines, swede

(f) Green. Finally, in this colour are spinach, asparagus, kale, broccoli, cucumber, avocado, green peppers, kiwi, bok choy, Brussels sprouts, celery, cabbage, edamame beans, peas, green beans, rocket, Swiss chard, apples, okra, mangeout, leeks, watercress

Be Aware of Medicinal Herbs

Many medicines are plant-based. A few examples here are appropriate: morphine is from poppies, aspirin is from willow bark, and digoxin is from foxgloves. Although medicinal herbs are not regulated in the same manner as pharmaceutical drugs, this lack of regulation does not detract from the fact that herbs can have beneficial effects on one's body. Some of the herbs which may provide some health benefit are these:

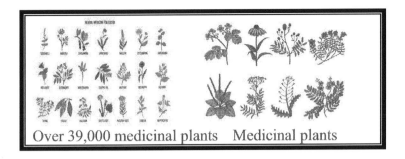
Over 39,000 medicinal plants   Medicinal plants

(a) **Neem**. This is a well-known Ayurveda herb in India. It has antibacterial, anti-parasitic anti-fungal properties. It has been useful for some people with dry, itchy and red skin conditions.

Neem   Aloe vera

(b) **Aloe Vera**. This herb is useful to treat burns. It has been found to have antimicrobial properties which provide potential benefits in the management of ulcerative colitis and diabetes.

(c) **Ashwaghundha.** This is known as the Indian ginseng. It was used as part of Ayurveda medicine for boosting mood and vitality. It provides benefits in reducing anxiety. An interesting study showed improved male hormone levels (DHEA) and testosterone. This accounts for its reported benefits in treating fatigue.

Ashwaghundha   Amla (Indian gooseberry)

(d) **Amla**. This is known also as Indian gooseberry. As an adaptogenic herb, it can balance your immune system. A double blind randomized controlled trial indicated that using 500mg twice daily could also reduce cholesterol and triglycerides in people with high blood lipids. Many benefits have been found in preclinical trials, which included liver protective and anti-diabetic effects.

(e) **Boswella**. This is known also as Indian frankincense. It is an herb that is used to reduce inflammation, not to mention that it can be an effective painkiller.

Boswella   Berberine (best metformin alt.)

(f) **Berberine**. This is a compound that can be extracted from many plants. It is most commonly consumed by the mouth for diabetes, high levels of cholesterol and other fats in the blood (hyperlipidemia) hypertension (or HBP). There are many ways how it can reduce the body's inflammatory pathways. Animal trials have revealed benefits for reducing the severity of heart attacks and heart failure.

(g) **Turmeric**. It has been used in India as a medicinal spice for over 4,000 years. There are multiple potential benefits. This is due primarily to its anti-inflammatory and antioxidant effects. It is beneficial for metabolic syndrome, can provide pain relief, and is helpful for managing inflammatory and degenerative conditions. To be effective, turmeric must be used with a little black pepper as the peperine in it helps in the proper absorption of the curicumin in the turmeric.

Turmeric powder   Sigisbeckia

228

(h) **Sigisbeckia**. This Chinese herb is useful for the relief of arthritis, back ache, joint and muscle pain. In pre-clinical trials, it has been shown to reduce inflammation to the cartilage within joints with similar modes of action to anti-inflammatory painkillers. No gasgastrointestinal side effects were reported.

(i) **Mushrooms**. There are many mushrooms with general health benefits. This is partly due to their beta-glucans content. As in the case of oats, these soluble fibres assist in improving cholesterol, heart health and blood sugars. The reishi type which has been nicknamed "mushroom of immortality" is attributable to its immune system protecting polysaccharides. It has been shown generally to reduce inflammation and to calm the mind. Although considered a vegetable, mushrooms are neither a plant nor animal food. They are a type of fungus and contain the substance called ergosterol. This can be transformed into vitamin D with exposure to ultraviolet light.

Mushrooms

Dairy (Milk)

Milk is a good source of calcium and nutrients, but there is no biological reason why humans require it from another species after weaning. However, drinking cow's milk is common. The ability to digest the lactose in this milk is known as "lactose persistence", though some people lack this ability after being weaned from their mothers' milk.[389] Today, the place of dairy in a balanced diet is increasingly being questioned. This is partly attributable to intensive farming practices and the environmental cost by the dairy industry. The human health benefit is also being re-evaluated.

There is no direct link between milk consumption and the reduction in the risk of bone fracture, according to some studies. Some studies indicate that fracture of bones and premature mortality are more prevalent where people consume more milk. A sugar found in milk tends to induce

---

[389]A study in 2017 indicates that the global prevalence of lactose intolerance due to lack of lactose activity is 68%. Those affected by consuming dairy products suffer from diarrhoea, bloating, cramps, nausea or headaches.

oxidative stress and chronic inflammation.[390] The latter is linked to heart disease, cancer, bone and muscle loss.

Also, dairy is linked to increased rates of prostate, breast and ovarian cancer, according to some studies, but colorectal cancer appears to be less with dairy consumption. Other serious bowel conditions could be adversely affected by dairy. The bacterium in milk releases a molecule that prevents blood cells from killing E.coli. It is the same bacterium that is responsible for the development of Type 1 diabetes.

The recent Canadian Dietary Guidelines have removed diary products entirely from their dietary recommendations. Also, as already mentioned, many people in some advanced countries are rejecting diary for environmental reasons.

You do not need to rely on calcium from dairy products as plants are an excellent source for it. Calcium is important for healthy bones and teeth, in addition to other roles for regulating metabolism, muscle function, a normal blood flow, nerve transmission and the release of hormones. Some 99% of the body's calcium is stored in the bones and teeth. The daily intake of calcium for those aged 19 to 64 is 700mg, while the figures are 800 to 1,000mg for those aged 11 to 18 years, 550mg for 7 to 10 years, 450mg for 4 to 6 and 350mg for those aged 1 to 3.

Most fruits and vegetables have been shown to provide calcium and to increase bone health and density. Some vegetables contain oxalates, which is an organic compound that makes it hard for your body to absorb the calcium. Your body may only absorb 5% found in high-oxalate vegetables, such as spinach, rhubarb and Swiss chard. Boiling them has the effect of reducing the oxalate levels by 30 to 80%, though it diminishes nutrients like vitamin C. Brussels sprouts, kale, okra and broccoli are particularly rich in calcium and low in oxalate. Plants containing calcium include lentils, peas, beans watercress cabbage, tahini, cauliflower, broccoli, bok choi, kale, collard greens, soy-based foods, calcium fortified plant milk, cereals and juices, various types of nuts, seaweed, fresh and dried fruits and seeds.

PLANT DRINKS (MILKS) This is in Chapter16 on Hydration

These drinks are not really milk in the true sense of the word, though plant substitutes for milk. The most environmentally friendly to produce are soy and oat milks, while almond milk and rice milk require much water to produce. Half the quantity of water is used to produce the equivalent

---

[390] What causes inflammation are trans fat, animal fats, high fat diet, stress, smoking, sleep deprivation, obesity, excessive calorie intake, sugar sweetened drinks, high sodium diet, low fibre consumption and excessive alcohol

quantity of cow's milk. There are many plant milks to choose from what is available, either sweetened or unsweetened. See Chapter.16.on Hydration.

> "Nothing will benefit human health and increase the chances for survival of life on Earth as much as the evolution to vegetarian diet."
>
> Albert Einstein

NUTRITION UPDATE ON PLANT FOODS

> "I hope that Oprah Winfrey, who knows the benefits of a vegan diet, will use her new partnership with Weight Watchers to create a program – like the 21-day Vegan Kickstart – geared toward plant-based nutrition."
>
> Neal Barnard, MD.

Plant-Based Diet for All Chronic Illnesses

Many physicians globally are not stressing the importance of this diet. It should be the first treatment for most illnesses. This could be attributable to a lack of awareness of these diets. In this day and age, such a deficiency has no excuse. In the US, there are national guidelines for active living and healthful eating.[391] In the interest of your health, your plate of food should contain 50% plant foods comprising mainly no starchy vegetables and fruits, 25% whole grains or unprocessed starchy food, and 25% lean protein.

A plant-based diet can have many favourable biometric outcomes on hypertension (high blood pressure), diabetes, and lipid profile. This can be within a 3 or a 4-month period. A person who does not have many chronic illnesses can see dramatic improvements from the quality of his new diet. The aim of a plant-based diet is to increase your consumption of nutrient-dense plant foods while at the same time reducing processed foods, oils, and animal foods (of all types including dairy products and eggs). What you should eat are these:

(a) a great deal of vegetables, raw and/or cooked;
(b) fruits of different types and colours;
(c) beans, peas, lentils, and soybeans; and
(d) small portions of seeds and nuts (generally low in fat).[392]

There are many proponents in the field; they have varying opinions as to what comprises the optimal plant-based diet. Dr Deen Ornish and a few

---

[391] www.ChooseMyPlate.gov

[392] Blaney D, Diehl H. The optimal diet: the official CHIP cookbook. Hagerstown, MD: Autumn House Publishing; 2009. Jan 1,
McDougall JA, McDougall M. The new McDougall cookbook: 300 delicious ultra-low-fat recipes. New York, NY: Plume; 1997. Jan 1, 1997.

others recommend some animal products such as egg whites and skimmed milk in small quantities.[393] Some doctors, including Dr Esselstyn at the Cleveland Clinic Wellness Institute, are of the view that all animal-based products as well as soybeans and nuts should be avoided, particularly if severe coronary artery disease is present.[394] Although there are minor differences, the evidence is that a broadly defined plant-based diet has many health benefits. It should be pursued.

Interchanging Terms

The term, *plant-based*, is sometimes used to mean a *vegetarian* or a *vegan* diet. These different terms are probably adopted for ethical or religious reasons. What is important is to know the specific diet and to ascertain the details of a patient's diet without making any assumption of one's diet. The following is a summary of diets that restrict animal products. Note carefully the information below shows what a diet excludes, but the plant-based diet is defined by what it includes. Here are 7 diets:

(a) Whole-foods, plant-based, low-fat diet: This diet encourages plant foods in their whole form, especially vegetables, fruits, legumes, and seeds and nuts (in smaller amounts). To experience maximum health benefits, this diet excludes animal products. Total fat is generally restricted.

(b) Mediterranean diet: This is similar to (a) but allows small amounts of chicken, dairy products, eggs, and red meat once or twice per month. Fish and olive oil are encouraged. Fat is not restricted.

(c) Vegan (or total vegetarian): It excludes all animal products, especially meat, seafood, poultry, eggs, and dairy products. However, it does not require consumption of whole foods or restrict fat or refined sugar.

> "A vegan diet is one of the best things you can do for your health and the well being of our planet."
>
> Robert Clarke

(d) Raw food, vegan diet: Same exclusions as for (c) as well as the exclusion of all foods cooked at temperatures greater than 118°F.

---

[393]Ornish D, Brown SE, Scherwitz LW, et al. Can lifestyle changes reverse coronary heart disease? The Lifestyle Heart Trial. Lancet.1990 Jul 21;336(8708):129–33. DOI: http://dx.doi.org/10.1016/0140-6736(90)91656-U. [PubMed].
Ornish D, Scherwitz LW, Billings JH, et al. Intensive lifestyle changes for reversal of coronary heart disease. JAMA. 1998 Dec 16;280(23):2001–7. DOI: http://dx.doi.org/10.1001/jama.280.23.2001. [PubMed].
[394] Esselstyn CB., Jr .Prevent and reverse heart disease: q & a with Caldwell B Esselstyn, Jr, MD [monograph on the Internet] Lyndhurst, OH: Prevent and Reverse Heart Disease; [cited 2012 Oct 6]. Available from: www.heartattackproof.com/qanda.htm.

(e) Lacto-vegetarian diet: It excludes eggs, meat, seafood, and poultry but includes dairy products.

(f) Ovo-vegetarian diet: It excludes meat, seafood, poultry, and dairy products but includes eggs.

(g) Lacto-ovo vegetarian diet: It excludes meat, seafood, and poultry but includes eggs and dairy products.

Ketogenic Diet. A picture in Chapter 1 shows that the Keto diet contains 75% fat, 20% protein and 5% carbs. It is a very low carb, high fat diet and shares similarities with the Atkins and low carb diets.[395]

Lifestyle Changes in Relation to Certain Ailments

This part of the chapter shows the benefit in making lifestyle changes to get rid of certain problems. The goal is to improve health by adopting a vegan, vegetarian or Mediterranean diet. In particular, what are looked at are obesity, diabetes, heart disease and hypertension.

Obesity

A vegan or vegetarian diet is effective for losing weight and solving the obesity problem according to many doctors.[396] As reported in the footnote below, many doctors also found that those who consume vegetarian diets have lower rates of heart disease, high blood pressure, diabetes, and obesity. Mention is made in their review that weight loss in vegetarians does not depend on physical exercise. Their weight decreases at a rate of about 1 pound per week. In addition, a vegan diet results in more calories being burnt after meals. This can be contrasted to non-vegan diets which may cause fewer calories to be burned. This is because the food is being stored as fat.[397]

Vegetarian diets may be better for weight management, and it has been suggested that such diets may be more nutritious than those that include meat.[398] Also, it has been shown that vegetarians were slimmer than

---

[395] The Ketogenic Diet: A Detailed Beginner's Guide to Keto.
https://www.healthline.com › nutrition › ketogenic-diet-10
[396] As reported in *Nutrition Reviews* .Berkow SE, Barnard N. Vegetarian diets and weight status. *Nutr Rev.* 2006 Apr;64(4):175–88. DOI: http://dx.doi.org/10.1111/j.1753-4887.2006.tb00200.x. [PubMed].
[397]Berkow SE, Barnard N. Vegetarian diets and weight status. *Nutr Rev.* 2006 Apr;64(4):175–88. DOI: http://dx.doi.org/10.1111/j.1753-4887.2006.tb00200.x. [PubMed]
[398]Farmer B, Larson BT, Fulgoni VL, 3rd, Rainville AJ, Liepa GU. A vegetarian dietary pattern as a nutrient-dense approach to weight management: an analysis of the national health and nutrition examination survey 1999–2004. *J Am Diet Assoc.* 2011 Jun; 111(6):819–27. DOI: http://dx.doi.org/10.1016/j.jada.2011.03.012. [PubMed].

those who consumed meat. Further, many vegetarians were found to have more magnesium, potassium, iron, thiamine, riboflavin, foliate, and vitamins but less total fat. The reason for this as suggested is that vegetarian diets are nutrient dense and suitable for losing weight without compromising on diet quality.[399] A study also reported a large difference in age-adjusted BMI (body mass index) with meat eaters having the highest BMI and vegans with the lowest.

The Oxford component of the European Prospective Investigation into Cancer and Nutrition assessed changes in weight and BMI over a five-year period in meat-eating, fish-eating, vegetarian, and vegan men and women in the United Kingdom. During the five years of the study, the mean annual weight gain was lowest among individuals who had changed to a diet containing fewer animal foods. The study also reported a significant difference in age-adjusted BMI, with the meat eaters having the highest BMI and vegans the lowest.[400] There are other studies as well that support a lower BMI with a vegan or vegetarian diet. Also, such a diet is suitable for controlling obesity in children.

Diabetes

There is an advantage of plant-based diets over other diets with regard to the prevention and management of type-2 diabetes. Vegetarians have about half the risk of developing diabetes compared with non-vegetarians.[401] It was reported in 2008 that non-vegetarians were 74% more likely to develop diabetes over a 17-year period than vegetarians.[402] In 2009, it was found that the prevalence of diabetes in individuals on a vegan diet was only 2.9%, compared with 7.6% in the non-vegetarians.[403] A plant-based diet low in fat with none or little meat may help to prevent and treat diabetes. This is possible by improving insulin sensitivity and decreasing insulin resistance.

---

[399] *Ibid.*

[400] Rosell M, Appleby P, Spencer E, Key T. Weight gain over 5 years in 21,966 meat-eating, fish-eating, vegetarian, and vegan men and women in EPIC-Oxford. *Int J Obes (Lond)* 2006 Sep;30(9):1389–96. DOI: http://dx.doi.org/10.1038/sj.ijo.0803305. [PubMed].

[401] Snowdon DA, Phillips RL. Does a vegetarian diet reduce the occurrence of diabetes? *Am J Public Health.* 1985 May; 75(5):507–12. DOI: http://dx.doi.org/10.2105/AJPH.75.5.507. [PMC free article] [PubMed].

[402] Vang A, Singh PN, Lee JW, Haddad EH, Brinegar CH. Meats, processed meats, obesity, weight gain and occurrence of diabetes among adults: findings from Adventist Health Studies. *Ann Nutr Metab.* 2008;52(2):96–104. DOI: http://dx.doi.org/10.1159/000121365. [PubMed].

[403] Tonstad S, Butler T, Yan R, Fraser GE. Type of vegetarian diet, body weight, and prevalence of type 2 diabetes. *Diabetes Care.* 2009 May;32(5):791–6. DOI: http://dx.doi.org/10.2337/dc08-1886. [PMC free article] [PubMed].

In a study it was shown that those on the low-fat vegan diet reduced their HbA1c levels by 1.23 points while those on the American Diabetes Association (ADA) diet reduced theirs by only 0.38 points. Also, 43% of those on the low-fat vegan diet were able to reduce their medication, compared with 26% of those on the ADA diet.[404]

Heart Disease

Dr Deen Ornish in his Lifestyle Heart Trial found that 82% of patients with diagnosed heart disease who followed his programme had some level of regression of atherosclerosis.[405] A lifestyle change can bring this about within one year. In Dr Ornish's plant-based regimen, 10% of calories came from fat, 15 to 20% from protein, and 70 to 75% from carbohydrate, while cholesterol was restricted to 5 mg daily.

In a prospective, randomised, secondary prevention trial, de Lorgeril found that his intervention group (at 27 months) experienced a 73% decrease in coronary events and a 70% decrease in all-cause mortality. This group's Mediterranean-style diet contained more plant foods, vegetables, fruits, and fish than meat. Canola oil margarine replaced butter and cream, while Canola oil and olive oil were the only fats recommended.[406]

While vegetarian diets are linked to lower risk of several chronic diseases, people consuming different types of vegetarian food may not experience the same effects on health. What is important is to focus on eating a healthy diet, not simply a vegan or vegetarian diet.[407]

---

[404] Sabaté J, Wien M. Vegetarian diets and childhood obesity prevention. *Am J Clin Nutr.* 2010 May;91(5):1525S–1529S. DOI: http://dx.doi.org/10.3945/ajcn.2010.28701F. [PubMed].

[405] Ornish D, Brown SE, Scherwitz LW, et al. Can lifestyle changes reverse coronary heart disease? The Lifestyle Heart Trial. *Lancet.* 1990 Jul 21;336(8708):129–33. DOI: http://dx.doi.org/10.1016/0140-6736(90)91656-U. [PubMed].

[406] de Lorgeril M, Salen P, Martin JL, Monjaud I, Delaye J, Mamelle N. Mediterranean diet, traditional risk factors, and the rate of cardiovascular complications after myocardial infarction: final report of the Lyon Diet Heart Study. *Circulation.* 1999 Feb;99(6):779–85. DOI: http://dx.doi.org/10.1161/01.CIR.99.6.779. [PubMed].

[407]Fraser GE. Vegetarian diets: what do we know of their effects on common chronic diseases? *Am J Clin Nutr.*2009;89(5):1607S–1612S. DOI: http://dx.doi.org/10.3945/ajcn.2009.26736K Erratum in: Am J Clin Nutr 2009 Jul;90(1):248. DOI: http://dx.doi.org/10.3945/ajcn.2009.27933. [PMC free article] [PubMed].

High Blood Pressure

The Dietary Guidelines Advisory Committee reviewed literature to identify articles on the effect of dietary patterns on blood pressure in adults. It has been found that vegetarian diets were linked to both lower systolic blood pressure and lower diastolic blood pressure.[408] This could mean that by eating a plant-based diet over many months the need for medication can be dispensed with.

Mortality

In a literature review, it was found that plant-based diets were linked to a reduced risk of cardiovascular disease and mortality compared with non-plant-based diets.[409] The benefit relating to the reduced risk of mortality may be primarily due to a lower consumption of red meat.[410] Low meat intake has been associated with longevity. Seven studies with a combined total of some 124,706 persons were analysed, and vegetarians were found to have 29% lower heart disease mortality than non-vegetarians.[411]

Some Health Concerns About Plant-Based Diets

These concerns relate to a possible deficiency in proteins, iron, calcium and vitamin D, vitamin B12 and fatty acids. However, except for vitamin B12, all these items are available from plant-based diets,[412] including brown rice with beans, and hummus with whole wheat pita.

Proteins. These are made up of amino acids available from plant of various types as well as from animal products. Soybeans and any food made from

---

[408]*Report of the Dietary Guidelines Advisory Committee on the dietary guidelines for Americans, 2010: to the Secretary of Agriculture and the Secretary of Health and Human Services.* Washington, DC: Agriculture Research Service, US Department of Agriculture, US Department of Health and Human Services; 2010. May.

[409] *Ibid.*

[410] Singh PN, Sabaté J, Fraser GE. Does low meat consumption increase life expectancy in humans? *Am J Clin Nutr.* 2003 Sep;78(3 Suppl):526S–532S. [PubMed].

[411]Huang T, Yang B, Zheng J, Li G, Wahlqvist ML, Li D. Cardiovascular disease mortality and cancer incidence in vegetarians: a meta-analysis and systematic review. *Ann Nutr Metab.* 2012;60(4):233–40. DOI:http://dx.doi.org/10.1159/000337301. [PubMed]

[412] *.Nutritiondata.self.com [web page on the Internet]. Soybeans, mature seeds, raw.* New York, NY: Condé Nast; 2012. [cited 2012 Oct 6]. Available from: http://nutritiondata.self.com/facts/legumes-and-legume-products/4375/2.

soybeans are good sources of protein. Soybeans may help lower levels of low-density lipoprotein in the blood and reduce the risk of hip fractures and some cancers.

There is no need to worry if a well-balanced, plant-based diet is eaten as it will provide enough of essential amino acids and, therefore, will prevent protein deficiency.

Iron. This can be obtained from plant-based diets, but the iron in plants has a lower bioavailability than the iron in meat. Plant-based foods rich in iron include kidney beans, black beans, soybeans, spinach, raisins, cashews, oatmeal, cabbage, and tomato juice.[413] According to the American Dietetic Association, iron-deficiency anaemia is rare even in individuals who follow a plant-based diet.

Vitamin B12. This vitamin is required for blood formation and cell division, and its deficiency is a cause for concern. The deficiency can cause macrocytic anaemia and irreversible nerve damage. Vitamin B_{12} is not produced by plants or animal products but by bacteria. For this vitamin, there is a need to take a supplement for the deficiency or consume foods fortified with vitamin B_{12}.[414] The labels on the food can be checked before purchase.

Calcium and Vitamin D. Eating a well-balanced, carefully planned, plant-based diet will cater for any calcium and vitamin D deficiency. People who ignore this and do not eat plants that contain high amounts of calcium may suffer from the risk of impaired bones and fractures. This risk is similar for vegetarians and non-vegetarians. Adequate calcium intake is necessary, irrespective of dietary preferences.[415] Significant sources of calcium can be obtained from tofu, mustard and turnip greens, spinach, bok choy, and kale. However, calcium from spinach and some other plants does oxalate and because of this is poorly absorbed.

With regard to vitamin D, it is a deficiency which is common in many people, especially who lack the benefit of sunshine. Some plant-based

[413] Waldmann A, Koschizke JW, Leitzmann C, Hahn A. Dietary iron intake and iron status of German female vegans: results of the German vegan study. *Ann Nutr Metab.* 2004; 48(2):103–8. DOI: http://dx.doi.org/10.1159/000077045. [PubMed]

[414] *Dietary supplement fact sheet: vitamin B12 [monograph on the Internet]* Bethesda, MD: National Institutes of Health, Office of Dietary Supplements; 24. Jun. 2011 [cited 2013 Jan 31. Available from: http://ods.od.nih.gov/factsheets/VitaminB12-HealthProfessional/.

[415] Appleby P, Roddam A, Allen N, Key T. Comparative fracture risk in vegetarians and non-vegetarians in EPIC-Oxford. *Eur J Clin Nutr.* 2007 Dec; 61(12):1400–6. DOI: http://dx.doi.org/10.1038/sj.ejcn.1602659. [PubMed]

products such as soy milk and cereal grains may be fortified with vitamin D to provide an adequate source. Those who are at risk are recommended to take a supplement.

Fatty Acids. Humans must ingest fatty acids for good health as their bodies do not synthesize them. There are only two such essential fatty acids: linoleic acid (an omega-6 fatty acid) and alpha-linolenic acid (an omega-3 fatty acid). Another 3 fatty acids are only conditionally essential. They are palmitoleic acid (a monounsaturated fatty acid), lauric acid (a saturated fatty acid), and gamma-linolenic acid (an omega-6 fatty acid). Any lack in essential fatty acids may be revealed by skin, hair, and nail abnormalities.[416] Refer to Chapter 10 on Dietary Fats for some detail.

People consuming vegan diets are likely to be deficient in omega-3 fats (n-3 fats). The plant version of omega-3 fats, alpha-linolenic acid, is also low in vegans. This can be remedied by consuming n-3 fats which are linked to a reduced incidence of heart disease and stroke. Appropriate foods as sources of n-3 fats include ground flax seeds, flax oil, walnuts, and canola oil.

A great deal of planning is required by those who wish to follow a plan-based diet. Reading labels before the purchase of any food is required. It is necessary to have a variety of fruits and vegetables. Avoid or limit animal products, added fats, oils and refined, processed carbohydrates. By following a plant-based diet, the major benefits for most people are these:

(a) the likelihood of reducing or eliminating a number of medications taken to treat many chronic conditions;
(b) lower body weight (reducing obesity);
(c) avoiding or decreasing the risk of cancer of various types; and
(d) possibly a few other benefits.

A plant-based diet is especially suitable for those with obesity, type-2 diabetes, high blood pressure, lipid disorders, or cardiovascular disease. The benefit is relative to how serious a person is in changing to this diet. Low-sodium, plant-based diets may be prescribed for individuals with high blood pressure or a family history of coronary artery disease or stroke. Severe obesity may require counselling and initial management with a low-calorie diet.

Special restrictions may apply to those with kidney disease. In this regard, fruits and vegetables that are high in potassium and phosphorus should be consumed. But people with thyroid disease will need to be careful

---

[416]Rosell MS, Lloyd-Wright Z, Appleby PN, Sanders TA, Allen NE, Key TJ. Long-chain n-3 polyunsaturated fatty acids in plasma in British meat-eating, vegetarian, and vegan men. *Am J Clin Nutr.* 2005 Aug;82(2):327–34. [PubMed].

when consuming certain plants that are mild goitrogens, These plants include soy, raw cruciferous vegetables, sweet potatoes, and corn. These people should be told that cooking these vegetables inactivates the goitrogens.

What is important for consideration is that too often doctors ignore the potential benefits of good nutrition in preference to the prescription of medication. Patients should be advised how to cure themselves by following healthy eating and active living.

A cultural mindset of doctors is required. Doctors need to be weaned from the powerful influences of the pharma industry. They should align themselves to good ethics and the welfare of their patients rather than thinking only in increasing their bank balance. Whether the sentiments in the US Sunshine Act will be followed to the letter of the law still remains to be seen as there are various ways of bypassing the law on "kickbacks" from the pharma industry and the medical device industry.

Table Showing List of Vegetables and Health Benerfits

Vegetables	Health Benefits
Bok choy	Aids in preventing cancer, fights inflammation, lowers risk of heart disease, full of antioxidants, Vitamins C & E, beta-carotene, selenium may slow growth of tumours, full of fibre
Broccoli	Phytochemicals: anti-oxidant, fibre & protein, iron, potassium, calcium, selenium & magnesium. Vitamins A, C, E, K & B vitamins, including folic acid.
Kailan (Kale)	Rich in calcium, Vitamin C, Vitamin A, fibre, folic acid, vit. K. Good source of chlorophyll and VitaminK
Lettuce	Vitamin A, B1, B2, C, folic acid, manganese & chromium
Celery	Antioxidants, reduces inflammation, supports digestion, rich in vitamins & minerals, low glycemic index
Choy sum	Foliate, Vit B6, beta-carotene which can be converted to Vit A
Cabbage (red, green)	Vitamins C & K, improves digestion, combats inflammation
Cauliflower (white/purple)	Nutrients, antioxidants that reduce inflammation, protects against cancer and heart disease
Pumpkin	Highly nutritious & rich in Vitamin A, antioxidant, boosts immunity, nutrient density & low in calories
Carrot	Vitamin A, beta-carotene, lutein good for eyes
Radish	Rich in antioxidants, minerals like calcium &

	potassium
Beetroot	Essential nutrients, fibre, foliate, manganese, potassium, iron & Vitamin C. Lowers blood pressure
Turnip	Fibre, Vitamins K, A, C, E, B1, B3, B5, B6, B2 & foliate, manganese, potassium, magnesium, iron, calcium & copper, phosphorus, omega-3 fatty acids & protein
Long bean, French bean, flat bean	Vitamins A & C, rich in phyto chemicals & antioxidants, good in fighting cancer and delays aging
Mung bean sprouts	Nutrients, antioxidants, lowers LDL, rich in potassium, magnesium and fibre
Okra/ladies finger	Rich in magnesium, foliate, fibre, antioxidants, Vitamins C, K1 & A, good for heart health & blood sugar control
Chayote	Good for antioxidants, heart health, blood sugar control, anti-cancer, liver function & and may slow aging.
Onions	Contain antioxidants & compounds that fight inflammation, decrease triglycerides & LCD cholesterol, improves immunity, can improve vision
Cassava	Calorie rich and plenty of carbs, vitamin C
Parsnips	Rich in antioxidants, Vitamins C & K, foliate, insoluble fibre
Shallots	High in antioxidants, improve blood sugar levels
Leeks	Rich in flavonoids, anti-cancer & ant diabetic properties
Lemon grass	Relieves pain, swelling & fever, improves levels of sugar and cholesterol in the blood, contains antioxidant properties
Bamboo shoots	High proteins, amino acids, carbs, many minerals & vitamins A, B6, & E, thiamine, niacin
Cucumbers	Many important vitamins and minerals, balanced hydration
Corn	High fibre, B vitamins, essential minerals such as zinc, magnesium, copper, iron and manganese
Eggplants (aubergines)	Many vitamins and minerals, aids digestion, heart health, prevents cancer, improves bone & brain function, prevents anaemia
Zucchini	High in Vit A and antioxidants. Good for heart health, digestion & vision, reduces blood sugar levels & improve heart health

CONCLUSION

A diet rich in vegetables and fruits can lower blood pressure, reduce the risk of heart disease and stroke, prevent some type of cancer, lower risk of eye and digestive problems, and have a positive effect upon blood sugar.

Vegetables and fruits contain important vitamins, minerals, fibre and plant chemicals. There are many varieties of vegetables to choose from. You can eat them as part of an overall healthy diet. You will benefit by a reduced risk of some of the chronic diseases, as alluded to above.

Some of the most nutrient-dense vegetables are spinach, carrots, broccoli, garlic, Brussels sprouts, kale, green peas, Swiss chard, among others. Refer to the table showing many other vegetables. Amongst fruits are these: oranges, blueberries, apples, avocados and bananas. There are many more to choose from. Fruits are an excellent source of essential vitamins and minerals, and they are high in fibre. They also provide a wide range of health-boosting antioxidants, including flavonoids.

Nuts and seeds are good sources of protein, healthy fats, fibres, vitamins and minerals. They regulate body weight as their fats are not fully absorbed and they regulate food intake. They contain unsaturated fats and other nutrients that protect against heart disease and diabetes.[417] To improve the immune function or digestive health, choose almonds. For a better heart, brain health or a little mood boost, go for walnuts. Pistachios should be chosen for losing weight and is the biggest antioxidant boost.

> "There are virtually no nutrients in animal-based foods that are not better provided by plants. Plant foods have dramatically more antioxidants, fiber and minerals than animal foods."
>
> Dr T. Colin Campbell

> "New 'Heart-Healthy Food Recommendations for Hospitals' from the American College of Cardiology:
> - At least one plant-based main dish will be offered and promoted at every meal.
> - Processed meat will not be offered."
>
> Physcians Committee

> "A plant-based diet is like a one-stop shop against chronic diseases."
>
> Anonymous
>
> "Came from a plant, eat it; was made in a plant, don't."
>
> Michael Pollan

End

---

[417] https://www.betterhealth.vic.gov Nuts and Seeds – Better Health Channel

AUTHOR'S OTHER BOOKS AND A BRIEF BIOGRAPHY

1. Law of Compulsory Purchase and Compensation, Butterworths 1984, 338 pages.

2. Law of Real Property and Conveyancing in Singapore, Longman, 1986, 447 pages.

3. Singapore Property Tax, Longman – Law & Valuation, 1988, 299 pages.

4. Law of Real Property & Conveyancing, Longman, 2nd Edition, 1991. 722 pages.

5. Development Control and Planning Law (main author), Longman, 1991, 434 pages.

6. Taxation Relating to Investments in Real Property, Longman, 1993, 378 pages.

7. Compulsory Land Acquisition, Butterworths, 2nd edition, 1994, 388 pages.

8. Strata Titles, Butterworths, 1995, 604 pages.

9. Law of Real Property & Conveyancing, Financial Times – Law & Tax, 3rd edition, 1996, 1085 pages.

10. Peasant Farmer to Professor & Beyond, eBook, Amazon KDP, 2012, over 375 pages.

11. Teaching & Study Skills in Higher Education, eBook, Amazon KDP, 2012, 643 pages, print length 423.

12. Wills & Estate Administration, eBook, Amazon KDP, 2012, 2nd Ed 2014, 256 pages, print length 205 plus 16 pages. Revised in 2016 and is given a new title: Make your Own Will. It was revised again in 2021 with the original title restored.

13. Taxation of Income & Capital, eBook, Amazon KDP, 2012, 2nd Ed 2014, 526 pages, print length 500. Revised in 2016 and a slight change in the title following a suggestion from a five-star reviewer.

14. India: Wisdom & Achievements, eBook, Amazon KDP, 2014, print length 381 plus 6 pages.

15. Revived Expectations, eBook, Amazon KDP, 2014, 192 pages, print on demand version as well.

16. Landlord and Tenant Law, eBook, Amazon KDP, 2015, 396 pages print on demand edition (revised 2016).

17. India: Invasions, Foreign Rule & Eurocentrism, eBook, Amazon KDP, 2016, 430 pages print on demand.

18. India: Foreign Atrocities & Plunders, eBook, Amazon KDP, 2017, 413 pages, print on demand edition as well.

19. India: Discovery of the Truth, eBook, Amazon KDP, 2018, 345 pages, print on demand version as well.

20. India: Ancient Influences and Superiority, eBook KDP, Amazon, 2019, about 375 pages, paperback version as well.

21. Transmigration of Souls - Reincarnation - Amazon KDP, 2019, About 260 pages, print on demand as well.

22. Law of Trusts, Amazon KDP, 2019, eBook, about 425 pages, paperback 415 pages.

23. Guyana: Border Disputes, Politics and Oil, eBook on Amazon KDP, 2019, about 350 pages, paperback 330 pages.

24. An Unusual Life Story, Amazon KDP, eBook about 350 pages, 2020, also available as a paperback.

25. Health and Nutrition, Amazon KDP, 2021, eBook and paperback, 323 pages.

26. Food As Medicine – Plant-Based Diet - Amazon 2022, eBook and paperback, 197 pages

27. Plant-Based Diet for Better Health, Amazon 2023, eBook and paperback, 243 pages.

The books 1–9 are of seminal importance in uncharted areas. A reputable UK University examined six of these books together with five refereed papers in a submission for a higher doctorate degree (DSc). The eBooks are also available as paperbacks.

The author also single-handedly produced six study manuals in Hong Kong on Real Property Law, Landlord & Tenant Law, Administrative Law, two Volumes on Questions & Answers in Applied Valuations for the RICS Final Year Examinations, and Taxation of Income and Capital (Revenue Law).

About the Author

Dr Khublall has acquired half a dozen qualifications of some distinction by stringent examinations. He holds a higher doctorate degree (DSc).

He has had a varied career over 55 years in a number of countries. He entered full-time university teaching in 1974 and attaining professorial status in 1988. He left academia in 1996 to practise as a barrister in England and Wales over period of 15 years.

He has written a total of 33 books of a varied nature and 33 academic papers. Nine of his textbooks were published by highly reputable international publishers, including Butterworth, Longman and Financial Times – Law and Tax. His last 17 books are available on Amazon as eBooks and paperbacks. Some of his papers were published in refereed journals, and he presented a number of papers at various international conferences and symposiums in Australia, the USA, Germany, Spain, Malaysia, Hong Kong, the Netherlands, the UK (University of Oxford) and Singapore.

Printed in Great Britain
by Amazon

32688410R00137